THE
OWL
CRITICS

The
Owl-Critic

James
Thomas
Fields
(1818–1881)

"Who stuffed that white owl?" No one spoke in the shop:
The barber was busy, and he couldn't stop;
The customers, waiting their turns, were all reading
The *Daily,* the *Herald,* the *Post,* little heeding
The young man who blurted out such a blunt question;
Not one raised a hand, or even made a suggestion;
    And the barber kept on shaving.

"Don't you see, Mister Brown,"
Cried the youth with a frown,
"How wrong the whole thing is,
How preposterous each wing is,
How flattened the head is, how jammed down the neck is—
In short, the whole owl, what an ignorant wreck 'tis!
I make no apology;
I've learned owl-eology.
I've passed days and nights in a hundred collections,
And cannot be blinded to any deflections
Arising from unskillful fingers that fail
To stuff a bird right, from his beak to his tail.
Mister Brown! Mister Brown!
Do take that bird down,
Or you'll soon be the laughing-stock all over town!"
    And the barber kept on shaving.

• • • •

"Anatomy teaches,
Ornithology preaches
An owl has a toe
That *can't* turn out so!
I've made the white owl my study for years,
And to see such a job almost moves me to tears!
Mister Brown, I'm amazed
You should be so gone crazed
As to put up a bird
In that posture absurd!
To *look* at that owl really brings on a dizziness;
The man who stuffed *him* don't half know his business!"
    And the barber kept on shaving.

"Examine those eyes.
I'm filled with surprise
Taxidermists pass
Off on you such poor glass;
So unnatural they seem
They'd make Audubon scream,
And John Burroughs laugh
To encounter such chaff.
Do take the bird down;
Have him stuffed again, Brown!"
    And the barber kept on shaving.

• • • •

Just then, with a wink and a sly normal lurch,
The owl, very gravely, got down from his perch,
Walked round, and regarded his fault-finding critic
(Who thought he was stuffed) with a glance analytic
And then fairly hooted, as if he would say:
"Your learning's at fault *this* time, any way;
Don't waste it again on a live bird, I pray.
I'm an owl; you're another. Sir Critic, good-day!"
    And the barber kept on shaving.

THE
OWL
CRITICS

ALFRED T. VOGEL

THE UNIVERSITY OF ALABAMA PRESS
UNIVERSITY, AL

ACKNOWLEDGMENTS

Throughout my career as a teacher, I have been indebted to a great number of colleagues and several generations of students who, in direct and subliminal ways, shaped my attitudes in education. They are, regrettably, too numerous to be singled out by name. I can, however, express my gratitude to certain persons whose encouragement and counsel have been most helpful.

It was in an article—"Can Critics Change the Schools?"—in the New York University *Education Bulletin* (Fall, 1972), written by Dean Daniel E. Griffiths, that I was delighted to find a viewpoint that exactly mirrored my own thinking at the time. In subsequent discussions, this feeling was confirmed by Dean Griffiths' continuing support of my work in progress.

My daughter Jane, a professor of English at Ithaca College, was the first to read my manuscript and to point out ways to strengthen the texture of my prose.

James Travis and Francis Squibb, editors of the University of Alabama Press, were always ready to give me the benefit of their expertise at every stage of the process by which a raw manuscript is transformed into a publishable book.

And my wife Signe earned my special gratitude by tolerating the ceaseless clatter of my typewriter when I knew she would have preferred to be evoking more pleasing sounds from her beautiful violoncello.

ALFRED T. VOGEL

Library of Congress Cataloging in Publication Data

Vogel, Alfred T   1906-
    The owl critics.

    Bibliography: p.
    Includes index.
    1. Educational innovations—United States. I. Title.
LA217.V63   370'.973   79-4550
ISBN 0-8173-9112-6

CONTENTS

Dedication:
To Signe

PREFACE

Few human institutions have received as much criticism as American public schools. Intermittently until 1940, and consistently since 1950, the schools have been subjected to attacks—often vicious attacks—on virtually every aspect of their functioning. The critics have appeared in many forms and represent all segments of America life: journalists, businessmen, teachers, clergymen, naval officers, university professors, militants, and just plain ordinary people. No one, it seems, can resist the temptation to lambast the schools.

While the critics have been numerous, the defenders of the schools have been few. On the occasion of a national convention, a school superintendent or professor of education will defend the schools, but until now there has been no articulate champion of the public schools. Alfred T. Vogel fills that gap. *The Owl Critics* is the work of a learned man who has had a distinguished career in the New York City public-school system. He is thoroughly familiar with the critics' work and brings to his analysis of that work a finely honed mind and a priceless background as a teacher. Vogel *knows* the schools—a statement that does not hold for the critics.

Why is there more criticism of public education in the United States than in the rest of the world? One can only speculate. It could be that the way public education got started in this country and the way in which it developed explains the plethora of critics.

As early as 1647, the Massachusetts Colony mandated a school for young children for each township with fifty or more families. These schools were not only to teach students to read, write, and cipher but were to cultivate the moral and religious values necessary to live in the colony. In the same legislation, called the Old Deluder Satan Act, townships of one hundred or more families were ordered to open a grammar school to prepare youths for higher education. The students were periodically quizzed by committees of citizens and, if they did not measure up, steps were taken to improve schooling.

Although the form of education varied with local conditions, the Massachusetts Colony set the mode for public education in the United States. Education was a local concern. Schools were to prepare children in basic literacy and in the accepted values of the community. The work of the schools was to be monitored by the citizens themselves. Those who taught were not accorded the independence, respect, or status conferred on ministers, lawyers, or doctors. While the present organizational structure of public education is far more sophisticated and its size and scope has expanded greatly, the United States still holds public education in the same view as the colonists did.

Public education is held accountable to the citizens formally through their elected or appointed boards of education, but every citizen still feels, as did every colonist, that he may criticize the schools and bring about changes in what happens in them. Therefore, no one feels incompetent to judge or impotent to bring about modifications. And there is no strong profession of teaching, such as that which exists in other countries, to ward off the critics and to resist change. Another way of putting the case is that public schools in the United States are tightly coupled to the society. The schools are what the public wants, and what the public wants is often what the critics say it wants.

Callahan's *Education and the Cult of Efficiency* documents one aspect of this thesis.[1] He studied the social forces that shaped the administration of the public schools in the first half of the twentieth century and summarized his analysis as follows:

> I am now convinced that very much of what has happened in American education since 1900 can be explained on the basis of the extreme vulnerability of our schoolmen to public criticism and pressure and that this vulnerability is built into our pattern of local support and control.[2]

Thus, he points out, school administrators responded with undue haste to the criticism that followed the launching of Sputnik, and that schoolmen welcomed and quickly adopted James B. Conant's recommendations for change in the high schools.

In more recent times, the schools have been under constant attack, and they have undergone numerous alterations. Most likely the critics did not directly and personally cause the schools to change in the last twenty years, but they did create a public climate that not only supported innovation but demanded it. Friedenberg's outspoken call for alternatives to traditional schools is one example;[3] Silberman's endorsement of open education is another;[4] Kozol's plea for equal opportunity is yet another.[5]

One cannot read Friedenberg or Kozol and not believe that there is a great deal wrong in the conception of the teacher's role, in regard to how the teacher lives in the school and to the relationship between teachers and their superintendents, principals, supervisors, and students. Kozol's relationship with supervisors indicated that teachers had no authority to teach what they thought desirable. Considering that Kozol started teaching "with no training in education and no experience as a teacher" this may not have been unreasonable. But the same rules also restricted those who were well prepared.

Teachers, however, have taken matters into their own hands in the past decade, and the situation is changing, though probably not in a way envisioned by the critics. The emergence of strong local teachers' unions and associations has had a tremendous impact on the way teachers feel, live, and work. Salaries have been raised, working conditions improved, and relationships with administrators modified to the point that many principals now lack any authority at all. The hand of the critic in all of this can be discerned, but lightly. It is there nevertheless.

The prisonlike atmosphere of secondary schools has been described and condemned. These judgments now appear to be having an effect. Students in many high schools no longer need passes, can leave the campus when they do not have classes, use the library and lounges without "permission," and exercise a great deal of control over their own behavior. In fact, liberty has gone a bit far in some cases.

In the fifteen short years since Kozol taught in Boston and the twelve years since *Death at an Early Age* was published, there has been such a deliberate effort to compensate for and remedy the conditions of blacks in large northern cities that this book, like Friedenberg's, is already dated.

The most obviously successful critic is Charles Silberman, whose *Crisis in the Classroom* has had a tremendous impact on elementary schools in this country. His advocacy of the English "open classroom" has been, if anything, too successful, for many teachers have climbed on the bandwagon without stopping to understand the concept. Silberman should not be blamed for this excess, since he cautions against uncritical acceptance of the idea. Yet, if one wants evidence of the power of the critic, look to Silberman.

There is, then, a clear picture of criticism and response in American public education. The stronger the criticism and the more prestigious the critic, the quicker the response. Since 1900 this pattern has produce some desirable as well as undesirable changes in the schools. But, as Callahan has said, "the real point is that this is an inadequate and inappropriate basis for establishing sound educational policy."[6]

Callahan is, no doubt, correct in his conclusion. But what would it take to establish education policies on a more rational basis? Several developments would have to take place. First, the field should not be left to the critics as it is now. Whenever a book or article about the schools is published, it should be subjected to scholarly analysis by informed professionals such as Mr. Vogel. But this, of course, is not enough. The reasons why the critics are so successful must be removed. This means that the teachers and administrators who staff the schools must themselves become critics, discovering and attacking from the inside the elements of the schools that should be improved. The teaching profession must develop a more self-critical attitude about itself and in this way improve practice within the system.

In order for the teaching profession—including superintendents, principals, guidance counselors and the like—to develop enough independence to feel free to criticize the schools, the way in which schools are financed must be changed. It is virtually national practice that schools are operated on an annual budget voted by local taxpayers. If this styem is not

employed, then the annual budget is approved by some local governmental unit such as the Finance Committee in Connecticut or the City
Council in New York City. The source of funds, with some exceptions
such as Delaware and Hawaii, is the local property tax. What this leads to is
an extreme case of local control in which school personnel are placed in a
very vulnerable position. As Callahan has said so well, "So long as schoolmen have a knife poised at their financial jugular vein each year, professional autonomy is impossible."[7] The dangers of local control must be
alleviated by moving the responsibility for financing schools from the
local to the state level. Further, funding should be assured for terms
longer than one year. It is only when school people can develop a feeling
of professional autonomy that they will be able to withstand criticism and
make public educational policies on a more rational basis.

There are other aspects of the problems presented by the critics and so
well put before us by Mr. Vogel. Even if local control is diminished to a
degree, the professional educators must themselves be of such an intellectual quality that they can accept useful and constructive criticism and
reject that which is useless and/or destructive. Much that is advocated by
some of the critics is nonsense, but unfortunately many in public education are unable to recognize it as such. The teaching profession must
constantly upgrade itself so as to do a better job of education, to win public
respect, and to handle better the thrusts of the critics.

The development of self-criticism on the part of professional educators, a diminution of local control, and an improvement in the quality of
the education profession would do much to balance the power of the
critic. The critics will always be with us, and we should learn how to endure
them.

School of Education,   DANIEL E. GRIFFITHS
Health, Nursing, & Arts   Dean
Professions, New York
University
August, 1979

REFERENCES

1. Raymond E. Callahan, *Education and The Cult of Efficiency* (Chicago: The
University of Chicago Press, 1962).

2. Ibid., preface

3. Edgar Z. Friedenberg, *Coming of Age in America* (New York: Random House,
1963).

4. Charles E. Silberman, *Crisis in the Classroom* (New York: Random House,
1970).

5. Jonathan Kozol, *Death at an Early Age* (New York: Bantam, 1967).

6. Callahan, op. cit.

7. Callahan, op. cit.

FOREWORD

Of school reformers there is no shortage, nowadays. They are legion—
and articulate. They do not wear saffron robes or shave their heads, but
everywhere we hear their monkish chant, "In-no-va-tion," as a mind-
numbing ritual. They have a simple creed—to anathematize every established educational policy and proclaim the virtue of its opposite.

The reformists charge that teaching procedures in the classroom are
locked in sterile routine. They draw the caricature of thirty-five pupils
fixed in five rows of seven seats each with the teacher sitting woodenly in
front of the room, and they demand greater mobility: movable desks, no
stifling routines, spontaneity, pupil self-direction. Then, when the Summerhill ballet degenerates into chaos, bickering, waste of time, nonlearn-
ing, and a drift toward insolence and apathy, the drug culture, and
mysticism; and, in a narrower focus, scholarship and reading and writing
approach the zero-limit, and there develops a worship of body language
and direct communion without the medium of words, the alarm sounds in
high quarters and the Hyman Rickovers and Arthur Bestors clamor for
order and structure and the restoration of learning. It is a parody of the
Hegelian cycle of thesis and antithesis.

In one sense, the reformists' insistence on fundamental change is a
matter of definition. Some equate the surface of things, the spatial patterns that a camera can capture on film, with the essence. They elevate
physical self-expression—children moving about or playing with colorful
objects or older students pressing buttons on electronic gadgetry or star-
ing at one another in circles—above the infravisual mental activity that is
necessary to develop mature minds. They blur the distinction between
two kinds of processes, the inorganic and the organic. Inorganic changes
are those that alter the physical conditions of learning: modification in the
architecture of school buildings, modular programming of the day's
schedule, variations in the length of the semester, the greater use of
programmed teaching machines, and so forth. Such improvements in the
conditions that facilitate teaching or remove obstacles to learning can be
adopted for what they are worth, that is, as tools that may or may not be
advantageous for education. Organic changes, on the other hand, are
those that go to the heart of the teaching-learning process: changes in
curriculum, teaching methods, and textbooks. It is likely that policy in
these areas will more profoundly affect the outcomes of schooling and
indeed the future of our society.

As an illustration of the kinds of innovative programs that are being
publicized today, there is the movement toward "schools without walls"
and "classrooms without doors." Certain schools are cited with approbation for their experimentation with a program in which students are

released from the compulsion of class attendance and dependence on secondary sources of information in textbooks in order to acquire the essentials of social studies firsthand by working in community institutions—the courts, museums, the police and fire departments, factories and insurance offices. Other schools give academic credit for independent study projects or work projects off campus. Schools and colleges have encouraged a variety of self-directed community activities—participation in political campaigns or civil-rights movements—as the equivalent of academic courses in a traditional setting. These are interesting developments, with suggestive values that might well be incorporated experimentally in curricular design.

On the other hand, there are currents of innovation that are highly disturbing. One such proposal that received much publicity recently concerned lesson planning. One would think that planning lessons at least a few days in advance is as necessary to teaching as it is to architecture or road building. Not so. The *New York Times,* in a March 7, 1971, editorial entitled "Teacher, Drop That Plan," argued feelingly for the abandonment of lesson planning on the ground that the teacher who thinks out in advance the aims of his lessons and the pedagogic means of reaching them is likely to kill "spontaneity." The converse proposition would seem to be that unplanned teaching must indeed generate spontaneity in abundance. This is precisely what seems to guide the thinking of some innovators, among them John Holt and Ivan Illich. The vision of a highly motivated and self-directed class group, with an adult present as a resource person or moderator or facilitator, not as a teacher in the traditional sense, is offered as an attractive alternative to the developmental lesson and the always-boring lecture.

One reason for the ascendancy of the new reformism is the energy of its proponents. The attack on conventional ways of teaching and learning is launched unremittingly and is directed against every vulnerable facet of the educational establishment. The defenders of the citadel must stretch their resources to the breaking point. Compulsory school attendance is derided as a form of tyranny; and curriculum, no matter how flexible and imaginative, is brushed aside; the teacher's authority, no matter how effective his methods of communicating with his pupils may be, is challenged. Finally the very existence of schools is questioned. To support their derogation of the schools, the reformists have mobilized a battery of psychological and sociological theories that cannot easily be grasped, and sometimes they have hidden the operative premises of their reasoning from view, thus blurring attempts to defend the schools rationally.

The sweeping claims of the reformists, moreover, are difficult to refute because any judgment about the outcomes of an educational program is not easily proven. Most educators believe the effectiveness of a curriculum can be gauged by some form of testing, whether set up by the teacher or the department or by some outside agency such as the Educational Testing Service or a state board of regents. In the longer view, however, they know the success of an educational program must be measured by the kind of adults it produces—literate, intellectually efficient, socially responsible members of society. Similarly, the shortcomings of our society—materialism, decaying moral standards, a vulgarized and shallow culture—can in part be attributed to the failings of our schools. Our newspapers and best-selling novels and most popular television programs also provide an index of the quality of our schools. Any effort to quantify the long-range effects of schooling faces the bewildering task of matching an infinite number of variable causes—students, teachers, materials, curricula, and so on—with an infinite number of social effects. At best, then, a statistically valid assessment of the educational process is beyond our reach. Add to this the fact that the judgments of the more extreme reformists are conditioned by certain assumptions about our way of life that are often suppressed in their public statements, and it becomes apparent that the hope of fruitful dialogue with them is illusory.

The purpose of this book is to examine and perhaps to throw light on some of the "progressive" ideas now being thrust upon educators, public officials, and the public at large. My thesis is that the rejection of tradition and standards by the reformists is based on inadequate information about what the schools are now doing and on unacceptable assumptions about the nature of teaching and learning. In some cases, the negativism of the reformists is a symptom of an underlying malaise or a political ideology that is not always apparent. It is my conviction that America's schools have always been responsive to fresh currents of thought and have assimilated changes in structure and direction throughout the years. Their basic programs, however, have rested on organized courses of study and planned instruction in classrooms. The appeal of "open" and "free" schools is understandable, but such peripheral developments are still experimental and must be evaluated critically before being established within the matrix of school programs. They may be thought of as mutations in an evolutionary process that have yet to demonstrate their contribution to the needs of students and, more broadly, to the needs of our society. It is my contention that the goals of acculturation are best served by what may be called, for want of a more precise term, traditional education.

THE
OWL
CRITICS

1

THE
OWL CRITICS

The poem "The Owl-Critic" tells of a young man waiting his turn in the barbershop who sees what he takes to be a stuffed owl perched on a shelf and makes sneering comments about the clumsy workmanship of the taxidermist, criticizing the shape of the owl's head and the unnatural angle of its beak. At the end, to the discomfiture of the patron, so smug in his convictions about what an owl should and must be, the owl flaps its wings and flies off its perch. The moral of this poem, written in the 1860s as a gentle satire on the muckrakers of that time, might well be applied to the flourishing host of detractors of our public schools today.

The Owl Critics of our generation—ranging from Jonathan Kozol and Ivan Illich on the Left to Paul Goodman and Edgar Z. Friedenberg somewhere near the center, together with such volatile crusaders as John Holt and Neil Postman—have had the ear of the public for some time. They have performed a legitimate service in bringing into the foreground the critical issues that beset the schools in this troubled period, and for this we should be grateful. But we cannot have confidence in judgments that are based on faulty evidence and, indeed, gross misrepresentation of the facts. The reports on the educational establishment published by the critics I have mentioned are neither accurate nor perceptive. What they have done, in fact, is to transform the proposition that our educational institutions should be hospitable to new ideas into the dogma that our schools have degenerated into sterile, reactionary organisms that must be excised at the root. What began as a questioning of values has become a ritual chant.

No publisher's list is complete nowadays without at least one title that dramatizes the failings of our schools and offers bright prospects for the future, if only we will dismantle the present structure and replace it with some newly designed—or deliberately undesigned—system. In contrast to the stifling atmosphere that is said to pervade our schools, these books offer a number of seemingly attractive alternatives suffused with infinite promise and exhilarating hope. The publishers have packaged their offerings, too, in containers with beguiling Madison Avenue labels—*Crisis in the Classroom, Education and Ecstasy, Death at an Early Age*, and *The Great School Legend*. So persuasive have the detractors been that anyone who defends the curricula and teaching methods prevalent in all but a handful of schools today is regarded with the contempt that was heaped, with some justification, on the Squeers and Ichabod Cranes of the past. The critics have succeeded in undermining public confidence in the schools and in bewildering teachers and administrators to the point of distraction.

It is time that the realities of our educational system should be viewed in rational perspective, so useful discussion of its philosophy, structure, and content will be possible. With the facts distorted out of all resemblance to the truth, it is unlikely that sound decisions can be arrived at. To get at the truth, we must strip away extraneous and specious layers of distortion by examining closely the substance of the charges leveled at the schools.

For one thing, the Owl Critics seem to be under the impression that they are pathbreakers in an uninhabited wilderness. They write as if the history of reform in education began with their entrance on the scene. When Jonathan Kozol relates his experience with the slum children of Boston, describing how he got to the children by reading to them Langston Hughes's "Ballad of the Landlord,"[1] he implies that the idea of motivating pupils through the use of contemporary materials close to their experiences was something unheard of among his mindless colleagues. Neil Postman's proposal that multimedia resources should be used as a replacement for printed textbooks ignores the fact that audiovisual materials have been in widespread use in the schools for many years. Look at the British informal schools, they say, if you want to see what inventive educators can do to break the deadly pattern of teacher-dominated lessons, but they shut their eyes to the progressive child-centered methods of early education here at home. The smugness of their pronouncements is matched only by their inaccuracy.

They would have profited from a chastening experience I had during my visit in 1933 to the Soviet Union with a group of British educators to get, among other things, a firsthand knowledge of the schools in a socialist state. At that time, like many other intellectuals, I was sympathetic toward the social experiment that was being undertaken in the Soviet Union and especially interested in its implementation—abandoned later—of John Dewey's "radical" educational ideas, the genesis of "progressive education." As a tourist, I was somewhat dismayed by the general shabbiness of the people's clothing, the run-down condition of most buildings, and the meager offerings in store window displays, but I consoled myself with the thought that these austerities were unavoidable during a period when the government was concentrating on building up the nation's heavy industries.

Among the things the Intourist guide proudly showed us were crèches—day-care centers and nursery schools—for the children of working mothers. Here, surely, there was something to applaud as clear evidence of the concern of a benevolent government for its people. A few weeks later, when I had left the Soviet Union and was traveling by train across the Netherlands, I got into a political discussion with the other occupants of the compartment and brought up the crèches as an indication of the progressiveness of the Soviet Union in contrast to the backwardness of the Western democracies. I thought I had made an unanswerable point, but I was soon put right by the lifted eyebrows and indulgent smiles of the group. "But, of course," one of them said, "we have had crèches in Holland for many years."

A comparable naïveté is shown by Charles E. Silberman in his discussion of current educational trends.[2] He describes at length the radical innovations adopted by a number of school systems, notably the Parkway School in Philadelphia (which uses the city's cultural resources as its textbook) and the John Adams High School in Portland, Oregon (in which unstructured teaching is the norm). Although he is cautious in his evaluation and suspends judgment about their value, he is obviously impressed by these experiments. It is surprising, however, that he should regard these programs as unusual and unprecedented, considering the many similar and equally bold experimental programs undertaken in the past. The fact is that the innovative direction of American public education has been evidenced from the time of its founding under the aegis of Thomas Jefferson's vision of "diffusing knowledge more generally through the mass of the people." Throughout our history, educators have challenged the established curriculums and methods of instruction whenever they were convinced of the need for change. The Laboratory School in Chicago (1896), the Gary Plan in Indiana (1908), and the Dalton Plan in Massachusetts (1920) are only a few of the many ventures in creative design that served as models to the nation at large in revitalizing the schools.[3] As far back as 1935 John G. Granrud, superintendent of schools in Springfield, Massachusetts, carried out a radical transformation of the educational program in that city to make it more relevant to the changing ethnic pattern of the community. The goal of the Springfield Plan was to foster intercultural understanding and to integrate the schools more closely with the community—in John Granrud's words, "to build a bridge to span the chasm between our material resources and our social relationships." The Springfield philosophy had a seminal influence on schools throughout the nation in developing child-centered and community-oriented educational projects.[4] I cite these examples—others are discussed later—to suggest the likelihood that some latter-day reformists are uninformed about the realities of the school picture when they issue their blanket pronouncements.

I do not mean that Charles E. Silberman is ignorant of history. On the contrary, *Crisis in the Classroom* is a model of massive research, documented in redundant fullness, larded with references to and quotations from authorities in every field of scholarship. What I do mean is that

Silberman is handicapped in his appraisal of his material by the fact that he is not a teacher but rather an encyclopedist, an omnivorous journalist surveying his subject from the viewpoint of an outsider. He must rely on secondhand reports, impersonal surveys, inorganic observations of class-rooms through glass doorways. He cannot evaluate a teacher's method of instruction until it has been labeled as traditional or progressive and placed in one of his neat categories. This limitation can be seen, for example, in his uncritical acceptance of his research assistants' anecdotal reports, which are scattered throughout his text under the rubric of "Items," and in his superficial and distorted picture of the high-school curriculum, notably the English program (to be discussed later in detail).

Moreover, Silberman's underlying hostility to educators who question the value of some proposed innovative programs leads to errors of judg-ment. His references and citations are selective and chosen largely for their correspondence with his own biases. One of his major themes, namely, that the constructive energy that infused American education in the past has lost its sense of direction and purpose today, can be attributed to his reliance on value judgments emanating largely from advocates of radical reform. This lack of perspective can be seen in such intemperate statements as: "Indeed progressivism was more widespread in this coun-try than in England in the 20s and 30s—a fact that contributed to its demise in the decades following when the approach was vulgarized be-yond recognition by teachers, principals, and superintendents who mouthed the rhetoric but understood neither the spirit nor the underly-ing theory."[5]

The point is whether education in the United States is responsive to the urgent problems generated by the technological advances, the social unrest, and the political ferment of the present era. I would say all educators are in general agreement about the need for adaptation and change. The decision that must be made in weighing the validity of the reformists' proposals is: (1) whether they are based on a sound appraisal of existing educational policies, and (2) whether they are likely to fulfill their visionary promises. The answers to these questions are the substan-tive theme of this book.

For the sake of clarity, let us begin with a very simple point. One specific charge made by Silberman—echoing Holt and Kozol and Goodman—is that the public schools crush children's individuality by "petty and de-meaning regulations."[6] He refers to the rules that require students to move through the halls between classes in prescribed patterns, to keep close to the walls in passing along corridors, to talk in whispers if at all, to use the up and down stairways properly, and to carry passes when leaving the room. The Owl Critics assert that these regulations are an infringe-ment on the students' personal dignity and a means of infantalizing adolescents. They imply that these rules were devised by insecure and mean-spirited or, more charitably, incompetent pedagogues as a means of asserting their aggressiveness against those least able to resist and of easing the unwelcome burden of controlling energetic children. Jonathan Kozol hints, and not too subtly, that teachers in urban schools are motivated by their animosity toward students of low socioeconomic status, especially the blacks and other minorities.[7] Edgar Z. Friedenberg adds to the litany of abuse by declaring that "teachers have a genuine hostility to these students, often expressed as contempt, solidly based on fear."[8] Silberman's appraisal of the regulations is couched in a clumsy witticism: "These petty rules are necessary not simply because of the importance that schoolmen attach to control—they like to control what comes out of the bladder as well as the mouth—but also because schools and school systems operate on the assumption of mistrust."[9]

I reject this glib psychologizing as totally false. Of course school regulations exist, varying in strictness from school to school. They are not imposed, however, for the reasons suggested. It is precisely because teachers believe individual children should be treated with respect that they approve of and enforce disciplinary rules. Teachers know that the best means of ensuring good behavior in their classes is by developing interest in class activities. If a student is doing something that matters to him, he is likely to be self-disciplined. When a class is absorbed in a project—making costumes for a play, taking part in a panel discussion, listening to a recording of *Hamlet*—the students will behave themselves at least as well as adults do in large groups. But no school can function without striking a delicate balance between individual rights and the performance of its primary task. There may be a Rousseaunian garden somewhere in which children can work together and move in an orderly manner from one area to another without controls, but it is unrealistic to take for granted that this would work out in the matrix of mass education.

It is not being cynical to recognize that the opposite of order is often not liberation but chaos. Can any group of people of any age whatever come together without some rules of conduct? Civilized life requires the acceptance or the imposition of rules that make possible decent human relations. Shoppers take their places in line at the supermarket checkout counters, just as theatergoers do in buying tickets. On the other hand, traffic rules must be enforced or traffic would come to a standstill on city streets and highways. At public meetings, audiences listen quietly to speakers with a common understanding that certain overt responses are permissible and others are not; and the recent experiences of community school board meetings in New York City reduced to a shambles by choral heckling and the invasion of the platform by political activists should be convincing proof of the tenuousness of the sanctions that govern our collective behavior.

Why should schools be different? The school day must be organized on a schedule signaled by bells or other recognizable sounds. In the absence of controls, young children in groups are likely to rush and crowd thoughtlessly and get in one another's way, and stronger and more aggressive youngsters will sometimes tyrannize others. For older students, who must change rooms hourly as they go through the day's schedule, the traffic flow during the passing period (usually no more than five minutes) would be unmanageable unless students were habituated to follow certain traffic patterns. As for the "demeaning" room passes, common sense suggests they are for the protection of children, enabling teachers to know where the students are and serving as a means of identifying intruders. No school administration imposes these restrictions mindlessly.

A more damaging count in the Owl Critics' indictment is that classrooms are "prisons"—this is the usual epithet—in which young people are constrained to receive unwillingly the dictates of their warden teachers. In the current lingo, students are turned off by conventional instructional methods. Charles E. Silberman depicts the typical classroom as an airless chamber in which dull tasks are imposed on children sadistically. "In most classrooms," he writes, "the teacher sits or stands in front of the room, dispensing inert ideas to his passive students as if they were so many empty vessels to be filled."[10] This surrealistic vignette is repeated by the other critics—in fact, it is their stock in trade. They speak disparagingly of the lecture, presumably dull, as the standard method of instruction in the colleges and contrast it with the more stimulating and effective method of interaction and discovery. Perhaps they do not know that the lecture, whatever its value may be, has been virtually unknown as an acceptable teaching method in the secondary schools for time out of mind (although it is now being revived, interestingly enough, in team-teaching programs), and that the developmental lesson, which has been widely adopted as one of the standard methods of teaching, is indeed a "method of discovery." Neil Postman strains our confidence in his judgment and grasp of reality when he reiterates the cliché that most high-school teaching consists of the feeding of dry facts to students to be regurgitated on examinations.[11] The truth is that, ever since the 1930s, curriculums and teaching methods have been designed explicitly to foster critical thinking and to train students to use observable data, that is, hard facts, as the basis of sound inductive reasoning.

There are, to be sure, certain inescapable conditions of classroom teaching that the critics have seized on to make their point. No one can deny that the teacher "sits or stands" at the front of the room. Nor do teachers demur to the charge that a respect for facts (such as names, dates, language patterns, and definitions) is part of what they want their students to acquire. Drill, homework assignments, testing, and grading are indeed inseparable from teaching, in the judgment of most educators. The reformists' proposals to downgrade or eliminate these measures may have some merit or validity in a school setting totally different from what we are familiar with—in a Summerhill or minischool set up to meet the needs of atypical students. But the assertion that these practices are "destructive" is no more pertinent to a rational appraisal of existing schools than would be a description of a violin recital as the scraping of catgut strings with a bow made of bleached horsehairs. These are the external conditions, not the substance, of teaching and learning.

Studies are cited by Silberman and others to indicate that, in most classes observed, the proportion of time during which the teacher was talking or lecturing was excessive, with the result that the individual student had little opportunity to express his own ideas or even to ask questions.[12] The inference drawn from these studies is that conventional teaching is impersonal and repressive of individual self-expression. To doubt the stopwatch allegations of researchers would, of course, be invidious, and I have no intention of doing so. It is to be hoped that alert supervisors would be able to take appropriate steps to remedy the situation. I would merely raise the question of whether the content and quality of the observed lessons served valid educational aims; this would be more significant in evaluating the lessons than the recording of time segments.

Teacher domination, the *bête noire* of doctrinaire pedagogic theory, does not now seem so heinous an offense as it was once thought to be. After all, the advocates of team teaching favor the lecture as an instructional method, and during a lecture it can be presumed that 100 percent of the hour is teacher dominated. Nor are those who favor the broader use of television in the schools disturbed by the fact that students facing the screen are passive auditors and spectators. The crucial point is whether a specific method of communication is appropriate at a given moment in the lesson. A more or less extensive exposition by the teacher of a difficult concept, a series of pivotal questions by the teacher to clarify and reinforce certain elements of the subject, open-ended class discussion of controversial issues, the use of audiovisual aids to extend the subject matter into a nonverbal dimension—all of these teaching methods have a legitimate place in the classroom. It is the teacher's responsibility to be resourceful in adapting these variables to the shifting patterns of the lesson. Within this framework, teacher domination is an acceptable concept.

The failure of mass education to recognize and serve the needs of the individual student is another of the allegations of the reformists. Kozol cites the example of a student who was stigmatized by one teacher after another as a nonlearner because he was sullen and disobedient and black, and was shunted from one class to another by unsympathetic administrators.[13] Holt describes a bright, eager girl who was suffocated by pedestrian assignments in literature and became an avid reader only when released by Holt's personal interest and his encouragement of free reading.[14] These children, and a host of other victims of the impersonality inherent in mass education, are exhibited with the same intense condemnation as Charles Dickens projected in his portrayal of the plight of orphans in *Oliver Twist*. How can teachers be so callous to the sensitivities of Tom and Maria and Luis, who enter their classes with eager curiosity and are bludgeoned day after day into sullen passivity?

The answer is that administrators and teachers are very deeply and genuinely concerned with Tom and Maria and Luis. Administrative policies are redesigned, courses of study revised, new teaching methods developed, for the very purpose of providing as favorable an environment and as extensive a variety of experiences as is possible in the school situation to meet the students' predictable needs. At the same time, educators cannot ignore the practical obstacles to the immediate full attainment of individualized instruction.

The goal of adapting a school's program to the individual needs of students is a guiding principle that can too easily become a fetish. Every child is, of course, a separate physical entity and every child's psychological makeup is indeed unique. But it would be pretentious for any teacher to think he can understand each child in his class or, for that matter, know any one child in depth. To catalogue the intellectual aptitudes, the patterns of reaction, the subconscious motivations, and the emotional coloration and moods of any child is beyond the capacity of the child's teachers and even that of his parents. Therefore, the commitment to individualized instruction must mean something other than gearing instruction to the individual child's unique nature.

Teachers must work on the assumption—until modified by experience—that a given tenth year class in English or mathematics or any other subject is composed of students who have in common the normal drives and interests of adolescents in their age group. In the class context, traits of personality that are not germane to the role of the learner must be excluded from the foreground of consideration for the time being. Out of the infinite number of possibilities, the behavior patterns and dispositions that are functional in classroom activities are the only ones that matter at the moment. Attention to one thing means literally inattention to others.

Too much is made of serving the individual child. Schools serve groups of children. Does this mean the individual child is ignored? Not at all. When a lesson is being well taught, every student in the class shares much the same experiences—he becomes aware of an interesting problem, he discovers and follows the steps likely to lead to a solution, he reaches an intellectually satisfying conclusion. Of course, students grasp the material at varying rates of comprehension, and here it is the teacher's skill in adjusting the lesson to individual differences that comes into play. The range and variety of perception are probably more constricted in mathematics and the sciences than in English and social studies, where the subject matter lends itself more readily to individual interpretation and originality of thought. But in all cases the perceptions of each student are uniquely his own, just as members of an audience listening to a Beethoven symphony register the musical sounds as an infinity of subjective images and fantasies. Mass education is not inconsistent with individual self-fulfillment.

What in fact happens in a classroom in a conventional school following a traditional program? The answer is refreshingly simple. Teachers do their best to interest their students in specific areas of scholarship by asking questions, presenting problems, opening up directions for inquiry; and students engage in reading, research, discussion, and other activities to find answers and solutions. The problem may be that of framing a precise definition: to describe the characteristics of living things. Or it may be a political problem: to determine how the Bill of Rights functions in our democratic institutions. Or it may be a matter of literary understanding: to explore Dickens's use of satire in his novels. Students' activities are not limited to mastery of a textbook, although most often the textbook is an irreplaceable instrument for efficient learning. They do library research to prepare reports; in groups, they present forums and panel discussions on timely, significant topics; they enact scenes from plays or improvise sociodramas; they work in laboratories and shops; they make posters, produce newspapers and magazines, rehearse orchestral and choral pieces. The classroom is an arena of creative activity as much as it is a center of formal instruction.

The Owl Critics, however, seem to be unaware of how teachers conduct their classes in the schools of today. They have revived the stereotype of the school teacher as a bumbling eccentric, a petty tyrant, a dull pedant. Silberman lards the text of his book *Crisis in the Classroom* with a number of anecdotal exhibits that reflect this stereotype. These "Items," as they are labeled, purport to be actual happenings observed in classrooms. The reader is asked to accept these incidents as authentic and typical. One Item depicts an elementary teacher whose pupils are eagerly crowding around the turtle tank in their science corner petulantly ordering the children back to their seats because her plan for that day was to teach about the life cycle and habit of crabs.[15] Another Item describes a suburban school—referred to as a school "of the future" in architectural design, with the classrooms arranged around a central library core—in which the children are permitted to visit the library for only one period a week, and then only "to practice taking books from the shelves and replacing them." They are forbidden to read the books, we are told, because the spelling teacher, who doubles as the librarian, prefers neat little spelling drills to the demanding task of getting children to become readers.[16] This kind of spurious fiction, suggested as typical of what happens in our public schools, can only be attributed to Silberman's guilelessness or malice. (For one thing, the term *spelling teacher* is a nonexistent category in any school system I have ever heard of.)

There is one Item that must be quoted in full to show the acrimonious undertone of Silberman's indictment:

> A sixth grade class in a racially mixed school. A black girl calls out an answer to a question that the teacher had asked of the entire class. "Don't you call out," the teacher responds. "You sit where I put you and be quiet." A few minutes later, when a blond-haired, blue-eyed girl calls out an answer to another question, the teacher replies, "Very good, Annette, that's good thinking."[17]

On the face of it, this is nothing short of a clumsy libel.

The readiness of the pubic to accept this distorted picture of teachers and schools as the truth stems in part from the impact of two bestselling novels of the recent past: *The Blackboard Jungle,* by Ian Hunter, and *Up the Down Staircase,* by Bel Kaufman.

Hunter's novel pictured a school in disarray—uncontrolled violence everywhere, defiance of authority, contemptuous hostility to learning, total disintegration and chaos. Millions of readers accepted this work of fiction as a factual representation, and the motion picture made from the novel affected its viewers deeply. As a work of fiction, *The Blackboard Jungle* made legitimate use of exaggeration, dramatic highlighting of details that supported its thesis, and distortion of the realities of conditions in schools generally. The book was received, however, as a documentary account of conditions in New York's vocational high schools and, by extension, high schools everywhere. The term *blackboard jungle* came to be synonymous with the breakdown of urban schools in slum areas. Ian Hunter's grim symbol of decay became part of America's folklore. The result is that most people have uncritically accepted Hunter's fictional construct as the truth, assuming that his appraisal of school conditions was authentic. The fact is that Ian Hunter's credentials for making a valid judgment about the schools were minimal. It is no derogation of his literary achievement to reveal that he taught in the English department of the Bronx Vocational High School for no more than a few months and that, on resigning from his post, he wrote a grateful letter to the chairman of the English department expressing his appreciation for the professional help he had received and the pleasant relationships he had formed with his pupils and fellow teachers. Hunter's novel must be regarded as a potboiler lacking in authenticity, grist for the Hollywood money mills.

Bel Kaufman's book *Up the Down Staircase* has a more insidious disqualification as a guide to an understanding of the truth about urban education. It is a very funny and clever and entertaining book and its portraiture of students and teachers is disarmingly perceptive. However, it is essentially a collection of comic-book drawings of the more vulnerable qualities of school personnel. There is, indeed, much to be satirized in the reams of mimeographed directives that school administrators issue, often expressed in a wordy and opaque jargon that has come to be known as *pedaguese.* But Bel Kaufman's impatience with the creaking machinery of school management leads her to represent all but a handful of the school staff as utter fools—the principal, the chairmen of departments, the guidance counselors, the administrative assistants, the school nurse, the teachers, and the parents. She reserves her sympathy for two teachers, one a thinly disguised self-portrait, the other an idealistic, uncorrupted innocent who beats her wings bravely against the walls of official stupidity. Moreover, despite her compassion for the students and her awareness of their insuperable problems and handicaps, Kaufman uses them—I should say, exploits them—for literary rather than humane purposes. She records their barbarisms in speech and writing for laughs. She calls attention to their pathetic illiteracy in a manner reminiscent of low-grade vaudeville, "Amos and Andy," and the parlor jokes that poke fun at Jewish and Negro dialects. The readers of *Up the Down Staircase* come away with a lasting impression of the futility of public education and the incompetence of its managers. Long after the book has been laid aside, its subliminal influence lingers.

I have worked in the New York City schools for forty years as a teacher and supervisor of English in the high schools. Neither I nor my colleagues were blind to the conditions Hunter and Kaufman describe. We knew, however, of the constructive efforts of deans and guidance counselors and the Bureau of Child Guidance to deal with the stubborn problems of alienation and delinquency, and we were heartened by the variety of educational programs—the More Effective Schools, Higher Horizons, College Discovery—that were being developed to cope with the problems of disadvantaged students. We were concerned: we talked education at faculty conferences, committee meetings, and even in conversations over the lunch table. We took pride in our vocation. Good teaching was an art to be mastered by intelligence and sustained effort. Within the dust-edged walls and behind the impersonal windows of school buildings were men and women who could get excited about lesson plans and motivational devices and new approaches to our subjects.

Those of us who were in English strove to work out what we thought were ingenious ways of getting our students involved. We scoured the library and consulted the English journal for fresh reading materials. Most of us did not question at the time whether Shakespeare and Dickens and Hawthorne were suitable for the average student; the movement to downgrade the great books was then without support. Our job, as we saw it, was to find ways of making the classics meaningful and enjoyable and, innocents that we were, relevant. We played recordings of John Gielgud doing Macbeth and Robert Frost reading his own poems. We attended the demonstration lessons sponsored by the Association of Teachers of English on Saturdays, where we watched classes—conducted by volunteer teachers for volunteer students—being taught paragraph writing or poetry appreciation or propaganda analysis and spent hours discussing the strengths and weaknesses of the observed lessons. We served on committees at the Bureau of Curriculum Development to construct fresh syllabus materials for advanced placement classes, reading clinics, and electives in specialized areas. We were far from being Silberman's mindless pedants who stifle the curiosity of children and give them "little opportunity, and no reason, to develop resolute ideas of their own about what they learn."[18]

This book is an attempt to justify the ways of teachers to those they serve.

2 AND GLADLY TEACH

The heckling chorus of "Down with the Teacher" goes on unabated. We hear it in Charles Silberman's description of the dullard who "sits or stands in front of the room, dispensing inert ideas to his passive students." It is echoed in John Holt's supercilious remark that "in more cases than not, it is the act of instruction that impedes learning."[1] The target of these smug pronouncements is, of course, the archetypal teacher as seen in the flawed mirror of the Owl Critics' perception, the fictional teacher who crushes individuality and blights the growing mind. This portrait, however, has little resemblance to what teachers are really like.

First, the stereotype is not borne out in students' evaluation of their school experience. Is it true that the schools are in fact joyless and repressive? Any number of surveys of students' feelings about their education indicates the contrary to be true. A 1971 study by *Life* magazine showed that about 85 percent of the students interviewed, coming from all parts of the country, liked school and valued their educational experience. It would be naïve, of course, to think that students are never bored and frustrated in class—as all of us are at times with our jobs, our families, our social life. Perhaps we can say of schooling what Winston Churchill said of democracy: "A democratic society is probably the least efficient type of social order, with the exception of all other types."

Second, the stereotype does not account for the diversity in competence and attitude observable in any teaching staff. No two lessons are ever conducted in identical ways. There is no standard lesson in mathematics or English or any other subject, although most lessons on a given topic may converge toward what may be called a model lesson. Students are quick to discover the different styles and idiosyncrasies of their teachers, and as they move from one class to another in their day's schedule, they learn to adjust their expectations to each teacher's varying methods and standards. In a very real sense, the students' exposure to these variables of intellect and personality is part of their education. If the stereotype does exist, it is a well-kept secret.

The prevalence of "inert ideas" in the curriculum, as charged by Silberman and others, must also be challenged. Any objective evaluation of the content of standard courses of study would reject Silberman's epithet as specious. The "idea" that stones and feathers fall to earth at equal rates of acceleration; the "idea" that the New Deal was a watershed in the political history of the nation; the "idea" that the white whale in Melville's *Moby Dick* may be interpreted as a complex symbol—these are typical of the kinds of ideas disseminated by teachers in classrooms. In the hierarchy of ideas, some are undoubtedly more significant at a given moment than others, but the inertness and dullness that are seen by Silberman as the norm of curricular content probably exist only in the mind of the beholder.

The implication in John Holt's statement that "it is the act of instruction that impedes learning" is similarly a distortion of the teacher's role. It is true, to be sure, that much is learned by children (by adults as well) without the formal intervention of any other person, whether parent or teacher. Linguistic patterns and certain behavioral adjustments seem to be acquired without instruction, although it is probable that the parent plays more than a peripheral role in the process. When we speak of teachers as acting *in loco parentis,* we mean that they must exercise control and establish standards of conduct while offering encouragement and emotional support—as biological mothers and fathers do. Like parents, teachers perform their vicarious role in different ways—some are more directive and some are more permissive. But teachers in school have a specialized function, that is, to provide the tools of intellectual growth—something as concrete as knowledge and skills and something as intangible as concepts and appreciations—that most likely would not be acquired without formal instruction. To relinquish this responsibility in the fatuous hope that somehow children and adolescents will acquire intellectual skills and basic knowledge through their self-directed efforts is unthinkable.

Teachers know that the classroom is not the only learning environment in the school. That is why schools provide a setting for informal learning in extracurricular programs—clubs, teams, the school newspaper and literary magazine, science fairs, school plays and concerts. In these activities, the teacher can relate to students more like an indulgent uncle or doting aunt than a demanding parent. The impersonality of class instruction gives way to informal conversation, whimsical humor, and a general loosening of restraints. Here learning takes the form of experiment in self-discovery and social adjustment, an extension of the kind of natural education that takes place uninterruptedly outside of school. Education is, indeed, the function of every breathing moment of a child's life. The street, friends and playmates, birthday parties, experiments with training pets and growing radishes in the back yard, building things with hammer and nails, discovering new worlds through the eyes of Walt Disney and Jules Verne—all of these experiences weave the fabric of our minds.

There are, too, the unexpected encounters within the school setting by which we become aware of our emotional selves without the intervention of parents or teachers or anyone else. I can recall, aged nine, being appointed as monitor to guard the entrance doors of the school (Public School No. 84 in the Brownsville section of Brooklyn) during the lunch period, when students were required, after eating at home, to remain outside the building until the bell. One day a tough kid tried to push his way past me with a drawn knife—it was really a small pocketknife—and somehow I summoned up enough courage to grab his wrist and force him out, my heart pounding with fear. My graduation from elementary school was tarnished—and perhaps memorialized—by the sight of a beggar standing piteously in the doorway of the school building as my parents and I were leaving, my proud moment turned to guilt-ridden dust. I recall, too, the hectic and exhilarating day at Townsend Harris High School when, seized by some tribal impulse, the student body, ordinarily models of academic conformity and docility, walked out of school and staged a noisy demonstration to protest the monotony and tastelessness of the fare in the school lunchroom.

But the classroom is certainly one of the vital centers of our formative years, and teachers play significant roles in our expanding perceptions, often unappreciated by the egotism that besets all children and adolescents under the imperatives of their little comprehended emotional drives. In retrospect, I am certain the question of whether they were traditional or innovative teachers or what schools of educational psychology or methodology they subscribed to had no meaning for any of us. They were simply there, sitting or standing in front of the class, and in our eyes they were patently endowed with omniscience and omnipotence. On the whole, I think my teachers were splendid men and women.[2]

Miss Heckman, a slim, towering figure, was our teacher in the fourth grade. I remember nothing about her skill in teaching or her personality except for one instant of revelation she somehow contrived in the course of an otherwise forgotten semester of lessons. One day, in the drawing period—call it art appreciation, esthetic sensitizing, development of creative skills—Miss Heckman displayed a sheet of white cardboard in the shape of a circle held vertically facing the class and asked us to draw what we observed. Dutifully, we attempted to produce our approximations of circles freehand, certainly not as perfectly as Michelangelo did with easy expertise for Pope Julius, but accurately enough, I suppose. Then she pivoted the cardboard disk toward us halfway from the vertical position and asked us once again to draw what we saw. I don't know how the other pupils fared, but for me nothing was observable except the same circular Euclidean form, and that is what I drew. I vividly recall Miss Heckman, after some inspection of our creations, drawing on the blackboard a bold ellipse, which, to our astonishment, was indeed an accurate representation.

Finally, she rotated the cardboard until its edge, held at eye level, faced the class. What was the shape we now saw? A circle? An ellipse? A curved line? This was a moment of crisis—none of us could supply the right answer. Then Miss Heckman gave us the answer: it was a straight line. This was impossible—and yet, when we looked again, the white cardboard disk did really look like a straight line, although, I imagine, some students must have had secret reservations about this simple truth.

In the following days we created myriads of circles, ellipses, and straight lines based on models of whitish-gray cylinders and cubes and pyramids set before us. We diligently, and I suppose happily, filled our coarse-grained drawing pads with a variety of still-life representations. I suppose none of us even remotely thought of the relevance of our activities to educational principles or curricular aims, but in fact we were the beneficiaries of a planned educational program devised by bookish professors of educational psychology or pedagogy at some Olympian research institution and formulated by bureaucrats at the Board of Education as part of the fourth grade art syllabus. How could we know that Miss Heckman was teaching us the concept of visual perspective?

Years later, in a lecture hall at City College, New York, I was one of about three hundred chemistry students who were listening with various degrees of attention to a lecture given by Professor Baskerville, a lean, intense figure at the lectern, expounding the theory of periodicity of the chemical elements. It was about halfway through a harrowing semester and we had already listened, read, experimented clumsily in the laboratory, studied for weekly tests—in short, we had experienced the drudgery of rediscovering, as generations of students had done before us, the grandeur and mystery of the physical universe. Not that all of us thought of the course as a metaphysical or esthetic experience—it would be foolish to think so. Nevertheless, we were impressed, if even occasionally and subliminally, by this glimpse into the secret workshop of nature that scientists were exploring and reducing to something like order.

But this lecture by Professor Baskerville was a revelation of such magnitude as to transform my conception of the universe forever. I remember the huge chart on the wall behind the lecturer—the Periodic Table of Chemical Elements—on which were the symbols of all the known chemical elements arranged in the increasing order of their atomic weights. The first six elements—beginning with H (Hydrogen)—were placed on the first horizontal line, and the seventh was placed under the first, and so on. The result was a neat arrangement of the symbols in six vertical columns, and lo and behold! all the elements that fell into each vertical column had similar properties, forming a pattern of geometric symmetry. These vertical columns—I recall only some of them: the inert elements, the halogens, the acids, the metals—constituted for me a startling demonstration of the underlying uniformity that governs the world of nature. Man's probing exploration of the nuclear structure of the atom would range infinitely farther in the next few years, far beyond the rudimentary

conceptions we were acquiring, but the pattern of the search for knowledge and truth that constitutes the method of the sciences was made
visible to me in this great moment of revelation.

There were other teachers who impressed me in a less momentous way,
even though most of the things that happened in their classes have faded.
I remember Mr. Kovar, whose mission as a teacher of the children of
immigrants was passionately undertaken, teaching some point in formal
grammar—I think it was the objective case of pronouns—and at one point
turning to the class as if pleading for understanding: "You see it, boys,
don't you? It's the objective *whom*. Think. Think." There was the urbane
Mr. Coleman, who once slashed the salutary comment "too ornate" across
the phrase "the ebon shades of night" in a composition of mine describing
an evening scene in the city. There was Mr. Abrams, testy and energetic,
who had a passion for mental arithmetic and flung out addition and
subtraction problems to my confusion and embarrassment, until one day I
suddenly caught on to the secret of digital placement. I recall, too, with
mixed feelings, a teacher of English at City College, known for his extraordinary respect for Walter Scott's historical romances, who one day
challenged his unconverted class, consisting in those days of committed
radicals and devotees of Theodore Dreiser and Upton Sinclair, to come
up one by one before the class and present a rational critique of his idol, as
if it were possible to do so.

Some of my teachers were martinets and some were gentle souls; their
methods of teaching varied widely and were probably hammered out of
their experience rather than derived coherently from pedagogic theory.
But they believed in their vocation, underpaid as they were, for they were
among the dedicated company of those who, like Chaucer's Clerk of
Oxford, "would gladly learn and gladly teach."

The growing tendency in recent years to describe teachers as practitioners of a somewhat less than professional craft has been given cre-
dence in part by the disparaging comments of Edgar Z. Friedenberg. His
opinion rests on the assumption that those who enter teaching are limited
by their "timid and constrained" personalities and by the inadequacy of
their preparation in liberal arts colleges or teacher-training institutions
where standards of scolarship are minimal.[3] This judgment has been
strengthened by studies that show college students who indicate their
intention to major in education have lower-than-average scholastic aptitude. It is not easy to assess these judgments. But this much can be said:
the art of teaching, like that of medicine or law, is so complex an act that
any theoretical preparation can do no more than acquaint the prospective
teacher with the rudiments of his profession. The teacher must learn
nine-tenths of his craft on the job, testing his theoretical knowledge by its
success or failure in the arena of daily encounter with children. During his
training period at college or graduate school he is required to take part in

a student-teaching program, and in his probationary years in the class-room he reinforces his experience by required in-service courses, work-shops, or graduate courses related to his specialty. Moreover, the teacher, especially at the secondary level, is a scholar in at least one area of the curriculum and, in a well-managed school system, is motivated to keep closely in touch with the most recent developments in his field.

Most teachers enter the profession because they have ideals, a social conscience, a desire to mold the minds of youth. They have conviction about the importance of their work. They are not unwordly—they know what's going on in the world of the arts and sciences, politics, and sports. They do not fit into any of the stereotypes set up for them. They are not sycophants or puppets who tremble at the pull of the string; on the contrary, they are individualists, self-assertive, defensive. They do not pretend to be psychological therapists who have a cure for every student's hangups. They are not nice guys who never scold or lose patience. They are tolerant of divergent viewpoints in others and especially in students, but they are not tolerant of opinions based on ignorance of facts. Some indeed may be hostile toward insolent, lawless, and self- and other-destructive students. Fundamentally, they are committed to the principle that youth cannot grow to a healthy maturity without guidance and direction.

Teachers formed in the mold of the image proposed by the Owl Critics will presumably have a very different conception of their role. They will pride themselves on being as much in the dark as the students they deal with; they will have no answers to the questions they raise or that they encourage their students to raise. They will never express their own opinions for fear of stifling curiosity. They will not require homework or impose drill exercises since they are wedded to the theory of self-expression as the ultimate value. They will never test their classes because they believe testing is a form of adult tyranny and shows distrust of children. They will compensate for their self-imposed passivity in the classroom by pretending to be merely children or adolescents writ some-what larger on the physical scale. They will drift comfortably with the current of impulse and whim because they have been schooled in the temples of antiintellectualism, beating the drums of relevance, contem-poraneity, and innovation endlessly to shut out the clamor of the busy marketplace and the marching feet of men.[4]

No institution in which human agents play a major role is immune to the failings of human nature. We have not yet constructed a brave new world in which stupidity, laziness, and venality do not exist. The courts, the civil service, the corporate hierarchy—all are impaired by the weaknesses of men and women on the job who perform their duties perfunctorily or negligently. The schools, too, have their share of incompetents and timeservers who have resigned themselves to apathy and face-saving routines, and there are many sincere teachers who are handicapped by their inability to communicate with the new breed of students. Reforms in curriculum and methodology can be no more productive than are the teachers and administrators who carry them into classroom practice.

One of my earliest experiences as a chairman of a department made me conscious of this truth in an ironic way. When a supervisor is newly assigned to a school, the teaching staff goes through the trauma of being jolted out of their comfortable habits, and teachers await the first official visit of the new chairman to their classes with apprehension. The teachers in my department—the English department at Seward Park High School in New York City—did not realize that the inspectorial visitor to their classrooms was as insecure and as immobilized by tension as they were. Nevertheless, formal observations had to be carried out. In most cases, the classes observed were orderly and obviously engaged in serious work; and my portentous appearance in the doorway was signaled by nothing more than a momentary turning of heads in my direction.

In one instance, however, things were different. Miss M's class was in a state of utter chaos. Students were out of their seats, standing around in noisy groups, some at the windows, a few with tabloid newspapers open at their seats, and others milling about in various patterns of horseplay. The teacher was seated at her desk, apparently working at a heap of test papers or compositions, her red pencil poised. The startled look on her face as she noticed me entering the room was like that of the Queen as Hamlet spoke to her—"Amazement on thy mother sits," said the Ghost—and even the cacophony of the disorderly students was stilled momentarily as if they had been frozen into immobility by the Medusa's stare. This was a critical moment. But Miss M. rose to the occasion with an aplomb that earned my everlasting admiration. With perfect poise, she announced: "Children, this is Mr. Vogel, the chairman of the English department. Now, please go on with your group projects."

I was reminded by this experience of an episode in the television series *Room 222,* which, unlike most portrayals of the schools, depicted an urban or suburban school with a degree of honesty and understanding. The episodes were sometimes sentimental in the portrayal of character, but the main thrust of the classroom scenes seemed to be in the direction of presenting the teaching-learning situation as a serious and demanding business. The history teacher, on whom the camera was most often focused, was not dogmatic, overbearing, or rigid. His great strength was his awareness of the need to teach history as a way of throwing light on the problems of today. He drew parallels between the past and the present, and he encouraged a close critical examination of shibboleths and commonly held assumptions about the nation's enshrined leaders.

In one case his class was discussing the attitude of Abraham Lincoln toward Negro slavery, and the students were guided in their analysis of documentary evidence—letters, speeches, state papers—to discover a certain ambivalence in the troubled soul of the Great Emancipator.

Now the scriptwriter for *Room 222* was probably sensitive to the currents of change in the educational scene and felt obliged to render lip service at least to innovative teaching method if only to avoid being charged with bias in favor of musty conventional practices. So, when he depicted his history teacher in the middle of one episode conducting a recitation on the Civil War and actually quizzing his motley class on the facts of the early military campaigns of the war, the writer faced a dilemma. He must have realized that the initial question: "What was the first battle of the Civil War?" is the kind of question no enlightened and progressive teacher ever puts to his classes. The second question was even more suspect: "What was the outcome of the Battle of Bull Run?" The scriptwriter must have become aware at this point that he was treading on slippery ground and should provide a way to undo the damage he was causing to the image of his "innovative" classroom. The solution he found was a happy one.

The long-haired student who was asked the second question fidgeted and sputtered but could not supply an answer—this was not a matter of opinion but a hard, cold fact. So the teacher came to his rescue—and to the rescue of the scriptwriter's self-esteem—by admonishing the student in these words: "That's too bad. Apparently you haven't done your research on the subject sufficiently." Research, indeed! Not old-fashioned homework or study, but research, a concept more dear to the hearts of reformists.

These and other similar observations have convinced me that there is no magic formula for good teaching. All efforts to mold a staff into neuter exemplars of approved methodology are bound to fail. Teachers will always be themselves, in speech and gesture, in their humor, in their tolerance or lack of it, and in their energy levels. A common denominator of commitment to teaching subject matter and developing intellectual skills must be inherent in their classroom behavior, whatever their diverse approaches may be. The one deadly sin in teachers is apathy, or indifference.

As chairman of a large department, I soon discovered that the best efforts of supervisors and administrators are bound to be thwarted by what may be called the irreducible quantum of individuality that teachers exhibit and will defend to the death. They will not be cast in a mold. It follows that uniformity of teaching method will not be insisted on by a pragmatic supervisor for, if it were demanded, it could not possibly be enforced. This was illustrated in the eccentric procedures of two members of my department that irritated me at the time. In retrospect, however, I think it would have been folly to attempt to change them.

Mr. P. never, or rarely, taught a lesson that was planned in detail or carried out in accordance with any recognizable method of procedure. He improvised and digressed at every point that offered a pretext for doing so. He was a brilliant raconteur, and took every opportunity to bring into the classroom his rich background of experience in the theatre and literary circles. He spread before his students a feast of reminiscence and anecdote derived from his direct contact with writers, actors, and bohemians whom he had known personally. Perhaps he was miscast as a pedagogue. He was a compulsive talker and would probably have been more comfortable in a Greenwich Village café with like-minded companions playing the part of Dr. Johnson to a coterie of Boswells. When I visited his classroom, I was entranced by his delightful stories about Edna St. Vincent Millay and Eugene O'Neill (whom he had known well), and I could not help feeling that his fortunate students were being drawn into an appreciation of literature as effectively as if they had been called on to analyze and discuss the texts of "Renascence" or "Beyond the Horizon" in exemplary lessons.

At the other extreme was Mrs. H., a large-framed, loud-voiced, stern disciplinarian. Through the years, she had acquired certain habits of class management that were unshakable. Nothing I said—or what authorities in the field preached in professional journals or expounded in texts on methodology—could dissuade her from her conviction that students had to be beaten into submission to be educated. She believed—not quite in the same sense as Jacques Barzun did—that "the teacher must not rest content with demanding attention—he must command it." I observed Mrs. H. on several occasions, and each time, whether the lesson was on grammar or poetry, her manner was equally imperious. When she taught grammar, every square inch on the blackboard was filled with illustrations of common errors, lists of spelling demons, and exercises in punctuation, to be converted into automatisms by ceaseless drill. With literature her attack was equally aggressive. What does this word mean? What is the figure of speech? And so on. There was no moment in her lessons when her resonant voice did not dominate.

This dogmatic trait was equally true of her manner at staff meetings and supervisory conferences. I recall most vividly the time Mrs. H. stormed into my office waving a written report I had made after a class visit in which I had suggested that she allow students to express their opinions at some point in the lesson. She flung the report on my desk with obvious contempt and bellowed, "Mr. Vogel, what kind of asininity is this?" I had no ready answer.

The leavening of a strong department by one or two such nonconformists is, on the whole, not unsalutary. Think of the possible alternative: teaching machines and programmed textbooks in which communication is reduced to robotlike signals. Breathing teachers can, at least, bring ideas to life in shared responses.

How boards of education find the men and women who are knowledgeable, empathetic, and committed varies from one community to another. Requirements of college and graduate degrees, a certain number of credits in education courses, student teaching or internship experience, together with some form of state certification, are usually taken for granted as minimal. In a few large municipal school systems, written examinations are administered to test scholarship and pedagogic concepts and interview tests are held to assess the less tangible qualities of applicants—speech, interpersonal skills, personality traits related to teaching in obvious and subtle ways.

It is a truism to say that college and graduate courses are less contributory as pragmatic preparation for the job than are student teaching and internship. Most important, it is generally agreed, is the teacher's probationary period in the classroom. Such apprenticeship, however, does not in itself assure professional growth. Its value depends largely on what policies are followed in the schools or school system to foster growth. Is there a supervisor—an assistant principal, or department chairman—who takes on the training function through class visitations, conferences, supportive services? Is there a program of curriculum development and syllabus construction in which teachers take a significant part? Are in-service courses and workshops provided for systematic refinement of concepts and techniques? Only under such a program of induction into the profession can teachers become fairly secure in their command of materials and methods and somewhat competent in dealing with interpersonal factors.

In the sixties, the preparation of teachers came under fire by a number of authorities, among them James B. Conant and Hyman Rickover, who noted that prospective teachers were likely to concentrate on courses in educational theory and techniques at the expense of courses in subject matter. The response of most school systems was in the nature of a reflex action, that is, the number of prerequisite courses for certification was reapportioned in some way. Concurrently, a National Teachers Examination was developed by the Educational Testing Service that could serve to assure minimum standards of selection.

Then, in the early seventies, the validity of tests was challenged by a number of critics in and outside the profession. "Does a high score on a qualifying examination insure successful performance in the classroom?" it was asked. The answer obviously had to be negative, although no responsible educator had ever asserted that tests in themselves could be predictively valid. However, when Judge Walter Mansfield of the federal court held, in a landmark decision in 1971, that there was no evidence of correlation between scores on tests for supervisors in New York City and their performance as principals and chairmen, the issue became a matter of national concern.

Judge Mansfield ruled that the tests administered by the New York City Board of Examiners—tests of scholarship in subject areas as well as administrative and supervisory skills—could not be shown to have predictive validity. Therefore, he concluded, the black and Hispanic applicants for licenses, who had brought the legal action, were justified in their complaint that the tests were de facto, although not deliberately, discriminatory. The result of the Mansfield decision was to bring to a grinding halt for six years all examinations for supervisors and administrators in New York City.

Encouraged by this decision, an applicant for a teacher's license brought a similar action to challenge the validity of tests for teachers (*Rubinos* vs. *The Board of Examiners,* 1976). Among the test items cited as inappropriate were questions on basic scholarship in English, mathematics, science, and history. In open court, the attorney for Rubinos, without the trace of a smile, presented the argument that there was no conclusive evidence that a teacher of mathematics, for example, need know more about arithmetic or algebra or geometry than his students did. There was no research study available, said the lawyer, to refute this proposition. No research, indeed, save the common experience of mankind from the dawn of civilization. Even if it is conceded that lawyers in their adversary role are obligated to promote their clients' causes with every sophisticated weapon in their arsenal, to advance so absurd an argument staggers credibility. Yet, as shown in later chapters, this is what in essence the Owl Critics—Carl Rogers and John Holt among others— have said.

Let it be said here that the most valuable ingredient in the process of education is the skill and dedication of the classroom teacher. All innovative restructuring of administration or curriculum is a meaningless charade without a staff of competent teachers at the center of things to awaken interest in and throw light on seemingly dull and remote areas of scholarship. Nor can teachers be successful unless they are ready to search out new materials and inventive methods of communication, humanizing the rigorous task of teaching the young by giving everything of themselves.

I have seen this in many classrooms. Teachers have learned to introduce the study of poetic figures of speech by showing how everyday language is enriched by metaphor and hyperbole and using rock 'n' roll recordings as a pathway to the appreciation of poetic imagery in Tennyson and Millay. In the hands of resourceful teachers, *Romeo and Juliet* gains a contemporary dimension by being linked with *West Side Story,* and *Julius Caesar* becomes a more exciting play when taught as an analogue of current political upheavals. On many occasions, I have seen teachers using ingenious devices for making literature exciting—in one instance, for example, making use of improvised sociodramas showing a parent

reprimanding a child, an employer scolding a worker, a principal admonishing a student, thus making vivid the theme of domination. The
teaching of spelling is unavoidably a matter of repetitive drill, but even
here teachers have discovered how to lighten the task by developing
pupils' interest in the origin of words. Grammar and the mechanics of
punctutation become more palatable when presented with a touch of
humor, as Maxwell Nurnberg demonstrated in his textbook *What's the
Good Word?* to the delight of generations of students.

These illustrations could be multiplied by the thousands. They have
been and continue to be the creative ways of teaching that refute the idea
that banality and mindlessness prevail in the schools of America.

3

THE DEAD HAND
OF CONSERVATISM

Perhaps the most pervasive criticism of the public schools, implicit in those already cited, is that the "dead hand of the past" prevents needed reconstruction. "What is mostly wrong with the schools," writes Charles Silberman, "is due not to venality or indifference or stupidity, but mindlessness—the failure to think seriously about educational purpose, the reluctance to question established practice."[1] This kind of blanket assertion, to be sure, contains a partial truth: all institutions have a certain inertia that inhibits rapid transformation of their structures even when there is recognized need for change. In the nature of things, proposals that involve far-reaching changes in policy are critically examined until there is ample evidence of the advantages of the new as compared with the known values of the established order. This cautious attitude, however, does not preclude responsive changes in institutions, either self-initiated or imposed, when there is patent evidence of their failure to carry out their assigned function. The schools, no less than other institutions, have anticipated outside pressure for reform by initiating and carrying out the most extensive reforms on their own.

It is a misconception, fashionable today in reformist circles, to think that the schools do not respond to the currents of doctrine that swirl about them. School administrators subscribe to *The Nation's Schools* and the *Harvard Educational Journal,* attend regional and national conventions, and read the books that trumpet the need for change. They are sensitive to the charges, repeated ad nauseam, that education "has failed to meet the challenge of this century" and that "the conventional curriculum structure corresponds far more clearly to the needs and opportunities of former generations than to our own." Above all, they are accountable daily to their students, their staffs, the parents and the community, the school boards—and to their own self-esteem as professional educators.

The Owl Critics seem to be blind to the fact that the schools of the United States have traditionally been hospitable to change. As a consequence, programs devised in past decades and embedded in educational practice for many years are now being proposed by the critics as "radical" solutions to today's problems.

"Many contemporary innovators," writes George M. Antonelli, pointing to this anomaly, "approach the persistent and recurring problems of educational improvement with the naïve belief that no one ever considered these problems before. Indeed, innovators of the past decade have attempted to solve these problems with scant attention to the historical dimensions of these problems. Consequently, many current innovations can be classified as revivals or reinventions."[2]

For example, the value of independent study for exceptional students is stressed in every school brochure as an innovative program. The student is released from class attendance to carry out a self-directed project of library research, interviews, laboratory experiments, or participation in a community institution under the supervision and guidance of a teacher-counselor. Recently, a number of colleges have sanctioned independent study by permitting students, among them working adults, to carry out individual study projects at home, only periodically, once a month or so, consulting with their instructors at the college. These are advertised as pioneer efforts to break the mold of conventional classroom instruction.

It is no disparagement of these programs to point out that their roots are imbedded in concepts and practices that existed at the turn of the century and perhaps earlier. The Dalton Plan and its affiliated programs (to be described later) involved a mode of self-directed study, and the Project Method, which was developed sometime in the twenties, encouraged students, individually or in groups, to investigate interesting aspects of the subject in greater depth than was possible in the class setting. In conventional teaching procedures, too, the assignment of topical reports and term papers provided opportunities for individual enrichment and creative fieldwork integrated with the content of a structured course of study. The lockstep formalism of traditional teaching methods is largely a myth based, as noted by Professor Antonelli, on lack of information.

Similarly, the "school without walls" shibboleth, now credited as a pioneer effort to break down the barriers between academic isolation and the teeming marketplace, is the outgrowth of concepts established long ago in American schools and still operative on a wide scale. One strain of this movement came from the Montessori doctrine of a designed environment with an array of stimulating learning materials as an effective means of early childhood education. A second source was the semantic theory that there must be an experiential component in any real understanding of the meaning of words and concepts. This was concretized by John Dewey in his doctrine of "learning by doing." A significant application of this principle was in the Cooperative Education movement, founded as early as 1906 at the University of Cincinnati by Herman Schneider, an engineering-faculty member, to "enhance self-realization and self-direction by integrating classroom study with planned and supervised experience in educational, vocational, and cultural learning situations outside the formal classroom environment."[3] Students were to spend part of their time—in alternate weeks or for entire semesters—

working in factories, business offices, or government bureaus to enrich their classroom learnings through experience in the world of reality. The Cooperative Education movement has been for many decades an integral structure in school systems and colleges in the United States.

Another of the guiding principles we have inherited from the progressive educators of the early century is the emphasis on the individual student as the focus of teaching. This had its roots in the sensibilities of philosophers such as Rousseau and Emerson and in the practices of the anonymous thousands of teachers who, like Mr. Chips, were more sensitive to each student's individuality than appeared in their dominance of their conventional classrooms. It made its debut here and abroad in the establishment of a number of experimental schools in the early decades of the century, largely in private schools, in which students were encouraged to design and carry through their learning activities with some degree of responsibility and independence. A comprehensive statement of the philosophy underlying the movement appeared as early as 1928 in Rugg and Shumaker's book *The Child Centered School*.

Failure to reach the individual child is a recurring point of attack on the public schools. The term *individual instruction* is not easily defined, but its polemic use is intended to suggest that conventional classroom methods fail to take into account the diverse characteristics of students or to respond to them with a personal concern for their needs. I have earlier pointed out the several distinct and overlapping meanings of the term, showing that a child in a class group does not thereby cease to exist as a thinking, feeling, socially reactive person and that good teaching gives ample opportunity for individual self-expression. What I want to point out here is that efforts to individualize instruction go back a long way in our schools.

Let me give one illustration. As early as 1920 an administrator in Dalton, Massachusetts, Helen Parkhurst, devised a plan in which each student was encouraged to assume responsibility for planning his activities and evaluating his progress.[4] Instead of being assigned to do each day's homework that evening for inspection by the teacher or in preparation for a test the following day, the student was given an extensive (usually a four-week) assignment in the form of a contract that he would undertake to carry out to completion. The extensive assignment had the advantage of giving the student an overview of a broad segment of the subject, let us say, the Industrial Revolution in New England or the structure of the solar system. He worked independently, within limits, with freedom to leave the classroom at any time to visit the library or the laboratory or to consult with any of his teachers. As he completed each problem, or each phase of the project, he submitted his work to his teacher-counselor for evaluation and further guidance. Once a week the class met as a group for reports on individual progress, discussion of common procedural problems, and debate on current issues. The Dalton Plan, as it came to be widely known, spread to other school systems, notably that of Winnetka, Illinois, under the sponsorship of Carleton W. Washburne.

One of the fruitful outcomes of the Dalton concept was the gradual development of the teaching unit, which today is a foundation stone of syllabus construction. The Dalton Plan involved the fusion of a number of subject areas, since the contract by definition embraced a topic as seen in broad perspective. The student who was working on Puritanism or the institution of slavery, for example, would have to deal with his subject in several dimensions—history, economics, sociology—and would make use of library techniques, map making, statistics, and the language arts in carrying out his project. Moreover, the teacher had to organize subject matter into broad conceptual units to assign contracts that would sustain interest over time. As the Dalton Plan gained currency among school administrators in the 1920s, its underlying principle, if not its concrete form, came to be accepted as a useful guide in syllabus construction. Thus, today, even in schools that have retained conventional teaching methods, the idea of planning instruction in extended units has been almost universally adopted. The legacy of Helen Parkhurst and Carleton W. Washburne has become so deeply rooted that we are hardly aware of its impact.

This brief résumé of some past developments should be enough to show that our public schools, far from being "reluctant to question established practice," have in fact been most hospitable to constructive change. The superficiality of the Owl Critics' derogatory judgments is abundantly clear when viewed in the perspective of the past five or six decades.

We are witnessing today a renewed skirmish in a battle that has been raging for many years. The conflict between "conservative" and "progressive" forces in education was as intense in the twenties and thirties as it is today. The innovative ideas of John Dewey, as implemented by William H. Kilpatrick at Columbia University's Teachers College, became influential at many of the more prestigious teacher-training institutions of that period. The new progressive education was based on the premise that children learn best when engaged in activities that are meaningful to them and thus congenial to their emotional and intellectual needs. In the lower grades, this meant informal methods of teaching, much manipulation of concrete materials, group activities and projects, a greater use of community resources—in short, the whole battery of child-centered activities recommended as innovative today. In the secondary schools, the new philosophy of learning was concretized in such developments as the project method, unit planning, the developmental lesson with its focus on problem solving, the expansion of curricular offerings, and a host of other concepts designed to serve the newly recognized needs of students.

In essence, the Dewey-Kilpatrick thrust was away from the imposition of inflexible curriculums and regimented instruction and in the direction of open-ended experimentation.

At conventions of professional societies, no topic of discussion generated more excitement than that of reconstruction of the curriculum. In the social studies and the sciences, in mathematics and foreign languages, and in every other field of scholarship, fundamental changes in policy were debated, formulated in resolutions, and recommended for action in the schools. In my own subject area this interest in fundamental issues led to a continual reexamination of the place of English in the total curriculum. In 1945 the National Council of Teachers of English appointed a commission to "study the place of language arts in life today, to examine the needs and methods of learning for children and youth, and to prepare a series of volumes based on sound democratic principles and the most adequate research concerning how powers in the language arts can be developed."[5] The findings of the commission, published in the 1950s, recommended a thorough reshaping of the course of study, among other things a revision of the literature course to include more contemporary works, a shift from formal instruction to a greater emphasis on student activity, the substitution of linguistics and functional usage for traditional grammar, and a stress on speech and the communication media. The spirit of these proposals was in due time influential in bringing about significant changes in the philosophy and content of English courses in the field.

In those years of ferment, an even more fundamental change was taking place in the area of school administration. John Dewey's credo—education for democracy and democracy in education—was becoming a visible reality, not only in teaching but also in school administration. Principals came to recognize the value of reaching policy decisions only after consultation with heads of department, teachers, and members of the community. Chairmen of departments came to regard their major responsibility to be that of developing in their staffs a professionalism that could be channeled in constructive ways. The adoption of new courses, the revision of syllabuses, the selection of textbooks, and the formulation of tests and grading standards were discussed at departmental meetings and implemented cooperatively by faculty committees. Democratic administration became established as the norm.

The philosophy of education that supported these reforms did not, of course, go unchallenged. Opponents of the Dewey-Kilpatrick doctrine spoke out angrily and scornfully on the erosion of scholarship they attributed to "progressive" education. Among these critics the most vocal were Arthur Bestor in his *Restoration of Learning* and Albert Lynd in *Quackery in the Public Schools*. The controversy flared into nationwide headlines in the *Pasadena* case in 1950 when the local school board dismissed Superintendent Willard Goslin on the ground that his progressive policies were responsible for the decline in scholarship and discipline noted in the district. Again, when the Russians launched Sputnik in 1957, the alleged inferiority of American education in mathematics and the sciences was attributed by some educators (among them Hyman Rickover and James B. Conant) to the neglect of solid learning and intellectual standards inherent in the practices of progressive education. As a result, a massive program with federal funding was launched to buttress the schools' offerings in mathematic and science, foreign language, and other areas,

Looking back, I am now convinced that the polemics of that era were infused with more factional heat than cold logic. The level of abstraction exhibited in such labels as "progressive" and "traditional" and "basic" made for endless and fruitless discussion since neither faction defined its terms precisely—and indeed they are indefinable. Those who stood for progressive education could preen themselves on standing in the vanguard of reform; at the same time, the traditionalists rested securely on their defense of scholarship in the humanities and the sciences as the bedrock of Western civilization. This adversary posture blinded everyone to the fact that the conflict was not between mutually exclusive principles. Progressive methods of instruction could well be used to implant traditional cultural values, and indeed were so used in schools such as the Little Red School, the Dalton School, and hundreds of public elementary and secondary schools throughout the nation. Conversely, such strongholds of conservatism as the preparatory schools and the more prestigious public academic high schools—Boys High School in Brooklyn and the Latin School in Boston—could justify their rigorous programs of study and their high standards of scholarship on the ground that they nurtured the student's intellect and capacity for critical thinking, an aim perfectly consistent with Dewey's vision of a society of informed, socially committed citizens.

The all-or-nothing stand of the extremists in the debate—William Kilpatrick on one end of the log and Arthur Bestor on the other—was not especially congenial to any number of teachers in the field. School staffs worked out their long-range programs and day-to-day decisions through discussion, consultation, and experimentation. In history, an emphasis on social problems supplanted a chronological framework not because a sense of the past was to be rejected as "traditional" learning but because teachers recognized the good sense of basing units of study on the immediate concerns of students. Teachers of English expanded their reading lists to include Ibsen, James Baldwin, and Arthur Miller because they were convinced these were important writers for students living amid the turmoil of the midtwentieth century, not because it was "progressive" or fashionable to do so. The Higher Horizons and College Discovery programs in New York City, which sought to expand the students' awareness of the real world through extensive out-of-school cultural experiences, were devised in response to the realization that some children lacked an apperceptive basis for learning because of a culturally improverished background, not for their correspondence to some formula.

The difficulty of defining terms is highlighted by the controversy over one of the key concepts in the discussion—*basic education*. In 1956 a group of educators in the colleges and secondary schools organized the Council for Basic Education, dedicated to the support of the traditional curriculum. In its statement of purpose, the council said in part: "Only by the maintenance of high academic standards can the ideal of democratic education be realized—that of offering to all the children of all the people of the United States not merely an opportunity to attend school, but the privilege of receiving there the soundest education that is afforded any place in the world."[6] On the surface this broad statement of principle may seem to be an innocuous, even bland, rephrasing of any number of similar manifestoes. But viewed in the context of the highly charged atmosphere of the period, the key concepts in the statement—high academic standards, the ideal of democratic education, the soundest education—take on the tone of an affirmation.

In a compendium entitled *The Case for Basic Education* (1959), edited by James D. Koerner, the council defended the rationale of the standard curriculum. The chapterheads indicate the conceptual framework of the council's aims: (1) Citizenship, History, and Geography; (2) English Composition and Literature; (3) Languages; (4) Mathematics and Science; (5) Some Electives—Art, Music, Philosophy, and Speech. These are the areas of scholarship that, in Clifton Fadiman's words, "are sanctioned not only by use and wont but by their intrinsic value."[7]

The term *basic education*, however, runs the risk of being equated with a static, unchanging cluster of narrowly defined school subjects—as in the demand by certain groups for a "return to the basics—reading, writing, arithmetic." Even so perceptive a critic of extremism in education as Professor Harry Broudy falls into the error of identifying "basic education" as an arid offering to this restless generation in search of new intellectual paths.[8] The fact is that the potential of adaptation to changing conditions is intrinsic to the concept. Especially today, the council's statement of basic principles serves as a timely corrective to the clamor of the radical reformists (John Holt, Neil Postman et al.) for the abandonment of large segments of the standard curriculum.

During the four decades that I worked in the schools of New York City, I saw a steady growth in administrative efforts to reshape curriculum and teaching method. Innovation is nothing new. Whatever seemed useful for the improvement of educational services was given consideration. If a proposed idea showed reasonable promise of meeting a problem constructively, it was discussed by concerned staff members, blueprinted by the Bureau of Curriculum Development, tried out as a pilot project, evaluated by teachers and consultants, and if it worked, incorporated into the body of school policy. If the promise of the new program turned out to be delusive, in the judgment of those in responsible positions, it was abandoned.

The attitude of most teachers toward innovation is one of open-mindedness tempered by caution. For one thing, their closeness to young people—clear-eyed, bursting with vitality, distrustful of pretense—makes them aware of the limitations of pedagogic theory. They would, to para-phrase Alexander Pope, not be the first by whom the new is tried, nor yet the last to cast the old aside. They have good reason to be suspicious of fads and panaceas and waves of the future. Nonetheless, on balance, it is fair to say that schools have shown a consistent trend in the direction of self-renewal and adaptation to the shifting demands of a burgeoning school population and changing conceptions of national goals. The "re-luctance to question established practice" observed by Charles Silberman simply does not exit.

Let me illustrate this by referring to three major developments in the past thirty to forty years that have helped meet the needs of individual students within the framework of mass education: ability grouping, elec-tive courses, and the refinement of teaching techniques.

Ability Grouping

In a class of hundreds of students entering high school, the range of abilities, traits, and interests is almost beyond codification. A few mea-sures are available: IQ,[9] reading grade, junior high school ratings, and anecdotal reports on attendance, behavior, and interpersonal relation-ships. A half century ago, when admission to high school was limited to gifted students (or at least those who aspired or were expected to go on to college), every entering class formed a more or less homogeneous group, and rigorous academic standards weeded out those who could not mea-sure up to prescribed levels of achievement. In the past few decades, however, high school attendance has become almost universal, and the disparity in ability and motivation among students has made it necessary to provide for marginal students as well as superior ones. In a great many schools, differentiated instructional programs have been provided for students of different abilities.

Ability grouping entails classification of students in three categories: the bright or honors group, the normal group, and the slow or remedial group. For the entering class, this allocation is usually based on lower-school records, but it is subject to revision as students' abilities are more accurately demonstrated in their progress through the grades. Honors classes and advanced placement classes are geared to enriched content, higher standards, and a stress on conceptual learnings. Slow classes, usually smaller in register, provide skills development, remedial instruction, and individual guidance in a setting conducive to personal relationships between the students and the teacher. Thus, ability grouping helps in a practical way to serve the needs of readily definable groups of students.

The theory of ability grouping is that learning is more efficient in classes in which the range of abilities is relatively narrow. Heterogeneous classes, differentiated only by age and grade, lead to a situation that may become unmanageable—the brighter students chafing at the reins when the lesson slows down for repetition or correction, and the slower students frustrated by the challenging pace set by the others. The situation resembles a Kafkaesque subway system in which express and local trains run on the same tracks. In earlier days, natural selection in the form of ruthless standards of achievement simply weeded out the less able, and even today the significant number of dropouts, although diminishing, indicates that similar pressures, complicated by a variety of economic and sociological forces, are still operative. Thus ability grouping is not a panacea. Even so, it does have value in removing some of the obstacles to efficient learning and feelings of self-worth.

Ability grouping was adopted, probably as an experiment at first, for what were considered sound educational reasons, and its evolution toward the more formal tracking system that is now in common use was probably not anticipated. However, the labels of "academic," "vocational," and "general" came to be attached to individual students while they attended school and even when they received their stigmatic diplomas at commencement.

Thus, the system of ability grouping, despite its obvious justification on pedagogic grounds, has become a paradigm of the divided society in which it exists. All the issues raised by the Jensen theory of genetic inequality, the Coleman report on the dominance of family background, and Jencks's assertion of the irrelevance of schooling to the establishment of an egalitarian society, are reflected in miniature in the policy of ability grouping. Today the tracking system is under attack as promoting racial segregation in schools with ethnically diversified populations. Surveys of urban schools reveal an excessive proportion of black and Hispanic students in slow and remedial classes. The criteria for designation to these classes may be applied objectively, but the result is what Judge Mansfield, in his landmark decision involving the selection of supervisors in New York City, called "de facto discrimination." Thus an educationally sound policy has come into conflict with an equally compelling civil-rights principle.

This conflict, it seems, is often somewhat overstated. Those who detect in the tracking system a taint of elitism or racial discrimination seem to blur the distinction between a social goal and a practical condition. Granted that egalitarianism and intercultural harmony are among the ultimate goals of the American way of life, it does not follow that these ideals must take precedence over other legitimate needs. Differences in intelligence, talent, aptitude, and cognitive skills are also compelling guidelines for educational policy. If black and Hispanic students, the first generation of the newly assimilated migrants to the great cities, have deficiencies in language skills, notably in reading, their predominance in remedial reading classes can hardly be avoided. These classes have a specific purpose—to raise the students' competence in language to a level that would justify their being transferred to regular academic classes. These same students, incidentally, may be in honors classes in mathematics and science and are likely to be involved in advanced music and art programs and athletic activities.

Jencks found no significant differences in the achievement of students in homogeneous and heterogeneous classes, segregated and nonsegregated classes, but he argues for placing students of a given age or grade in undifferentiated groups, despite their disparity in basic skills, in order to promote broad social goals.[10] Whatever social values such a policy might further, it is likely that it would defeat instructional aims and that the education of all children would suffer. *Hamlet* is beyond the grasp of slow readers, and the rigors of theoretical biology and physics are likely to frustrate nonacademic students even more than they frustrate academic students.

On the other hand, the Norvell study[11] of young people's literary interests suggests that limited verbal ability can be overcome by a strong interest in a given curricular area—that is, a student fascinated by the space program or by the strange forms of life on other planets projected by science fiction can read H.G. Wells or Ray Bradbury with a comprehension upredictable from his low reading grade; and an enthusiast of model airplanes or hot rods or gardening can successfully grapple with the physical and biological sciences with a competence that his record on standardized tests would belie. This suggests that differential grouping must take into account not only the cognitive skills measured by objective tests but also the drives and interests that are less amenable to measurement.

This is the rationale of elective courses in the high schools.

The Expansion of Electives

The vitality of our schools in adapting to recognized needs can be illustrated in no better way than by noting the expansion of elective courses as adjuncts to the basic courses of study. This trend, which began several decades ago, has now attained status as an integral part of the organization of most secondary schools. As a matter of fact, it was never correct to say that the schools imposed a uniform program on all students, for there was always the option of majoring in a given curricular area or taking a vocational or commercial course rather than an academic one or selecting one of several foreign languages, whether French, German, Spanish, Italian, or more recently Hebrew, Russian, or Chinese, as the global village expanded. Within the school, too, options were open to join the school orchestra or one of several choral groups or to try out for one of the athletic teams or dramatics workshops or publications. It was only in their *basic* course assignments that students followed trodden paths.

Outlets for special interests were provided in most schools in the extracurricular programs—in clubs, teams, squads, student organizations, and the like. Gradually, however, logistic considerations favored the transfer of these activities into the time frame of the day's schedule as cocurricular programs. The school orchestra rehearsed during the school day; the debating club became an elective course in the speech program. The obvious advantages of such specialized classes gave impetus to the development of electives on a wider and wider scale. It is now generally agreed that the opening up of elective options to all students in the various subject areas is educationally justified. It brings together in each class students who are highly motivated, have a background of prior experiences in common, and have developed an interest in specific areas of the curriculum—the contemporary theatre, the problems of the ecology, Afroamerican culture, and the like. Thus, learning in elective courses is likely to be more efficient, more extensive, and even more exciting than in classes differentiated solely on the basis of ability.

The elective concept may well be the talisman we have been searching for in our effort to reach the student of lower-than-average reading ability. Elective courses may provide an effective means of upgrading these students, supplementing and even partially replacing the clinical and remedial programs in widespread use. Our classification of students as nonreaders or slow readers is based on standardized and therefore coldly objective reading tests, and one of the shortcomings of such testing instruments is that the vocabulary items and the content of the reading comprehension passages are sometimes culturally biased, that is, remote from the experiential backgrounds of some students.[12] As I have indicated earlier, the fallacy of relying on reading tests exclusively is exposed in the Norvell and other studies; indeed, it is a key factor in the current controversy over the relative weight of genetic and cultural factors initiated by the Jensen report. Thus an elective program that might channel the energies of slower students into areas of study that interest them is theoretically of great pedagogic value.

When I was assigned as English chairman at Seward Park High School in 1949, there were three elective courses offered for especially talented and gifted students—Creative Writing, Journalism, and a Dramatics Workshop—all derived from what had been extracurricular activities. Shortly afterward, a course entitled Great Books was added to provide for seniors an intensive experience in appreciation of literary masterpieces. Since that time, the elective program has expanded dramatically, gaining momentum each year.

The grade location of the newly established elective program was initially the second half of the senior year. This was made possible at Seward Park by our decision, taken earlier for reasons unrelated to the question of electives, to accelerate the upper half of the entering tenth-year class by one grade, that is, assigning the brighter students to English 4 instead of English 3. We had done this for two reasons: first, to ease the demand for textbooks in each of these grades; and, second, to create more teachable homogeneous class groups. One of the unanticipated benefits of this plan was that a semester of study beyond English 8, ordinarily the terminal grade, was opened for some three hundred highly motivated and bright students. With the New York State Comprehensive Regents Examination behind them, these students were now free to venture into broader and more diversified fields of scholarship than they would normally.

After some discussion, it was decided by the department to designate English 9, a hitherto nonexistent grade, as a survey of contemporary culture, current issues, emerging literary trends, and whatever else in the immediate present students and teachers felt was worth exploring. Suggestions were crystallized in the form of six elective courses to begin with, leaving open the possibility of extending the offerings as far as our vision and resources could go.

The electives offered were as follows:

1. The Contemporary Theatre—the study of outstanding plays, from Ibsen to Tennessee Williams, with visits to the theatre on and off Broadway.

2. Great Books—literary masterpieces chosen by the teacher and the class and thus varying from term to term: Dostoevsky, Mann, Freud, Hesse, and so on.

3. The Literature of Controversy (initially called the Literature of Protest)—Thoreau, Bellamy, Upton Sinclair, Sartre, and so on.

4. Black Literature—the study of outstanding black writers such as Wright, Ellison, Baldwin, Hansberry, and Hughes.

5. Creative Writing—the study of contemporary trends in literature as the basis of original writing of stories, plays, and poetry.

6. Psychology in Literature—the psychological insights to be found in literature, as reflecting current theories of human behavior.

The response to this program was enthusiastic. Each teacher was free to conduct his course as he saw fit, and the range and inventiveness of teaching method observed in these classes was heartening—close textual analysis, open-ended discussion, dramatic readings, panel discussions, and formal developmental teaching and the loosest kind of seminar interaction. One index of the creativeness released by the program was the insatiable demand for the purchase of new textbooks and recently published books (in the form of paperbacks mainly) for the special needs of the new courses.

Invitations were extended by the teachers of these classes to other members of the faculty to serve as guest lecturers or discussion leaders on special occasions. Once I, as a representative of the school administration, was asked to make an appearance at a meeting of the Literature-of-Controversy class, having to answer questions about the oppressiveness of the establishment—Silberman's *Crisis in the Classroom* was then in the air—and face the unsparing challenges of this group of politically sophisticated and knowledgeable students, soon to be heard from on our college campuses. Some questions were about the English program. Why did we require students to read the "dead" classics like *Silas Marner* and *A Tale of Two Cities*? Why did our textbooks in American literature have nothing on or by black writers? (This was, let me say now, as I did then, a valid charge, and we had recognized it and were in the process of remedying the situation). Other questions related to school management. Why were students treated like children, requiring room passes and such, and why was there not a smoking lounge, for seniors at least? Why weren't students consulted more fully as a matter of policy when it came to making important decisions about school programs? Why did everyone have to endure twelve years or more of schooling just to earn a ticket of admission to the rat race of demeaning work? There was more, and I came away with renewed respect for our too often maligned young students—and a realization that there are no easy answers to their questions about established values.

In the next year or two, as enthusiastic reports of the elective courses filtered down through the school, we decided it was time to extend the program to earlier terms of English. By this time—about 1968—most of the high schools of New York City were experimenting with electives, and the interchange of ideas through our professional associations, coordinated by the Bureau of English at headquarters, gave us access to syllabus materials contributed by other schools. Thus we were able to map out additional elective courses with greater assurance than in the early stages of the project.

We chose English 6, a comfortable middle grade, as the locus of the new elective program, and decided at the same time to open admission to nonacademic as well as academic students. By polling the eligible classes the preceding term, we arrived at a set of thematic course titles in which the most interest was indicated. These were: the Literature of Sports, Science Fiction, Mythology, Black Literature, and the Entertainment

Media. Other themes that had come close in the referendum were set aside for later implementation, including: Women in Literature, Non-western [Asian and African] Literature, Shakespeare, Poetry, Linguistics, and (with undaunted optimism) How to Write.

The elective concept was not, of course, the invention of any one department or any one school system. It gained acceptance by reason of its obvious educational values. Administrators and teachers, taking a second look at the course offerings in their subject areas, discovered the topics in existing syllabuses that could best be extrapolated as elective courses. This resulted in the creation of a vast number of exciting variants in established curriculums that might well be described as a radical restructuring of the schools' offerings.

Item: By the year 1973–74, elective courses open to students at Seward Park High School included the following: Consumer Education, Film Making, Modern Dance and Ballet, Computer Theory and Technique, Medical Laboratory, Photography, Stagecraft, Sociology, Typing for College-Bound Students, Music Composition, and many others.

There is probably no better indication of the clouded vision of the Owl Critics than their apparent unawareness of the vitalizing impact of the elective concept.

The Development of Teaching Strategies

Neil Postman and Charles Weingartner are on record as subscribing to the belief that all teachers—or at least most teachers—do not know what should be taught and exhibit no observable skill in teaching. In *Teaching as a Subversive Activity,* they reiterate all the clichés about the "irrelevance" of school subjects, the imposition of sterile tasks on resistant students, and the fraudulent examination and grading system. Offering as an illustration an assignment given in a supposedly progressive school in a unit on ancient Greece, they pull all stops in excoriating this piece of "pretentious trivia" and assert, with intentional abrasiveness, that "the children know that none of the questions have anything to do with them." To Postman and Weingartner, existing curricula and methods of teaching constitute a stupid charade in which children are induced to take part by deceptive promises of future benefits.[13]

I would prefer at this point to limit my discussion of the issues raised in *Teaching as a Subversive Activity* to their bearing on teaching method and to deal with curricular implications elsewhere. It is difficult, however, to make this distinction for two reasons: first, that subject matter and teaching techniques are organically related to one another; and, second, that Postman's contemptuous attitude toward school subjects, no matter how they are defined, would preclude his assent to *any* justification of any given method of teaching, no matter how persuasively presented. That is, if what we teach is without value, our expertise in teaching is misdirected. A unit on ancient Greece, by Postman's standards, can have no possible educational value—therefore, why bother? On the other hand, a unit on the space program or racism or extraverbal communication (these are Postman's suggestions) would have obvious appeal to students no matter how presented, and, therefore, it would be pointless to devise methods of teaching these self-motivating and self-sustaining topics.

Putting aside the dilemma for the moment, I would suggest that teaching methods discovered and refined in the past twenty to thirty years enable teachers to arouse interest in and develop mastery of areas of scholarship that are relevant in the deepest sense to the needs of students and give them the essential tools of intellectual growth.

A number of such teaching methods are theoretically distinguishable:

1. The developmental lesson
2. The panel discussion
3. The demonstration lesson
4. The drill lesson
5. The lecture
6. The laboratory lesson
7. Committee meetings
8. The library lesson (in research methods)
9. The seminar
10. Audiovisual instruction
11. Supervised study
12. Individual guidance for independent study.

In practice, these types of lessons are interrelated and merge with one another in complex ways. Moreover, the subtle effects of personality and mood make for variations in the application of each type, and thus there remains an element of individuality and creativeness in teaching that is as undefinable as it is in acting or musical performance. With these qualifications in mind, I would like to describe how the application of one of these methods achieves important educational values

The *developmental lesson,* probably the most common type of structured teaching method in operation at the secondary level, has emerged, in a sense, as the matrix within which the other modes of teaching can be integrated. It is a logical embodiment of John Dewey's prescription for optimum learning, namely, the purposeful effort to solve a problem that has meaning for the learner. The developmental lesson involves students in valuable group activity and at the same time serves the goal of individualizing instruction. Moreover, it is a flexible instrument, adaptable to the varying content of different subjects.

Good teachers in the nineteenth and early twentieth centuries no doubt understood and applied the method of developmental teaching, as well as other methods, intuitively. A Horace Mann or a William James could readily see its advantage over a repetitive drill or the expository lecture if only as a stimulating departure from routine. The widespread adoption of the developmental method in the schools today came about in part through the intellectual ferment at certain teacher-training institutions; but the major impetus was in the schools. New approaches to teaching were hammered out at departmental meetings, supervisory conferences, and informal conversations among the staff. The testing ground was, of course, the classroom, and here every teacher had to discover for himself how the method worked or failed to work.

Essentially, the developmental lesson consists of a number of sequential steps:

1. Motivation, leading to the identification of a question or problem
2. The formulation of a relevant aim that is recognized as worthwhile by the students
3. Investigation of the question or problem through analysis and discussion structured usually by the teacher's questions
4. A concerted effort to arrive at a consensus, or to discover new questions for later exploration
5. Application of the concepts learned to a broader context of the students' experience
6. Reinforcement through related assignments, research projects, panel discussions, and so on.

If carried out with imagination and skill, the developmental lesson combines the advantages of teacher direction and optimum student participation.

The unit on ancient Greece (referred to earlier) was cited by Postman as an example of the irrelevance of the standard curriculum and the dull pedagogic routines that turn students off. One might readily conclude from his comment that the teacher was setting a mechanical task to be performed with little involvement, except perhaps as preparation for the inevitable weekly test. This is the impression Postman gives when he characterizes the unit as a piece of pretentious trivia, "a game of Let's Pretend," taking for granted that his putative readers, among them inexperienced teachers and college students, would have no reason to question the validity of his indictment or enough grounding in experience to recognize its flaws. An examination of the unit is therefore appropriate.

Here is the teacher's assignment, as cited:[14]

Ancient Greece

1. Who were the ancient Greeks? Where did they come from? How did the geography of Greece affect them?
2. Why was Athens the leading city in Greece? What is a city-state?
3. How many languages were spoken in Greece? How did this affect Greek life?

4. What sort of religion did the ancient Greeks have? How does this
   compare with that of the Egyptians?

The unit assignment was to be carried out by each student within five to
six days with the aid of a textbook and reference materials suggested by
the teacher. In addition to answering the questions, students were to
undertake research on their own or in cooperation with classmates. Presumably, class meetings during the span of the unit would be devoted to
close analysis of some of the assigned questions or other topics related to
the general theme of the unit. The teacher might conduct formal recitations on one or two days or might allow time for consultation with individual students or small groups, resolving their difficulties or suggesting
ways of working out their projects. Resourceful teachers would no doubt
find additional ways of making the unit a stimulating experience.

However this may be, we must still come to grips with Postman's charge
that all of this is window dressing, devoid of substance and value. Let us
see.

The first question to be clarified is why and how the class became
involved in the study of ancient Greece and early civilizations in general.
Was it a capricious decision on the teacher's part? Or was the involvement
perhaps initiated by the students themselves? Not very likely. The course
was probably a requirement in a two- or three-year sequence in social
studies. Increasingly today schools have have developed courses in ancient history, in the reasoned belief that a knowledge of man's past is
important to intellectual growth. The teacher was, then, following a
prescribed syllabus, planning the term's work so subject matter would be
covered with reasonable completeness.

From the first day, the teacher set out to develop interest in the content
of the course and nurtured that interest in each subsequent phase. The
gist of his approach might be phrased in some such statement as this: "We
owe a debt to the ancient civilizations of Egypt, Palestine, Greece, and
Rome for their contributions to our intellectual life, especially in science,
art, religion, and philosophy." Teachers of earlier generations, say at the
turn of the century, might have been able to assume that their students
had some background in classical studies, since Latin and Greek were
often required subjects and Milton's *L'Allegro* and *Il Penseroso,* steeped in
classical allusions, were still read in English classes. Today, however,
teachers must arouse and sustain interest in areas of scholarship that may,
as in this case, have no immediate appeal to students.

How, then, would the teacher approach the unit on ancient Greece?
The timing of the unit would give him certain advantages. In the first
place, he could count on the interest and understanding generated in
earlier units, that is, the study of Egyptian and Palestinian civilizations.
Second, he would know the extent to which the class was already
habituated to carrying out assignments with more than perfunctory com-

pliance. His lesson planning, then, would be geared to students already keyed up to a certain level of apperceptive alertness. At the same time, he would be realistic enough to take nothing for granted.

Thus, the teacher might see fit to initiate the study of ancient Greece with one or more of these motivational devices:

1. He might tell the story of Ceres and Persephone or the myth of Prometheus.

2. He might present a list of words derived from Greek roots: television, geometry, biology, tantalize, and so on.

3. He might display a picture of the Parthenon, together with photographs of the Capitol in Washington or the Metropolitan Museum of Art in New York.

4. He might seize on the fortuitous occurrence of the Olympic Games that year and explain their origin.

5. He might display a map of Greece and draw inferences about the effect of geographical factors on the economic life of a people.

Then in planning a specific unit—let us say on the religion of the ancient Greeks—the teacher might develop interest in the topic by asking such questions as these: "What natural phenomena seemed mysterious and unexplainable to you as a child?" Or "What natural phenomena do you think primitive man could not understand or account for?" The class would readily supply answers: day and night, the seasons, storms and thunder and lightning, birth and death, and a host of others. A second question would concretize the general theme: "How did primitive man explain these occurrences? The Egyptians? The Hebrews? These developmental questions would breathe life into the bland wording of the initial question in the assignment: "What sort of religion did the ancient Greeks have?"

The class is now ready to consider a focal question: the biological or psychological or societal basis of religion. Specifically, why did the ancient Greeks create a pantheon of gods and goddesses who were omnipotent and immortal and yet were not unlike earthbound men and women in some ways. To provide an answer to this question, the teacher has a number of pedagogic options. He can, for one thing, offer an authoritative exposition in the form of a lecture—a teaching method that can be effective on occasion in the hands (or on the lips) of a skillful lecturer. Or the teacher might conduct a formal recitation, that is, assign a section of the textbook for study and then, in class, clarify and reinforce the students' comprehension through questioning. This method, too, is valuable as a means of strengthening the students' grasp of concrete knowledge as a foundation for conceptual learning. Or, finally, the teacher might see an advantage in giving the students free rein, encouraging the class to assemble the relevant facts and come to a rational consensus inductively.

If a survey were taken at this moment of the teaching procedures being carried out in the classrooms of all the secondary schools in the nation (conducted, it must be assumed, by an omniscient deity assisted by a computer), I am certain it would reveal a bewildering variety of teaching methods in use. I am equally certain that the quality of the observed lessons would follow the curve of normal distribution more or less. What we call teaching method is an abstraction, to be fleshed out only by the teacher's creative imagination. The pedagogic patterns that teacher trainees learn to identify—those listed at the beginning of this section, for example—are merely ways of categorizing the complex flow of events and interpersonal messages that constitutes the teaching-learning experience. The terms *lecture* and *seminar* refer to contrasting methods of instruction but do not determine the boundaries of what is communicated. The developmental lesson is theoretically an instrument for efficient teaching, but its application in a routinized form can be as deadly as any other.

I would like to think that the teacher we have been following in his lesson on the religion of the ancient Greeks found a happy solution to his dilemma. As I have suggested, there are a few methods he could have used to good effect. Certainly, if he had been tempered by the trial-and-error of classroom experience, he would be aware that certain teaching devices work better than others (for example, showing visually is better than telling; the concrete example is better than the generalization; student activity is better than student passivity), and this realization would guide him in the later stages of his lesson.

Here are three possible activities that would be appropriate in the developmental framework of the lesson:

1. At the blackboard would be listed the names of the Greek gods and goddesses together with the ministry and function of each. The list would be drawn up cooperatively by the teacher and the students and would not pretend to be definitive or scholarly. Among other things, the names of the deities would be given in their Roman forms if these were more familiar, and the order of listing would be random.

Name	*Function*
Mars	War
Athena	Wisdom
Aphrodite (Venus)	Beauty
Ceres	The earth's fertility
Apollo	The sun; the arts
Zeus (Jupiter)	Kingly authority
Vulcan	Fire
Poseidon	The sea
Pluto	The underworld
Nemesis	Fate; retribution
Prometheus	Rebellion against tyranny

By analyzing this chart, students would be led to discover that the Grecian mythic world was peopled by divine beings endowed with human traits in some respects and embodying (1) the elements of nature, (2) the dominant forces in human society, and (3) the aspirations of mankind. That is, the Greeks seemed to project their own hopes and fears onto the Olympian stage and thus, in their ritual and drama, could identify with their gods. Once understood, even in a fragmentary form, this concept of the nature of Greek religion could be compared with other visions of the supernatural. The outcome of this activity might well be the formulation of a hypothesis governing the origin and nature of all religions.

2. As a departure from the conventional summary and application of the developmental pattern, the teacher might search for a way of transferring the concept to a contemporary setting. Thus he might raise the question of whether our technological, urbanized society has erected its own pantheon of gods not unlike those of the ancient religions. This would not be beyond the students' grasp—they have their own objects of worship and are not unfamiliar with the ceremonials surrounding the Oscar awards and the Miss America contests. They may have read Molnar's play *R.U.R.*, with its ominous theme of the revolt of the robots, and certainly have not fully outgrown their childhood exposure to animated-cartoon fantasies. Besides, students are ingenious in finding parallels between the most disparate things, and once the idea caught fire, they would come up with deities by the dozen. Here are some I have elicited from a class studying Greek mythology: the automobile (named Mustang, Maverick, Comet); the open road; the Pentagon; the Beatles and lesser demigods in the field of rock 'n' roll; the Big Brother of television; the magic carpet of mysticism and the drug culture; the private eye (Sherlock Holmes as the hand of retribution); and the golden idol of material success.

Seen in a new light, the concept of idolatry and worship becomes meaningful, close to the students' experience.

3. Finally, a creative-writing assignment, calling for an original way of interpreting the theme of the lesson, might prove to be a valuable learning activity. The assignment could, of course, be open-ended, but there is one thematic model that leads to imaginative if sometimes extravagant creations. The teacher retells the myth of Pandora's Box (a parable of the origin of evil) or Ceres and Persephone (an explanation of the seasons) or any other similar legend and asks students to compose myths or legends that will account for the existence of contemporary institutions and beliefs. The compositions submitted, it is hoped, will be varied, ranging in content from the trivial to the profound, reaching out to explain the genesis of "ships and shoes and sealing wax, and cabbages and kings." Whether the subject is traffic lights or earthquakes or nightmares, the project is certain to give students a deeper understanding of the mythic

process and a glimmering view of the pleasure to be derived from scholarship.

In general, projects that the students would undertake in this unit on ancient Greece would lead them to discover fascinating aspects of Greek culture: the story of the Trojan War; the wanderings of Odysseus; the utopian visions of Plato; the punishment meted out to the seeker of truth, Socrates; the fables of Aesop; the scientific gropings of Archimedes and Pythagoras. Perhaps in these days of women's liberation, students would be especially interested in the story of Lysistrata's war resistance or the worship of Athene as the goddess of wisdom. A lifelong possession of literary and anthropological and linguistic scholarship would grow out of these projects and others to follow. Sharing the heritage of the past does not make students any less concerned with the problems of the present but rather makes their concern more rational. Discovering how the ancient Greeks and Romans faltered in their search for a viable political system and how the revolutionary ferment of the eighteenth century led to the establishment of democratic institutions in the Western world makes them more resolute to take part in building a just and stable social order here at home in the twentieth century. Postman's dismissal of this unit on ancient Greece as "pretentious trivia" is merely eccentric.

The range and flexibility of teaching methods prevalent in today's classrooms present a challenge and an opportunity to teachers. Any method of teaching is a versatile instrument, not a formula that can be applied mechanically. Each lesson must be freshly designed to fit the ever-varying mold of each class group and the special logic of each subject area. The teacher must also take account of the intensely contemporary outlook of the children in today's schools, remembering that these children were not alive during the Great Depression of the 1930s or during World War II. The television generation that has watched men walking on the moon lives in a conceptual world that cannot be ignored. Whatever instructional tools, such as films and tapes other audiovisual aids, that are available for classroom use should be exploited to the full to make scholarship more vivid. The changing aspirations and the frustrations of emerging ethnic groups must be recognized as critical factors in determining curricular design and school policies. New concepts of group dynamics and redefinitions of the aims of education must be continually in the foreground of the teacher's consciousness.

The schools are facing these challenges clear-sightedly. Their readiness to adapt to changing conditions is a sign of inner strength and a cogent reply to those who talk of stagnation.

The three developing trends discussed here represent, of course, only a small sampling of the ways in which the schools have adapted their programs and teaching methods to recognized needs of children and youth. Nongraded schools, work-study programs, team teaching, a thousand experiments in core curriculums, as well as new concepts of scholarship embodied in the humanities, the new mathematics, and theoretical biology—all these are logical outgrowths of the educational philosophy that has been operative for many decades in America's schools. This philosophy, not easily defined, can be observed in the expansion of curricular offerings, the development of new teaching strategies, and, in general, a pragmatic, experimental approach to the challenges of a changing society—an attitude that belies in the deepest sense the invidious charges of the Owl Critics.

4 CURRICULUM— THE HEART OF THE MATTER

"The present curriculum," Alvin Toffler declares in *Future Shock,* "is a mindless hangover from the past. Its division into airtight compartments is not based on any well thought out conceptions of contemporary human needs."[1] John Holt and Neil Postman are equally vehement in disparaging what they label the sterile, subject-centered curriculum. These judgments are echoed by Charles Silberman with the smug comment that "the banality and triviality of the curriculum in most schools has to be experienced to be believed."[2]

Are these opinions valid? To answer this question, we must go back to fundamental definitions. What is the rationale of any educational program? Specifically, what are the criteria of curricular design? The answer is to be found in our assessment of the psychological needs of children and adolescents and of the roles they will be ideally expected to play in the adult community of work, civic responsibility, and leisure activities, or, as James B. Conant phrased it, the contribution of education to individual development and national needs. These are precisely the considerations that have determined curricular design in decades past.

Adolescents are curious about every aspect of life that touches them with immediacy: their bodies, their sexual development, their family life, their social group and peer relationships, sports, cars, clothing, jobs. They are searching, in Erik Erikson's phrase, for "self-identity," a sense of being recognized as "somebody" in the context of an impersonal and bewildering world. Within the framework of the curricular offerings of the schools, it is hoped that students will be able to find some clues to the resolution of their uncertainties.

The standard curriculum is a mirror of the real world. The sciences and mathematics make more intelligible the nature of the physical universe and the technology that has given man mastery over some of its forces. Social studies opens up the pageant of history, throws light on the dynamics of political institutions, and examines the myriad problems of contemporary society. The study of literature gives insight into psychology, philosophy, and ethics, answering the burning questions of youth in search of self-knowledge. Music and art sensitize students to their own creative powers and broaden their enjoyment of the many-splendored arts.

In recent years the curriculum has expanded to include life-centered areas of study, such as consumer education, family living, sex education, driver training, and the like. Fields of scholarship not explored in the past—Afroamerican and Latin American history and culture, for example—have been introduced, and courses in computer science, film making, psychology, Russian and Chinese, the ballet, and others have enriched the offerings of our schools immensely.

It is therefore difficult to understand what Toffler and Silberman mean by their disparaging commentaries. The humanities and the sciences are neither trivial nor banal! History, English, science, mathematics, languages, art, and music are the indispensable ingredients of the life of the mind. Courses in physical education, economics, law, accounting, secretarial studies, and the industrial arts serve the practical interests of youth. The comprehensive high school now being established on a broad scale will insure vocational training and technical experience in laboratories and shops for all students. Far from being a "mindless hangover from the past," the living curriculum is a model of renewal and adaptation.

Moreover, when Toffler or John Holt (or Neil Postman or Charles Silberman) refers to the "airtight compartments" into which school subjects are conventionally organized, he is deliberately exploiting the credulity of his readers. Such terms as "mindless hangovers" and "airtight compartments" are intended to generate emotional heat, rather than to shed light on the issue.

The persistence of the standard subject categories in the schools is logically justified by the fact that each area is distinctive in its underlying principles and content. Each subject, as Jerome Bruner has made clear, has its unique logical structure, its special methods of investigation, and even its own vocabulary.[3] In each field of study, mastery is dependent on a specialized step-by-step sequence of learning stages. In mathematics, the understanding of percentage and decimals is unattainable without a knowledge of certain elements of the decimal system, and the study of computer theory is impossible without a grounding in the binary number system. In biology, the theory of evolution cannot be grasped without a knowledge of the structural and functional differences between plant and animal life, the modes of reproduction, and the mechanisms of genetic transfer. The stages of scientific method—the observed phenomena, the tentative formulation of hypotheses, the process of verification or rejection—can best be appreciated through experiences in the laboratory or the field, that is, by means of courses in earth science, biology, chemistry, and physics. In the social studies, where inductive reasoning is equally applicable, the tools of research—documents, artifacts, contemporary reports—are examined with different techniques and evaluated by different criteria. Thus, the subject-area structure that exists almost universally in our schools can be tampered with only at the risk of debasing scholarship and depriving students of the essential tools of intellectual growth.

Moreover, the "airtight" compartmentalization that Toffler derides does not exist. There are—and always have been—natural links and correspondences between and among the separate disciplines that can be and are exploited fruitfully. I came across an illustration of this concept unexpectedly while reading E.M. Forster's *A Passage to India.* Mr. Fielding, who teaches in the British school in Chandrapore, breaks the unwritten code by making sincere efforts to communicate with the natives. At one point, he is talking with Dr. Aziz, a physician, who has remarked that one trait of the British he admires is their fearlessness. In response, Mr. Fielding says: "I can't be sacked from my job, because my job's Education. I believe in teaching people to be individuals, and to understand other individuals. At Government College, I mix it up with trigonometry, and so on. When I'm a *saddhu,* I shall mix it up with something else." (A *saddhu* is a hermit, an ascetic, which suggests that Mr. Fielding had something of Thoreau's temperament despite his secure job.)

The point is that it is impossible to teach any subject without "mixing it" with other things—a sense of history, an awareness of man's common destiny, and a deepened knowledge of one's self. Every subject must be placed in an expansive context, if it is to be taught well. Arithmetic is infused with drama when our familiar numerals are presented in the context of the Roman system of numeration, the ingenious Japanese abacus, and the Arabic invention of the cipher. The Pythagorean theorem—that the square of the hypotenuse equals the sum of the squares of the sides of a triangle—becomes more interesting to students when they learn that this was a pragmatic means of determining the boundaries of fields in the Nile delta—*geometry* means the measurement of land. Galileo's experiment with objects dropped from the Leaning Tower of Pisa and Isaac Newton's flash of insight when the apple fell are the kind of instructional materials that should be in a teacher's repertory (even though historians of science consider both stories apocryphal). Subject matter comes to life only when a teacher draws analogies, traces origins, shows that the immediately perceived event is closely interwoven with universal truth.

The resourceful teacher of American history does not present the Revolutionary War or the Civil War as monolithic blocks of military data—battles, sieges, campaigns, casualties—but rather as political crises with causes and consequences, infused with moral issues and human tragedy and nobility, paralleled in ancient and contemporary events. He enriches his lessons with the historical documents and the journalism of the period and with readings from Tom Paine, Jefferson, Lincoln, and Walt Whitman. History becomes a parable of moral and political truth.

The curricular area designated as English is in fact a cluster of fused disciplines that has evolved immeasurably beyond the rhetoric of the medieval trivium. The English class has become a laboratory for the study and use of language, the development of communication skills, and a seminar in ethics and psychology. The study of literature does not—and should not—merely inventory the contents of great books, but rather is—and should be—a means of developing insight into the nature of man and his social values. English cuts across the barriers of subject divisions shamelessly. Novels like Sinclair Lewis's *Arrowsmith,* poems like Robert Frost's *Mending Wall,* and plays like Lorraine Hansberry's *Raisin in the Sun* are not so much textbooks as they are windows opening on distant fields.

The natural correlations between subject areas are used routinely by teachers to clarify difficult concepts. Analogies are drawn with other subjects or with events in the outside world whenever it is appropriate in the course of a lesson. This is the bread-and-butter practice of teachers everywhere. Here, to illustrate, is a small sampling of such teaching devices that I have used myself or observed in the classes of others:

1. The function of punctuation marks is compared with that of traffic signals. Thus, the period is STOP; the comma is SLOW; the parenthesis is DETOUR.

2. The plot of a Shakespearean tragedy is represented by a graph. The line begins to rise slowly during the exposition; it turns up sharply at the point when the conflict appears; it climbs precipitately as the tension mounts; it reaches its apex at the climactic scene; then it moves rapidly downward with the falling action, the final resolution.

3. Vocabulary is taught by using an algebraic equation—thus: Courage is to Cowardice as Optimism is to X. This formula is used widely in testing vocabulary as well.

4. In discussing the possibility of a world government bringing an end to wars, the question of man's residual aggressiveness inherited from his savage ancestry must be faced. In demonstrating this point, the teacher draws a "time line" to represent the millions of years of man's existence on earth, thus showing in graphic form the brief span of civilization as compared with the eons of prehistory.

Apart from these informal devices for bridging the distance between subject areas, there have been efforts to combine certain subjects into fused or core studies. The natural affinities between English and social studies and between mathematics and the sciences have led to curricular designs combining these groups into single courses. For the past few years, too, an extensive project has been underway in New York State and elsewhere to develop a course in the Humanities, a fusion of literature, music, and the arts. These revisions of the traditional academic curriculum are indicative of the readiness of educators to explore new paths, but our experience with such formal attempts to regroup the standard subject areas has been insufficient to warrant any firm conclusions about their merits.

My own experience with core programs has been negative. At Seward Park, the chairman of the social studies department and I discussed at length the advisability of developing a syllabus for a core course in American history and American literature. The idea was attractive: it would enrich the content of both subjects, each throwing light on the other. But I felt there were obstacles in the fused course that could not be overcome. For one thing, the linguistic component of English would probably be neglected by social-studies teachers, and, conversely, history would be dealt with superficially by teachers of English. Literary works that did not reflect the political or economic forces in American history would be slighted in the core course, I feared. In the Revolutionary period, the writings of Thomas Jefferson and Benjamin Franklin would probably be examined, but what would happen to Washington Irving's tales and legends, so remote from the politics of the era? In studying the period of national growth and the looming conflict over slavery, how would the works of Nathaniel Hawthorne and Edgar Allan Poe be correlated with the historical events of the period? The westward movement would certainly be illuminated by the works of Mark Twain and Bret Harte, but their literary qualities would be scanted if they were taught as illustrations of vivid reportage of frontier life. These considerations led me to reject the plan.

I continue to believe that the standard curriculum, adapted to changing conceptions of social needs, contains the essential values that all educators, including the most strident critics, seek to achieve. The alternatives proposed by the Owl Critics would be damaging and corruptive.

What do they propose as substitutes for the standard curriculum? First, there are those who would do away with every form of curricular structure, trusting to the curiosity and the immediate concerns of students to provide learning activities that would be stimulating and constructive. Second, there are those who disparage traditional scholarship on the ground that expanding frontiers of new research—the so-called knowledge explosion—soon makes obsolete whatever is taught at any given moment. They see education as being limited to giving students the skills of learning, the tools of inquiry, the ability to identify problems and seek solutions. Third, there are those who are critical of the established curriculum because they believe that direct contact with the vivid reality of the contemporary world is more instructive than vicarious experience obtained from the printed page. There are in addition a number of minor variations on these themes.

A common thread runs through all these proposals, and I suggest that this provides a clue to the fallacy inherent in all of them. The reformists share a tendency to single out one element of the learning process and assume it will suffice without the other elements. This fallacy can be seen in their simple-minded advocacy of learning in the field, on-the-job internships, the city-as-school programs—all crystallized in the concept of "schools without walls." Let us examine the rationale of this trend.

In its classic definition, *scholarship* is the mastery of bodies of knowledge, concepts, systems of logic. Thus, a student is said to have acquired a measure of scholarship in physics or history or Shakespeare if he has learned these subjects satisfactorily as determined by achievement tests or other means of evaluation. But there is another conception of scholarship that must be taken into account. Take a very simple instance of what we call knowledge: the meaning of a word. We can define a *bicycle,* in dictionary terms, as a lightweight vehicle having a metal tubular frame, with two wheels one behind the other, handlebars for steering, and so on. But we do not *really* know what a bicycle is until we have experienced the anguish and exhilaration of learning to ride one. In the same way, knowledge of the Constitution, say the First Amendment, is not satisfactorily acquired by memorizing the words: "Congress shall make no laws abridging the freedom of speech . . ." but comes to us as a meaningful concept only when we have been stirred by the courage of Peter Zenger, watched or taken part in a demonstration in protest of some governmental policy, or perhaps served as faculty adviser to an activist school club or publication. Thus, an on-the-job intern whose assignment is in the criminal courts has an opportunity to gain a more realistic, if a less comprehensive, understanding of legal justice than an academic student who takes a conventional course in school.

The value of immediate experience in the learning process cannot be disputed. There are, however, two considerations that should be decisive in our appraisal of schools-without-walls programs as a substitute for organized courses within the school.

First, it is a fact that commonly practiced methods of teaching in the classroom include a component of immediate sensory experience. Provision is made for science laboratories, demonstration lessons, and audiovisual aids to supplement the abstract or merely verbal materials of study. Wherever possible, too, visits to museums, theatres, law courts, or welfare centers are arranged for the entire class or recommended for individual students on their own time. Good teaching, as we have seen, consists largely in concretizing the abstractions in textbooks.

Second, it is unlikely that experiences outside the classroom and the school in internships and the like can yield understandings and insights unless integrated into a total instructional program. What, for example, will the intern be able to observe in the courts if he is not equipped with a considerable measure of information about our judicial system in general, prevalent theories of criminal justice, the Constitutional safeguards that protect the rights of the accused? If the student's participation in the complex laboratory of our judicial system is not interpreted and reinforced in a course of study on juridical principles and social ethics, his observations in the field are bound to be superficial and perhaps misleading.

The fallacy of the reformists lies in their singling out one element of a complex organic process and claiming that it can function in isolation. They assume that the goose will lay its golden eggs even after it has been eviscerated. This kind of assumption, when applied to any field of thought, may be termed the abstractional fallacy. It is the fallacy of the school of abstractionists in art who separate the formal component from the esthetic substance of a painting, thus reducing the art to the level of solipsism and triviality. It is the fallacy of the so-called new criticism in literature, which views the novel or play or poem as a graph of intersecting force lines, rather than as an expression of human experience. Something of the same error is seen in Noam Chomsky's attempt to codify grammatical forms and syntactic relations in quasi-mathematical terms, with seeming indifference to the meanings and functions of words.

In education, the abstractional fallacy works in this way: You see a group of students in a classroom engaged in animated discussion of a book, a current issue, a problem in ethics. You conclude that the important value illustrated in the lesson is the enthusiastic interaction among the students, not the truth or value of the ideas themselves. You therefore set up the principle of discussion as a prescription for a total educational program. (Neil Postman does this.) Or you are excited by discovering the frontiers of scientific thought that challenge the truth of some of our conception of the physical universe—the quantum theory, the theory of discontinuity, the theory of uncertainty—and you conclude, as John Holt did, that nothing is worth teaching except the processes by which learning is acquired. Or, as we have seen, you recognize that a sound educational program should include an awareness of the world of things and nature and people as well as the world of books, and you therefore advocate an education that is entirely, or at least largely, derived from observation and experience, not from books.

Stephen Leacock, in his perceptive essay on education entitled "Oxford as I See It," pilloried this fallacy with disarming humor. He had visited Oxford to discover how this venerable institution, housed in ancient buildings, with a pitifully inadequate physical plant compared with American universities, with professors who lectured reluctantly and rarely and students who seldom attended the lectures, could produce so many cultivated and articulate graduates. He thought he found the answer in the tutorial meetings where small groups of students would get together with a teacher, usually a graduate scholar or junior instructor, in someone's room. There they would talk informally and endlessly, go over passages in

great books, debate philosophical and esthetic questions—while puffing
at their pipes and filling the room with the dense aroma of tobacco and
good talk. What, then, was the secret of Oxford's excellence? Leacock
went over all the possible explanations and solemnly concluded that it
must lie in the prevalance of pipe smoking. His prescription for a great
university was to provide an adequate library first of all, and then to
provide smoking rooms. Nothing else mattered.

The abstractional fallacy can be detected in a number of recent proposals for curricular innovation, among these the program known as Competency Based Learning (CBL) and the Questions Curriculum proposed
by Neil Postman. Both seem to reflect the doctrine of Carl Rogers and
John Holt that, in a world in which all fields of scholarship are undergoing
dramatic changes and moving in unpredictable directions, the only acceptable goal of education is "to facilitate the process of seeking knowledge."

Competency Based Learning is an experimental program supported by
the Fund for the Improvement of Postsecondry Education and now being
tried out in a number of small colleges.[4] In essence, CBL defines the goal
of education as mastery of a number of skills or abilities. Among these are:
(1) effective communication skills; (2) analytical capabilities; (3) problem-
solving skills; (4) ability to make independent value judgments; (5) facility
in social interaction; (6) awareness of the world in which the student lives;
(7) responsiveness to the arts and the humanities. This list is a sampling of
the competencies that are identified as indices of a well-rounded education. Standard courses in history, science, and literature are offered—no
doubt in deference to counsels of prudence—but these courses are used
merely to provide a setting for the development of the desired skills.
Students earn credit by demonstrating to examining panels their mastery
of "competency level units," that is, their levels of skill in making oral
reports, playing roles, analyzing problems, relating to others, and so on.

On the surface, CBL has some noteworthy features, namely, its stress
on student activity and its definition of the goals of schooling in terms of
abilities that contribute to vocational success and social adjustment. One
of the weaknesses charged to liberal education has been a certain vagueness in its formulation of goals, in contrast to the concreteness of aims in
vocational and professional courses. Apparently the purpose of CBL is to
remedy this weakness by dissecting the concept of a liberal education into
its nuclear elements.

The CBL program will be evaluated in due course, as all experiments
must be, but even in its prospectus there are certain theoretical features
that should be considered in weighing the probability of its success or
failure.

First, the psychological premise of the CBL program is questionable.

The existence of unitary skills and competencies, the basis of the program, rests on a theory of the human mind long since discredited, namely, faculty psychology. This theory posited a number of separate faculties—among them mental powers, reason, imagination, will, instinct—as an explanation of human behavior. CBL seems to assume the existence of disparate abilities without a clearly defined relationship to one another or any relationship to curricular content.

Second, the listed CBL competencies are not clearly differentiated from conventional statements of objectives found in every syllabus guide published in the past fifty years. The same terms are used—critical thinking, problem solving, communication skills, research techniques, and so forth. There is a striking difference, however, in their application. In conventional courses these aims are implicit in the study of a specific area of scholarship. For example, a term paper is judged by the significance of its thesis, the logic of its organization, the relevance of supporting facts and references. The paper could not be written without some degree of mastery of pertinent skills, that is, effective communication skills, the ability to make independent value judgments, and the like. But these skills are merely instrumental, as all skills are, by definition.

Abstraction of skills from the content of courses can only lead to artificial exercises and improvisations. This is borne out in a report on a CBL unit test in which it was required that a debate be staged by "a committee of Repocrat party members selecting a successor to a deceased State Senator from among three different nominees" as a demonstration of ability "to grasp the situation, to relate well to others, and to exert influence." It may well be asked whether there is any advantage in this method of testing skills in isolation as compared with a panel discussion on, let us say, the qualifications of three or four actual candidates for public office.

Finally, it is apparent that the CBL program, in its strained effort to codify all learning under the rubric of "competencies," does not avoid the trap of empty verbalism in its formulation of objectives. "Awareness of the world in which the student lives" is hardly to be called a skill or competency—in fact, it is nothing more than a euphemism for scholarship in the physical sciences and the social sciences. The term *awareness,* stripped of its connotations, is another word for "knowledge." Again, "responsiveness to the arts and humanities" can mean nothing more than "appreciation" of the visual arts, music, and literature, the stated aim of conventional courses in the field. "Effective communication skills"—conversation, formal speech, group discussion, written expression—are taught and tested every hour of the school year in English classes. But so complex and elusive a concept as "facility in social interaction" must be reserved for the judgment of the gods. It is pretentious to think that facility in interpersonal relationships, which is beyond most of us after a lifetime of experience, can be reduced to measurable units of competency.

It is not likely that a sound curriculum can be constructed on the shaky premises of the Competency Based Learning program.

The abstractional fallacy can likewise be seen in bold configuration in the educational program proposed by Neil Postman and Charles Weingartner in their book *Teaching as a Subversive Activity*. They would replace the traditional subject-centered curriculum with what they describe as a question-centered curriculum. The content of courses would consist entirely of problems or questions that were of interest to students at a given moment in a given social setting.[5] Students would be encouraged or guided to formulate questions on some aspect of the current scene—the ecology, the drug problem, race relations, civil rights—or whatever moral or social or philosophic problem seemed pressing for them at the moment. Postman (I refer only to Postman for convenience) contrasts the energy-releasing impact of topics such as the ghetto rebellions of the 1960s and our military intervention in Vietnam with the sterility of traditional school subjects. He envisages a new generation of teachers and students who will not be concerned so much with the niceties of grammar or geometry as with a genuine search for truth and justice.[6]

In a tentative appraisal of Postman's ideas, several basic limitations are immediately apparent.

First, there is the question of apperceptive readiness in students below the college level or at least the senior year in high school to understand the complexity of the problems recommended for study. Postman himself inadvertently concedes the need to view contemporary problems in historical perspective when, in suggesting campus riots and ghetto uprisings as suitable topics for investigation, he writes: "There is insurrection throughout the land, as there has been before, in 1776 and 1861. How do we know if this is one of man's deepest needs expressing itself (the language of the unheard, Dr. King calls it), or if it is a mindless aberration precipitated by summer heat and boredom?"[7] How indeed can students deal intelligently with the meaning of social upheaval and revolution without knowing something of European and American political history and of the struggle for human rights whose roots go back to the ancient world? And how are students to acquire such knowledge without studying history—perhaps even a bit of the history of ancient Greece, a subject singled out by Postman as an example of the sterility and irrelevancy of the standard curriculum? Awareness of contemporary problems must be developed in the schools, but to posit such awareness as the only meaningful concern of education and to hope that students will be able to deepen awareness without relevant information is fatuous and self-defeating.

Second, the kinds of topical problems that are recommended as substitutes for the conventional subjects tend to cluster in eddies of discourse that form a subject-area hierarchy of their own, centering on sociology and political science, and excluding mathematics, foreign languages, art, and music except when these subjects may have some tangential bearing on the problem being considered. They exclude history and literature as serious concerns, since the in-depth study of the past is by definition without meaning. Students will be turned on to the problems of today at the expense of being turned away from the sources of our culture.

For Postman, the one criterion of curricular value is relevance to "some identifiable and important purpose . . . that is related to the life of the learner."[8] He asserts, in his abrasive style, that most teachers "teach subjects such as Shakespeare, the Industrial Revolution, or geometry because they are inclined to enjoy talking about such matters." When they are challenged to justify teaching these subjects, they have no answer save the cliché that literature and mathematics and history are "good for their own sakes." To strengthen this canard, Postman draws the analogy of a comic-book conference of surgeons who decide to remove the gall bladder of a patient, although there is no medical need for the operation, because it's just "inherently good to remove gall bladders." He concludes that "what passes for a curriculum in today's schools is . . . largely designed to keep students from knowing themselves and their environment in any realistic sense; which is to say, it does not allow inquiry into most of the critical problems that comprise the content of the world outside the schools.[9]

Taking this highly arguable thesis as a proven truth, Postman proceeds to delineate the kind of curricular design he would like to see adopted by the schools, or at least by those courageous and disenchanted members of the teaching staff who go along with him. What should be the content of the teaching-learning process? Postman's answer is plain: it is "to have the entire curriculum consist of questions . . . that are responsive to the actual and immediate as against the fancied and future needs of learners in the world as it is (not as it was)."[10] Not organized bodies of subject matter, not science or history or mathematics, not great books or the biographies of great men and women—only a list of questions on whatever random puzzlement comes into the head of a student or a teacher at any given moment.

A sample list of such Postmaniac questions stretches across three pages of the text, some perhaps emanating from students, but most of them clearly imposed by adult teachers or by the authors themselves.

Here is a sampling of the kinds of questions Postman likes:[11]

What do you worry about most?

What, if anything, seems worth dying for?

What seems worth living for?

How can good be distinguished from evil?

Where does meaning come from? What does meaning mean?

How do you know when a good or live idea becomes a bad or dead idea?

What are the most obvious causes of change? What are the least apparent?

What conditions are necessary for change to occur?

What are the conditions necessary for life to survive?

Plants? Animals? Humans?

How might man's survival activities be different from what they are if he did not have language?

How many symbol systems does man have? How come? So what?

What's worth knowing? How do you decide? What are some ways to go about getting to know what's worth knowing?

This bewildering list of questions, set forth with straight face as the basis of a reconstructed curriculum, boggles the mind. Like the two clever tailors who deceived the emperor of China with the elaborate pretense of clothing him with nonexistent garments, Postman and Weingartner must hope to bemuse the academic world by their sheer audacity. Clearly, most of their their ill-assorted questions are only remotely relevant to the immediate concerns of youth. Some might lead to time-consuming talk for an hour or two in a bright class with a high degree of frustration tolerance, and some might serve as motivation for an assignment in creative writing or poetry. To comprehend the drift of many of the questions, much less to answer them, would require college courses in semantics, psychology, and anthropology. It is conceivable that these questions might be appropriate in a graduate course in curriculum construction to provide a basis for sorting out possible areas of instruction in the schools. In a high-school class or undergraduate class, however, the endless dissection of verbal subtleties inherent in these questions would engender confusion and frustration in most of the hapless students.

Let us look more closely at some of the questions. Take this: "What are the conditions necessary for life to survive?" Is this anything more than an introduction to a unit in biology, possibly appropriate as a motivational question? The question "What is good and what is evil?" is one of the profound philosophic problems that has engaged thoughtful men throughout the ages, and is the kind of question that would be more appropriate in a class that has studied such works as *Macbeth* and *Moby Dick* than in a contextual vacuum. The question "What is progress?" is probably unanswerable by anyone lacking a mature system of values based on much experience and reflection. "How many symbol systems does man have? How come? So what?" is an impertinence that would baffle and irritate anyone but a doctoral candidate fresh from immersion over his head in Noam Chomsky and Alfred Korzybski.

Postman's innovative curriculum is no better than a hoax. At best, it might serve as a footnote to the theory and application of the developmental or socialized recitation that occurs routinely in English, social studies, and science classes, the questions serving as motivation or medial summary. At worst, it would result in a breakdown of communication. Any method of doing anything, from baking a pie to writing a novel, requires by definition that the ingredients used exist apart from the act of assembling them or transforming them into the finished product. Postman's educational recipe is all process and no content. The lessons he envisages as being liberating and mind stretching are suspended in midair. They begin with spontaneous questions that have no anchor in an ongoing course of study and end in the quicksands of epistemological enigmas that neither the teacher nor the students are competent to deal with.

Consistent with his viewpoint, Postman bluntly dismisses the traditional concept of school subjects as artificial and dysfunctional. "There is no such thing as subject matter," he writes. "Subject matter exists in the minds of perceivers."[12] Since the events of history and the phenomena of nature have no objective existence, it follows that there is no body of disparate referents that can be labeled history or physics, and that a curriculum based on such subject divisions is meaningless. Postman's proposed Questions Curriculum transcends these artificial categories and concentrates on refining subjective perceptions of whatever it is that exists outside the human mind.

In support of this thesis, Postman summons up the ghost of Alfred Korzybski, founder of a dissident cult in the field of linguistics known as General Semantics. In his major work, *Science and Society,* Korzybski developed the concept that language is at best a faulty instrument for communication since it is based on a fallacious assumption about the relationship between the real world and the linguistic symbols we use to describe and control it. When we utter the simplest of declarative sentences—such as "It's a cold day" or "Tom has a bad temper"—we are trapped by the ambiguities inherent in language. A "cold day" and a "bad temper," for example, are subjective judgments, not objective facts. Much more significant, of course, is the ambiguity of abstractions such as: "Our freedom is threatened by recent decisions of the Supreme Court" or "The traditional curriculum is inherently irrelevant." Korzybski maintains that we must devise a new symbolic system to avoid this and other pitfalls. The model suggested for attaining the goal of linguistic precision is the language of science and mathematics, specifically, non-Euclidean geometry and Einsteinean physics.[13]

To go more deeply into Korzybski's theory would require an exposition of epistemological concepts that are beyond the scope of this book. It suffices for present purposes to note that the basis of General Semantics is the notion that language is a representation of our subjective perceptions rather than of the objective universe. We perceive the outer world only through the medium of our imperfect senses and therefore we cannot know what the extrasensory world is really like. Most of us naïvely assume that the painting or the typewriter or the face we perceive in front of us exists in the form that our vision (or any other sense) reports. How wrong we are!

The fact is that our sense receptors can only register the impact of extraorganic energy waves on our sensitive nerve ends, nothing more. The myriad waves are assembled and interpreted by the brain—a cortical computer mechanism—as disparate and visible "objects" to the degree that an awareness of their existence becomes crucial to our biological survival or social adjustment. As William James put it, the universe is a blooming, buzzing confusion to the infant until it gradually becomes sorted out into discrete and interrelated things—mother, bed, doll, stairs—through trial and error. Nothing teaches the child that the yellow flowers on the stove can be hurtful more convincingly than putting his hand close enough to feel pain. The early education of the child is a process of associating his perceptions or environmental constructs with the phonological patterns that constitute language. After a few years of intense exploration and interaction, the child has built for himself a relatively stable and controllable world in which he finds nourishment, love, warmth, and safe channels for muscular exercise and creative play and concomitantly acquires a vocabulary adequate to his need to control it.

In primitive societies, the process of acculturation goes on uninterruptedly in a world of resistant earth, swift-running animals, stubborn roots, and fearsome enemies. In our civilized world, as Thomas Henry Huxley showed brilliantly,[14] the means of accelerating and making more efficient the child's power to gain nature's rewards and to avoid her punishments is education. Parallel with the child's adaptation to the world of things is his acquisition of a code of signs and symbols—gestures, words, syntactic forms, expressive intonation and stress—that enables him to respond to the directives of others and transmit his own perceptions and wants to others when there is need of communication.

For semanticists, and particularly for Korzybski and his followers, language, while being a miraculous tool for mastery of the unknown, also has the potential of opening up a Pandora's Box of threats to survival. For the word is not the object it symbolizes, as Korzybski reminds us again and again, but only the symbol of an image within the consciousness of each individual. The danger is that the same word or constellation of words arouses slightly or markedly different images in different minds in the same way that an unfocused image on the television screen has a ghostly periphery that blurs the sharp outline of the picture. The danger may become critical in one's interpretation of the immediate environment, as when children visiting the zoo or adults in Yellowstone Park risk harm by associating the word "bear" with the woolly stuffed animal in the playpen or with the gentle, harmless protagonists of *The Three Bears* instead of recognizing the possible sudden emergence of nature red in tooth and claw. This is precisely the distortion of reality that may occur when we lard our journalism and public discussion with abstractions such as progress, freedom, law and order, and others, where the danger is less imminent but no less real.

Postman makes much of the semantic hypothesis, predicating his instructional program (the Questions Curriculum) on the premise that free discussion and a kind of loose Socratic dialogue are the most efficient means of clarifying the meaning of concepts and making more precise the verbal instruments used to symbolize them. Since nothing in the world exists except as it is perceived, and since language is the only means of sharing our perceptions, it follows that "languaging" (as Postman calls it) must be the one predominant activity of teachers and students.

How does this work in practice? To show how his curricular program would work out in the classroom, Postman describes a series of lessons on the meaning of the terms *right* and *wrong* in the separate contexts of etiquette, morality, politics, and grammatical usage. In one lesson, transcribed in the text of the book,[15] the teacher sought to have the class explore the unique sense in which rightness and wrongness applied to language and communication. To initiate the lesson, the teacher wrote on the blackboard the sentence, "It is right to say *he doesn't* instead of *he don't.*" In the discussion that followed, the students readily identified several criteria of "correct" usage and showed considerable ability to examine ideas critically. The teacher kept in the background, probing now and then for clarification. If a student said that such and such was an example of dialect, the teacher would ask, "What do you mean by a dialect?" The lesson was lively and stimulating and the students were apparently helped to understand the limitations of the dictionary as the final authority on matters of language use and aware of the complexity of terms such as correct usage, regional dialect, and levels of diction. No doubt the process of inquiry exhibited in this lesson would be instrumental in developing students' skills in critical thinking and communication.

But there was one glaring weakness in the lesson—its aimless drift. Each point raised during the discussion, whether relevant or not, was given equal attention. As much time was spent quibbling over whether a student was correctly quoted by another or whether he had or had not shown hostility over some unintended slur as was spent trying to define crucial terms. The teacher's refusal to make any contribution to the discussion (other than to serve as moderator) had the effect of preventing any kind of consensus. Of course, if the teacher had dogmatically insisted on the correctness of *he doesn't,* he might well have been criticized for imposing on his students a narrow standard of linguistic acceptability—and it is probably this kind of teacher domination that Postman seeks to disparage. The fact is, however, that the transcribed lesson went on and on aimlessly and led nowhere.

But what is most striking about the lesson is the fact that the rigorous semantic logic on which it was supposedly based should lead in practice to a methodology that is completely compatible with the standard teaching methods that Postman dismisses so caustically. The mountain labored and produced a mouse.

The kind of dialogue reported in this transcribed lesson occurs to a greater or lesser extent in thousands of conventional classrooms across the land. Student interaction, open discussion of contoversial issues, critical analysis of concepts—these are standard activities in contemporary schools. They are of value in clarifying the students' understanding of important topics in organized courses of study, not merely as intellectual exercises. No matter how well-intentioned, free discussion becomes an exercise in futility when students are not well enough informed or have insufficient background in scholarship to deal with problems knowledgeably. The rationale of the subject-oriented curriculum is that it serves to impart in some systematic way the factual information and the tools of logic that will enable students to grapple effectively with the political problems, the moral dilemmas, the scientific concepts, and the metaphysical uncertainties of our age of anxiety.

Even granting the semantic hypothesis that "words are only symbols and do not necessarily correspond with the external constructs they represent," it does not follow that we should limit classroom discussions to the kinds of topics that are recommended in the Questions Curriculum, even those that least depart from common sense. On the contrary, a proper appreciation of the semanticists' contribution makes it imperative that we extend the range of students' concepts and concerns to the greatest feasible limits, that is, we must help students gain a fuller understanding of "languaging" by a solid grounding in the historical, literary, and scientific foundations on which it rests.

Everyone would agree, I am sure, that the concept of a democratic (in contrast to an authoritarian) social order should be explored and examined fully somewhere in the social-studies course in the schools. In Postman's Questions Curriculum the topic might never be considered unless, perhaps, it came up by chance in the course of a discussion of the ecology or civil rights, when some student happened to say, "That shows how undemocratic our administration is," and the teacher-moderator asked, "What do you mean by a democratic administration?" On the other hand, the standard curriculum, as implemented in a course in American history or an elective in the literature of dissent, would raise the question at the moment when interest and apperception were at their kindling point, for example, in the study of the American revolution or in a unit on Soviet-American relations or in a reading of Thoreau's essay on civil disobedience.

The loose texture of Postman's curricular design would surely come unraveled under the strain of practical use. The question about democracy and totalitarianism might be raised during a discussion, let's say in the form: "Is a democratic society superior to a totalitarian society?" or "Why do you prefer a democratic form of government?" Assuming that the students were able to analyze the question and bring up a number of related subconcepts—such as freeaom of speech, equality under the law, civil rights, justice, respect for the individual, the stability of institutions—the discussion would inevitably reach a point where the students would realize they needed more background information on the subject. The class would flounder, as it did in the transcribed lesson on usage, until the teacher—using a textbook or reference books or current periodicals or films—provided the essential information. It would soon become apparent that the minimal procedure for transforming the biases and intuitions of the students into more informed and mature ideas would be to undertake a planned study of the Enlightenment, of Rousseau and Voltaire and Locke, the American and French revolutions, the Civil War; the doctrines of Marx and Lenin and Mao Tse Tung, and the social legislation of the past few decades in the United States. Thus, with inevitable logic, a course of study would come into being.

Postman's pretentious effort to bolster his thesis by relating it to the doctrines of current schools of linguistics does not diminish the value of their discoveries and insights. An understanding of the meaning of verbal symbols and an awareness of the abuses inherent in language are, of course, invaluable if productive communication among members of social groups or school boards or congressional committees is to be possible. This is recognized by educators as a primary task of the schools. There is, however, no consensus about the strategies and programs that will best achieve this goal. But one thing is certain: the Questions Curriculum is not the answer. For when the smoke is cleared away, the Postman-Weingartner restructuring of the curriculum turns out to be no more than a marginal comment on teaching method.

There is, unfortunately, an element of frivolity in Postman's blueprint for the future that makes suspect even his more acceptable proposals. In his book *Teaching as a Subversive Activity* he offers an agenda of sixteen proposals with respect to the teaching staff that he hopes will "change radically the nature of the existing school environment." Among these are the following:[16]

1. Declare a four-year moratorium on the use of all textbooks.

2. Have English teachers teach math, math teachers teach English.

3. Dissolve all "subjects," "courses," and especially course requirements.

4. Prohibit teachers from asking questions they already know the answers to.

5. Require all teachers to take a test, prepared by students, on what the students know.

I have deliberately selected the proposals that indicate an imaginative, if misguided, concern for innovation, however absurd and impractical they may be. I omitted the proposal to "require that all graffiti accumulated in the school toilets be reproduced on large paper and hung in the school halls"; and another that would require "every teacher to take a one-year leave of absence every four years to work in some field other than education (recommended occupations: bartender, cab driver, garment worker, waiter)." These proposals betray an irresponsible strain in Postman's impish personality that may endear him to the lunatic fringe among his entourage, but that casts doubt on the credibility of everything he says.

It is just a single step from the Questions Currriculum to the quicksands of total abandonment of any kind of planned educational program. The advocates of what is called unstructured teaching or student-initiated learning tell us that the teacher is really an obstacle to learning. They support their thesis by asserting that the only basis of true intellectual growth is self-motivation and self-direction. All learning must grow out of the student's immediate concerns and "felt needs."

Like all partial truths, this is a superficially attractive theory. Its faults, however, are transparent. They can best be exposed by examining the credos of two of the most important and influential standard bearers of this doctrine—Carl Rogers and John Holt.

5

PERMISSIVENESS AND THE HAPLESS STUDENT

The siren song of freedom and self-expression lures the unwary into the morass of "nondirective" learning theory. It is heard most alluringly in the confessional essays and lectures of Carl Rogers, assembled in his book *Freedom to Learn.*[1] Rogers qualifies as an Owl Critic by his considerable experience in psychotherapy and a modicum of firsthand experience in the classroom. It is likely that his ideas, filtered down through disciples such as John Holt and Earl C. Kelley, have provided the conceptual framework for a large segment of the newer theories of teaching and learning, the ideological foundation of the current drift toward open classrooms, unstructured teaching, and spontaneous learning.

The major premise of Rogers's thesis is a challenge to the teacher's legitimacy as initiator and director of classroom activities. The status of the teacher is to be diminished or at least transformed: he will become the consultant, the adviser, the facilitator—but he will not teach! Rogers probably found the model for his version of learning theory in his experience as a psychological therapist. Observing that a permissive relationship with individual patients and therapy groups leads to relaxed tensions and intimations of self-understanding, he advocated a similar strategy in the classroom. Students will choose their own area of study, initiate their own activities, and carry them forward with a minimum of supervision.

One version of this kind of unstructured learning calls for the complete absence of any syllabus or lesson plans. The classroom takes on the atmosphere of a happening in a Greenwich Village café theater. There is no scenario. The teacher opens the class meeting with the ritual question: "What do we wish to discuss today?" The class may sit in embarrassed silence for a while, but this does not mean that nothing is happening; in theory, at least, there is always an interval of creative silence during which ideas are germinated and sorted out. Finally, a suggestion or two may be offered and taken up in discussion until some interesting topic catches the fancy and initiates a momentary stirring of intellectual activity.[2]

This idyllic opening scene, however, may foreshadow a technical difficulty that will plague the dramatist in subsequent acts. How, for instance, is the interest of the students sustained? What occurs the next day and the next week? Does the class as a whole pursue the topic in some systematic way, or do a few students undertake follow-up and research on their own?

If there is further exploration of the topic extending over some period, the concerted planning that is indispensable to the completion of any project will necessitate the abandonment of unstructured teaching. The dilemmas inherent in the concept of unguided learning defeat whatever psychological values are to be gained by the release of initiative and creativity.

A schematic application of Carl Rogers's design for releasing student initiative is found in Earl C. Kelley's workshop plan. The title of his best-known book—*The Workshop Way of Learning*—signals his recognition of self-directed activity as a major principle of pedagogic method. "The most crucial learning at any given time," he writes, "has to do with the individual's current problems."[3] Therefore, he concludes, the classroom should be a workshop or seminar in which students will identify their "current problems" and find answers to them by thinking and talking them out. Group dynamics will replace instruction, the teacher playing the role of stage manager rather than director.

The workshop method is illustrated by Kelley in his account of a course he gave at Michigan State University for a group of experienced teachers.[4] At the first meeting of the class, after announcing the general format of the course, he asked the students to decide which problems they were most troubled by in their professional work. He then assigned them at random—"by counting off"—to exploratory "problem-finding" groups in which they were to identify their genuine problems, presumably not the kinds of conventional topics that might be discussed at faculty meetings. Each participant was assigned at the next class meeting to a discussion group that shared a major area of interest in common—guidance, curriculum, community relations, and so forth. Thereafter, the momentum of free discussion under the relaxed guidance of a teaching assistant was motivation enough to ensure worthwhile learning.

Something like the workshop way of learning has, of course, been in common use in the elementary and secondary schools for a long time. It is called the committee method. Groups of students are assigned to carry out various projects on their own—preparing a report, organizing a panel discussion, or planning an assembly program. But unlike Kelley's workshop, the committee method rests on an established syllabus in history or science or the humanities; it is a way of encouraging students to go more deeply into a subject, whether folklore, or colonial customs, or energy resources, than is possible in the classroom recitation. It is a form of enrichment.

The Kelley workshop design, like all other forms of undirected learning programs, assumes that students should be able to "invent" subject matter in response to their immediate concerns. It is possible that adults, such as the teachers in Kelley's course, with backgrounds of scholarship and professional experience, would be able to formulate problems and explore possible solutions on their own. It is not likely that immature students, with their intellectual and other limitations, could do so.

It is Carl Rogers who has done the most to propagate the theory that the teacher's role is not to instruct but merely to provide an environment in which self-directed learning activities are likely to take place. "Teaching," he once announced to an audience of teachers, "is, in my estimation, a vastly overrated function." To underline this shift of emphasis, Rogers suggested replacing the conventional title of teacher by that of "facilitator."

In support of his recommendation, Rogers questions the validity of all existing curriculums.[5] "As soon as we focus on the question of teaching," he writes, "the question arises, what shall we teach?" This is, of course, a question educators must face continually. Their deliberations assume the existence of a general consensus on the goals of education, and their responsibility, as they see it, is to redefine these goals in the light of current thinking and to make provision for responsive changes in school programs. Rogers, however, stands apart from this consensus by insisting that, because our basic assumptions are wrong, we must set aside everything that has ever been thought or said about the curriculum.

One of these false assumptions, Rogers asserts, is that there is a definable body of knowledge and concepts that should be transmitted to students. "I wonder," he writes, "if, in this modern world, we are justified in the presumption that we are wise about the future and the young are foolish. Are we really sure of what they should know?" Rogers's argument at this point strikes a familiar note: we are living in a rapidly changing world that demands new modes of response almost from day to day. "If there is one truth about modern man," Rogers tells us, "it is that he lives in a world that is constantly changing" and therefore "the goal of education must be the facilitation of change and learning." One might ask why education must facilitate change if the world is in a constant state of flux anyway—but that would be quibbling. The substantive inference Rogers draws is that the only thing that it is important for students to learn is "the process of seeking knowledge." Whatever factual or theoretical knowledge we now have is bound to become obsolete very soon; there is, therefore, no reason to teach or acquire such knowledge. Instead, the schools must gear their efforts in another direction, that is, primary emphasis must be placed on teaching the processes of acquiring knowledge so that students will be able to cope with the challenges of an unforeseeable future.

To underline this change of direction, Rogers suggests that the title of teacher should be replaced with that of "facilitator of learning." This shift of emphasis will result in more vital interpersonal relationships than are attainable in the conventional classroom. The "facilitator" will not impose his own ideas or the content of a prescribed syllabus but will establish an atmosphere of mutual trust in which the creative powers of students will be released. "The facilitation of significant learning." Rogers writes, "rests upon certain attitudinal qualities which exist in a personal relationship between the facilitator and the learner."[6] These attitudinal qualities are described at some length, and the portrait that emerges reveals the positive values Rogers wants to achieve as well as the shortcomings of his proposal.

The first qualification of the teacher-faciltator is "realness or genuineness." "This means, Rogers explains, "that he is a person to his students, not a faceless embodiment of a curricular requirement nor a sterile tube through which knowledge is passed from one generation to the next."[7] To illustrate what "realness" means, he cites a sixth-grade teacher who decided to try out an "unstructured or nondirective" approach in what had been a difficult class. "I began," the teacher is quoted as saying, "by telling the class that we are going to try an experiment. I explained that for one day I would let them do anything they wanted to do—they did not have to do anything they did not want to." The experiment apparently worked well and was continued for several days, eventually leading to the adoption of a "work-contract plan" in which each child was to choose from a checklist his or her activities for the day—reading, exercises, self-graded tests—and carry them out to completion. To Rogers, a latecomer to the educational feast, this was a new departure in teaching method; he was apparently unaware of its historic roots. But what mattered more than the teacher's method to qualify her as a real person in Rogers's eyes was her readiness to express openly her feelings of annoyance and anger when art materials were missing or scraps of paper were scattered on the floor.

Another "real" teacher in Rogers's estimation is Sylvia Ashton-Warner, whose extraordinary skill in relating to Maori children has become almost a legend in educational circles.[8] Miss Ashton-Warner's success was the result of genuine devotion to her pupils—she was indeed a "real" teacher—but it was also due in large measure to her insight into the nature of teaching method. For one thing, she discarded the vocabulary lists assigned by school authorities and based her lessons on the linguistic experiences familiar to children nurtured in a primitive society. Rogers praises her vitality, creativeness, and dedication as qualities that are not observable in the majority of "unreal" teachers who staff our schools, but he seems to underrate her skill in adapting teaching method to the needs of her pupils.

A second quality the "facilitator" should possess is labeled "prizing, acceptance, trust." These are indeed desirable attitudes in teachers (as well as in people generally) and would need no further comment but for the implication that most teachers do not prize or accept or trust their pupils. A genuine respect for children, a readiness to listen to them, a sensitiveness to their feelings—these are the supportive traits of all teachers. But teachers know that goodwill is not a sufficient basis for an educational program. A physician's bedside manner is less functional in curing a patient's illness than his use of the proper medical procedures. Rogers's characterization of the facilitator as empathetic and sincere is as marginal in dealing with the knotty problems of education as it would be in describing the qualifications of a lawyer, an engineer, or a psychotherapist.

How, then, are we to construe this "new" concept—facilitator of learning? Does it mean something different from the time-honored title of teacher? Teaching, one would assume, is nothing more than the facilitation of learning. The most conventional pattern of instruction attempts to promote learning by awakening interest in a subject, raising questions and setting problems, seeking answers through discussion and study, requiring exercise and drill to insure retention, and testing periodically the degree of mastery of skills and concepts. The guiding principle of these activities is to apply the psychological laws of readiness, purpose, and reinforcement in the classroom setting. The evocation of a new title—facilitator of learning—in place of the conventional term teacher does little to dminish the value of these basic principles and practices.

Still, Rogers insists that there would be advantages in the nondirective procedures that would become the norm in classrooms. Students, encouraged to think out solutions to problems on their own, would become adept in the processes of inquiry and research by which knowledge is acquired. "The only man who is educated," Rogers writes, "is the man who has learned how to learn—and who realizes that only the process of seeking knowledge gives a basis of security."[9] In other words, the product of schooling will be a highly motivated, self-directive individual who has acquired the ability to deal effectively with the problems he encounters in business, household management, community affairs, and other concerns of adult life. He will have learned to identify problems, weigh alternative solutions, discover the relevant facts, and evaluate the advantages and disadvantages of different courses of action.

I have no quarrel with this statement of objectives. In fact, it corresponds with the prevailing philosophy of educational objectives, as expressed many years ago by the Commission on the Reorganization of the Secondary Schools in a report entitled "The Cardinal Principles of Secondary Education."[10] "Education in a democracy, both within and without the school," the report states, "should develop in each individual the knowledge, interests, ideals, habits, and powers whereby he may find his place and use this place to shape both himself and society toward nobler ends." Perhaps the phrase "toward nobler ends" is a bit too ornate and idealistic for our tougher contemporary outlook, but surely we must agree with its intended meaning, namely, that the schools should develop literate, informed, socially responsible men and women, equipped with useful vocational skills and resources for rewarding leisure activities, and imbued with a degree of self-understanding and self-esteem. Rogers's definition of the educated man or woman is not inconsistent with that of the Cardinal Principles but is pitifully narrower in scope.

The eloquent wording of a goal, however, does not prescribe the best means of its attainment. It is one thing to preach the ideal of liberty and justice for all and quite another to carry it into practice through legislation, public debate, judicial intervention, social militancy, and, in the extreme case, civil war. It is the fate of much of our discussion of the goals of education to flounder in the snare of the glittering generalization. The promise of a brave new world to be created by free schools, open classrooms, and student autonomy cannot be accepted without critical analysis of their concrete application in the classroom. This pragmatic criterion must, of course, be applied to every theoretical system.

In short, Rogers's proposal to transform the teacher's role into the radically different function of facilitator of learning must be evaluated like every other pedagogic concept. Is the withdrawal of the teacher from an active, directive role in the classroom likely to promote or to defeat valid educational aims? How does the system work in practice? Rogers himself provides a number of anecdotal accounts of the application of his method, the most illuminating example being a description of how he conducted a course at the college level, an elective graduate course entitled "Values in Human Behavior (Including Sensitivity Training)," given at the California Western University.[11]

In a preface to his narrative, Rogers cautions the reader not to take his method of conducting the course as a model, since the concept of the facilitator's relationship with his students cannot be reduced to a formula and will accordingly vary widely in different classes. At the same time, he expresses confidence that the pattern of teaching he exhibited in the course, although somewhat affected by the fact that it was a graduate course for education majors, might well be used, with certain modifications, in the secondary and elementary schools.

The purpose of the course—"Values in Human Behavior"—as set forth in the college catalog was to "assist the student in achieving the following aims: (1) a better understanding and knowledge of human nature; (2) knowledge and understanding of the philosophies and principles of leadership; and (3) ability to translate this knowledge and understanding into patterns of effective leadership in education." A student reading these grandiose purposes would be faced with the problem of surmising what the specific subject matter of the course would be, but the promise of exploring human values would certainly be exhilarating, and the parenthetical tag (Including Sensitivity Training) would undoubtedly pique curiosity and arouse expectations of fresh and vital insights.

Professor Rogers himself approached the course with only the vaguest conception of what it would deal with. In a "Memo," (Rogers' word) to the students handed out at the first class meeting, he described his orientation to the teacher's role and responsibility in the following disarming message: *Values in Human Behavior (Including Sensitivity Training).* Wow! what a title for a course. To me it seems to be an opportunity to do anything we wish which will add significantly to our own learning. . . . Here are some of my thoughts for the course thus far. I have had relatively little time to think about the matter and all of these plans are subject to change if you wish."[12]

The colloquial tone and candor of this first part of the memo was intended—quite consciously, I suggest—to establish the kind of rapport with his students that Rogers believed in, that is, the teacher must be "a person to his students, not a faceless embodiment of a curricular requirement." It is possible, however, that at least one or two of the students were disturbed by Rogers's cavalier attitude toward the intellectual substance of the course he had undertaken to teach. They were probably a little dismayed, too, by the vagueness of outline in the description of course objectives implied in the statement: "an opportunity to do anything we wish. . . ."

Some students, I imagine, must have detected an element of deception in the Memo even at this point. For if the course was to be entirely unstructured (that is, to permit the group "to do anything"), the Memo should not have gone beyond a bare statement to that effect. The students would then be free to institute and carry through their own plans in accordance with their own wishes. But even this resolution of the dilemma created by the doctrine of student autonomy would not be satisfactory, for the problem of determining what the group wished to do would arise again and again to plague its inventor.

At any rate, the Memo did in fact go on to outline how the course would be conducted. After the first meeting, there would be two workshops, each extending from Friday evening through Sunday morning, during which there would be discussion in large and small groups covering such broad topics as: "What are the sources of my values?" and "What human values do I stand for?" Most of the time during the weekend sessions would be spent in basic encounter groups led by Rogers's assistants on the college staff, and suggestions for the topics to be dealt with in these discussion groups were formulated as follows: "Personal values as they relate to the meaning that one perceives in life; the values one regards as significant in one's personal behavior; values as related to sexual and family behavior; values in interpersonal relationships; values as they relate to the philosophy and the practice of the behavioral sciences; special value problems such as prejudice, ethnic attitudes, and the like. . . ."

There was, of course, no element of compulsion or restrictiveness in these suggestions; in fact, it was clear to the students that the encounter groups would be entirely unstructured.

The requirements for credit in the course, the Memo went on to say, would include, first, the reading of certain articles and books. Rogers presented this requirement only out of deference to the administration. "I was encouraged by the coordinator of the program," he informed the students half apologetically, "to prepare a broad-gauge reading list and I have tried to do this." But the reading requirement would be administered permissively. The students could read all the books on the list, or none of them. They could, if they wished, read any other books or articles bearing on the subject that they discovered on their own. They were not required to read any book through. They were assured that they would not be tested on their comprehension of any of their readings. They would, however, be asked to submit a candid statement of what they had read or, if such was the case, a statement to the effect that they had read none of the material.

The second requirement of the course was that "you write a paper which may be as brief or lengthy as you wish about your most significant personal values and the ways they have changed or not changed as a result of this course." Here we see the same kind of formlessness in guidelines and standards as in the reading requirements. Most students would be perplexed. What kind of paper did the professor want? Did he want a personal apologia in the form of a self-portrait, or did he want a carefully researched analysis of, say, the values of existentialism as compared with those of the Judaeo-Christian tradition? If it did not matter what one wrote in the required paper, why bother? Indeed, the serious student might well ask himself whether a researched and analytic paper might not brand him as a conformist, a square, or whatever else the current jargon might be. If the course was to be informal and undemanding, why pursue any kind of rigorous study of a philosophy or religion or ethical system? If all values are to be challenged, even the value of scholarship is open to question. Besides, neither the professor nor his assistants, according to the Memo, would evaluate the papers anyway.

The third requirement of the course, as explained with disarming candor in the Memo, was that each student turn in to Rogers a statement of his, the student's, evaluation of his own work and the grade the student thought appropriate. "If I find that my estimate of your work is quite at variance with yours," the Memo went on, "I will have a personal talk with you and we will see if we cannot arrive at some mutually satisfactory grade which I can in good conscience sign and turn in." One might wonder how Rogers could grade a student's work in the absence of defined aims, standards, tests, or any other criteria of progress and growth. How does one estimate intellectual or emotional growth when there is no lower or upper limit to achievement, no starting point, no goal? It is an Olympic contest in which each runner starts at whatever point on the track he wishes, and there is no timekeeper or referee present during the race, and—to carry the analogy further toward absurdity—every runner is declared the winner if, in his own judgment, he did creditably.

We are not given a transcript of the course, that is, a recording of what was said at the various meetings of the group. It would be helpful to have such a record. In fact, tape recordings or typed transcripts of the detailed proceedings in model lessons, whether conventional or innovative, would be most useful in discussions of teaching method in training and in-service courses. Rogers does, however, report the reactions of a number of students to their involvement in this experimental course, and most of the comments were favorable, indeed enthusiastic. The participants enjoyed their opportunity to enter a social milieu in which confession and self-analysis were encouraged. They were part of a group, not members of an impersonal lecture audience or isolated individuals deprived of emotional and intellectual nourishment on a campus whose tribal taboos inhibited self-expression. The students in Professor Rogers's class enjoyed and benefited from their experience.

Nevertheless, the theory of learning implicit in Rogers's method of conducting the course must be rejected. Can the unorganized, nondirective exchange of thoughts and surmises (no matter how insightful they may be) in a group encounter session or an unstructured lesson provide the useful knowledge students must have to adjust successfully to the adult world in which they will need competence and emotional security? The answer can be found by looking more closely at Rogers's belief that the methods of psychotherapy, a field in which he has some expertise, can be applied successfully in teaching.

Insight therapy, whether in the privacy of the analyst's office or in the group-encounter session, works by eliciting from patients the memories and insights that will, it is hoped, enable them to understand and thus gain mastery over the sources of their emotional disturbances. Persons seeking relief from sleeplessness, sexual inadequacy, intense anxiety, and other kinds of disabling obsessions place themselves in the psychotherapist's care. The patient is asked to talk out his problems freely or to take certain tests, among them word association tests and the Rohrschach inkblot test, to reveal to the therapist aspects of his psychic life of which the patient is unaware. Similarly, in the group encounter, each individual participant is encouraged to discover his subconscious feelings and motivations by uninhibited exposure to the group of his most secret experiences.

In recent years, however, a growing number of psychologists have become skeptical of the efficacy of insight therapy and its procedures. They point out that, after seventy years of use, there are still few indications that uncovering motives and expanding of self-understanding really confer much therapeutic power over most troubling symptoms. Perry London, in *Behavior Control,* a critical study of psychotherapy, notes that the effect on the patient is often quite different from the relief he is seeking. "The fact that intelligent, educated, sophisticated people tend to stay in therapy for a long time," he writes, "suggests that it works in some other sense which is not measured by most research into its effectiveness."[13]

It is this "other sense" that gives the clue to the fallacy of Rogers's theory. The unstructured lesson gives the student relief from the tensions of an organized program of studies; it is a stimulating experience, for a time at least, and may open up avenues for further exploration for him. Taking part in the free interplay of ideas, facing challenges from other minds, forced to define his own ideas and defend them, the student becomes aware of his strengths and limitations in an authentic social setting. But this heightening of consciousness, valuable as it is, is not what he came to school for or, more precisely, it is not what his parents sent him to school for. Nor is it what the collective wisdom of society—as embodied in the education law and in the massive appropriations for school buildings, educational equipment, and professional staff—hopes he will obtain from schooling. One's heightened consciousness is doubtless important, but it is unlikely that the elementary and secondary student, or even the college student, can construct the sciences and arts out of his consciousness, heightened or otherwise.

In the last analysis, the Rogers doctrine of facilitation cannot serve as a foundation for constructive reform of curriculum and teaching method. It is, at best, a salutary reminder that good teaching method should involve students intellectually and emotionally in class activities. It offers no guidelines for developing sequential units of study or a comprehensive school program. It prescribes no criteria for judging the value of a given course of study or for measuring its outcomes. If a course in Values in Human Behavior can be presented, as Rogers's course was, in a series of informal encounters and with virtually no direction or imposition of standards, we cannot avoid the conclusion that (1) the course is merely a pretext for self-indulgence and devoid of definable content, (2) the teacher-facilitator has no clear conception of what is worth knowing in the field, and (3) the values derived by students from the course have no intrinsic relationship to the prospectus of the course but are acquired incidentally.

Advocates of open classrooms and unstructured teaching assent to another of Rogers' doctrines without being aware of its weak logical basis. There is an attractive ring to the syllogism: (1) the world is changing; (2) the future is unknowable; (3) therefore, the schools must stress the processes of learning, not the substance of scholarship. One of the natural hazards of reading educational literature is this very platitude, set forth in the opening paragraphs of countless articles and books, informing us that we are living in an era of change in science, politics, religion, ethics, technology, and so on, ad nauseam. Those who utter this banality fail to recognize that change does not mean the replacement of existing concepts or structures or institutions by entirely new concepts or structures or institutions. For example, when we think of yearly model changes in automobiles, we mean that certain elements of design or engineering are different from those of earlier models. But 90 percent of next year's model will be identical with last year's model. Even when a rotary engine is substituted for the conventional internal combustion engine, most of the physical features that characterize the automobile remain unchanged. As to changes in life-styles, present trends are not so far-reaching as may appear on the surface: sexual emancipation has not freed men and women from moral and personal sensitivities, nor have changes in fashion—men's hair styles and women's miniskirts, for instance—had much effect on social life except, perhaps, to add variety to the scene. I am not even sure the revolutions that sought to bring about sweeping changes in the Soviet Union and elsewhere did in fact produce economic structures that are very different from those of the Western democracies, state monopolies functioning very much like the monopolistic corporations they were intended to improve upon. Continuity is a more significant factor in human affairs than change. The cliché—a changing world—must be viewed as a convenient substitute for exact definition, a catchy slogan used to establish rapport with an audience hungry for fresh solutions.

It should be noted that Rogers—not alone among reformists—implies that it is the "changing world" in itself that necessitates corresponding changes in social institutions, specifically in education. This is a classic example of non sequitur. Even if the world remained totally static, innovative designs in curriculum and methodology might be desirable. Conversely, a dramatically changing world might or might not justify radical changes in the schools. The value of any educational program—old or new—is appraised in the collective judgment of responsible persons in the schools and the community. Whether to include Chinese (or sex education or woodworking) in the curriculum is a decision that is based on an assessment of student needs, and adjustment to changing conditions in the social environment is only one of those needs. Even in a society that is changing rapidly, the abiding value of the sciences and the humanities is not diminished.

Rogers's statement, that "only the process of seeking knowledge gives a basis of security," is truly puzzling to me. We are asked to assent to the proposition that students should learn how to find answers to problems without having a solid background of information and scholarship. I am puzzled because I cannot conceive what is meant by *process* detached from *substance.* The proposition has an appealing quality because one of its two possible meanings corresponds with the hopes of parents and teachers everywere, namely, that students will be able to deal intelligently with the practical problems of adult life. The second implication of the proposition, however, is patently untrue, that is, the assumption that the basic cognitive skills and a smattering of research techniques are or will be sufficient for an understanding of the unpredictable future world. These skills and competencies are, as I have shown in connection with the CBL program, abstractions. It is not enough to know that inductive reasoning is a set of processes; what is essential is command of the specific data that go into the inductive process. Therefore, the outcome of Carl Rogers's proposed reforms, downgrading the basic curriculum and diminishing the teacher's role, is bound to be catastrophic.

There is one additional question raised by Rogers's plan. As a practical matter, what criteria can be devised for the recruitment and certification of teachers—forgive me, "facilitators"—if their qualifications are to be such characteristics as "realness" and "empathy"? Intellectual qualities—cultural background and scholarship in definite subject areas—will have no place in the selection of teachers. The facilitator will not be required to have expertise or even rudimentary scholarship in mathematics, foreign language, or social studies—or, if he does have such competence, he will be under pressure to conceal the fact. Boards of education will have to resort to intuition and clairvoyance in selecting their staffs. Certifying teachers on the basis of their emotional qualities alone would be equivalent to admitting lawyers to the bar because they are sincere believers in justice and civil rights or licensing physicians on the basis of their sensitivity to human suffering.

Mystics, fanatics, practitioners of one or another brand of psychotherapy, political extremists, intellectual charlatans—all these would be free to hawk their esoteric wares in the classrooms of our nation's schools. With no restraints provided by definite objectives and planned syllabuses, the practitioners of the unstructured teaching method would pursue their individual phantoms aimlessly. No matter how fascinating and provocative each class session might be, the sequence of topics that constitutes the conventional course of study in the major fields of learning and the expanding elective programs would dissolve into a series of whimsical pastimes, to the detriment of learning and intellectual growth.

6

JOHN HOLT, ROMANTIC

Among the reconstructionists, none is more articulate than John Holt, whose commentaries on the iniquity of conventional schooling have been in the public eye since the early sixties, when his books *How Children Learn* and *How Children Fail* made all of us do some agonizing soul searching. Here was a sincere, sympathetic teacher whose experience had convinced him that most of what the schools had been offering and most of the pedagogic methods in use were not merely ineffectual but positively damaging. For the last few years, in an unending stream of articles and lectures, he has disseminated his iconoclastic theory frankly and persuasively at home and abroad. He is clearly one of the most conspicuous standard bearers in the vanguard of reformism.

In an open letter addressed to a Dr. Bliss (presumably a troubled teacher who wrote to Mr. Holt in a spate of incredulity) and published in a miscellany of Holt's writings entitled *The Underachieving School* (1969), Holt set forth the guiding principles of his educational philosophy.[1] They are reproduced here in full (the numbering is mine):

1. I think children learn better what they want to learn when they want to learn it, and how they want to learn it, learning for their own curiosity, and not at somebody else's order.

2. I believe that learning would be greatly improved if we could completely or at least largely abolish the fixed curriculum in its present form.

3. I do not believe that testing and grading perform any inherent or useful function in learning; in fact, they corrupt and impede the learning process.

4. I am altogether opposed to any kind of ability grouping in school.

5. I think that in many more cases than not it is the act of instruction that impedes learning.

6. I think we need to find ways to get more people into the schools that are not teachers.

7. I would also like to see children encouraged and helped to use the resources of the world outside the school to further their learning.

8. I believe that compulsory school attendance no longer serves a useful function.

9. I think we have made education, which should be something that helps young people move into the world and do useful work there, into an

enormous obstacle standing in their way. In short, I am opposed to all kinds of credentials requirements as preconditions for doing work.

10. Everything we (teachers) say and do tends to separate learning from living, and we should instead try to join them together.

The common theme that runs through Holt's ten articles of faith seems to be that our schools, as they are organized at present, are repressive, rigid, counterproductive institutions, and that most if not all of their operative policies should be drastically changed or discarded completely. At the same time, it should be noted that Holt does not quite commit himself to any one course of action unequivocally. There are qualifying phrases in each article of his credo that must be taken into account in a critical assessment of his position. He does not say that children learn *only* what they want to learn when they want to learn it; he says they learn better when they are freed from teacher domination. He does not advocate abolishing the "fixed curriculum" entirely, but holds firm on largely abolishing it. In public discussion of Holt's position, however, such niceties are overlooked, and Holt himself, in some of his polemic writings, does not openly disavow the more radical or extreme interpretations of his views.

It should also be noted that some of his seemingly bold proposals concern matters of policy that educators working in the schools have already integrated into the schools' programs more or less widely. Ability grouping, greater versatility in teaching method, the use of community resources, and the recruitment of teachers without academic accreditation, especially in the fields of music and art, are not uncommon practices. These are policies in which either alternative proposal can work equally well under certain special conditions; whatever failings are discovered in their pragmatic application can be corrected. In Holt's agenda, however, there are a number of dogmatically stated positions that would, I am convinced, cause serious damage to the schools if adopted generally.

1. Holt writes: "I think children learn better what they want to learn when they want to learn it, and how they want to learn it, learning for their own curiosity, and not at somebody else's order."

It is unquestionably true that children (and adults) learn best when interest and motivation are high. Common sense and experience support this concept and few educational theorists would challenge its validity as a guiding principle of pedagogy. We put all our energies into learning to drive a car or play bridge or choose the right clothes when personal and social pressures make us eager to do so. When planning a trip, we study road maps and travel folders thoroughly. In preparation for my first journey abroad some years ago, I devoured every book on the history of art I could lay my hands on to pave the way for my projected visits to the Louvre and the Prado museums. When I taught *Hamlet* to an honors class, I reread every line of the text and reexamined the critical commentaries in the footnotes even though I had taught the play many times before. As for students in school, rehearsals for plays and concerts, team practice for interscholastic games, work on a science or art project, and even intensive study for an examination—all of these activities attest to the fact that the strongest motivation for learning is the immediate need or desire to learn.

Assent to this principle, however, must be qualified. The examples of purposeful learning activities cited above assume that the learner has an awareness of his goals and the means of attaining them. He may not, however, be aware of alternative goals and variant activities that might fulfill his purposes with greater reward and satisfaction.

For example, a child who loves to draw or paint will acquire a broader range of expressive skills and discover new outlets for creativity after he has been taught or introduced to the concept of visual perspective. Similarly, awareness of the reproductive function of flowers and their symbiotic relationship with insects and the summer breezes may literally be a revelation for children, opening up unsuspected avenues of further inquiry. In elementary mathematics, the use of the abacus and Cuisinaire rods reduces the enigmatic decimal number system to a logical pattern, making possible the exploration of the binary and duodecimal number systems and, later, their extension into higher mathematics and computer theory. Expansion of interests and goals cannot be left to transient curiosity. Holt's simplistic reliance on immediate interest is therefore less valid than the pedagogic principle that children's interests must be nurtured and extended in a sequential curriculum.

In the traditional classroom, Holt implies, the teacher directs his pupils against their will to learn things they have no immediate urgency or need to know—Ohm's law or decimals or a sonnet by Edna St. Vincent Millay. Silberman's anecdote about the teacher who stifled her pupils' curiosity about the turtles is an apt illustration. Holt cites a similar case: an arithmetic teacher who failed to take advantage of the interest generated by a fire engine that screamed past the building.[2] Both incidents were intended to suggest that teachers are inflexible in carrying out their planned lessons and thus are likely to repress children's natural curiosity. Whether these incidents are typical is hard to say, but I am sure most educators would agree that these teachers should have been more resourceful when unexpected happenings opened up opportunities for expanding their pupils' horizons.

But Silberman and Holt are saying something more fundamental. They are asserting that efficient learning cannot take place unless students have a natural desire to satisfy curiosity or resolve an inwardly felt tension. Interest, they say, must be spontaneous, growing out of the children's experiences in and out of school. But is the curiosity less real if the teacher contrives its emergence? A syllabus is simply an organized plan for awakening and satisfying curiosity, and its long-range aim is to develop more mature and complex interests than would likely exist in the absence of planned instruction.

Consider, for example, the subject of nutrition, a curricular thread that runs through the elementary and secondary grades. Every child is viscerally interested in satisfying his appetite with a lunch and a tasty snack as often as possible. His appetite does not usually discriminate between wholesome and nutritionally damaging foods. It is the responsibility of informed parents—and of teachers *in loco parentis*—to ensure that the child becomes concerned about sound eating habits and learns the basic principles of the science of dietetics. A teacher who sets about doing this by announcing bluntly: "This morning we will study nutrition" is a clumsy technician, but the teacher who lets children make their own discoveries haphazardly is irresponsible.

The good teacher will awaken the interest of the class by using some motivational device, perhaps keying his approach to the care and feeding of window plants or the cageful of hamsters in the science corner; or by having the children look as closely at the nutritional ingredients of dry cereals set forth on the carton as they do at the colorful cartoon figures; or displaying posters and photographs or a film depicting the victims of malnutrition in Uganda or Bangladesh. There are any number of additional ways of vitalizing the subject: in a multiethnic class, for instance, the black and Hispanic and Jewish children may be asked to bring to class samples of the foods indigenous to their cultural backgrounds. The series of lessons on nutrition (now at the center of consciousness) will include a study of the basic food elements—proteins, carbohydrates, fats, minerals, vitamins—using textbooks or pamphlets supplied by health agencies and including class demonstrations on the chemistry of these elements. As a culminating activity, teacher and class might cooperatively prepare a number of nutritionally well-balanced meals, write letters to parents or other classes or the school dietician, or plan an assembly program dramatizing what was learned in the unit. Thus the students' uncritical pleasure in eating has been expanded into a learning experience that extends far beyond the kind of curiosity Holt sees as the one motivating force.

Or consider the course in Euclidean geometry, which has persisted in the high-school curriculum for centuries. I'm not sure where it stands now, what with the several non-Euclidean geometries competing for attention and the growing disenchantment with formal disciplines. Recently geometry has been merged into a course entitled "Tenth-Year Mathematics," sharing the stage with algebra and trigonometry and other forms of gamesmanship. I have every confidence that students in this course are learning many things that we Euclidean purists did not even suspect the existence of. But one thing I know—none of us could possibly have had a spontaneous interest in anything like the amazing series of puzzles called plane geometry.

I do not remember exactly how we were introduced to the study of geometry. I have vague recollections of being asked by the teacher the very first day to buy a straight rule (we called it a ruler) and a pair of compasses. For a few days, we did nothing but erect perpendiculars, bisect lines, and construct triangles of various shapes. Some of us were ingenious enough to create intricate arabesque designs with the compasses. It was not until we were familiar with the mystery of geometric forms that we were plunged into the intellectual bath of formal geometric logic. We journeyed patiently through the maze of postulates, axioms, theorems, and corollaries that constituted the fabric of plane geometry, not quite sure what we were doing but buoyed by a peculiar satisfaction in being able to affix the magic formula *Q.E.D.* to a completed proof as a benchmark of our pride in accomplishment. Our attitude toward geometry was probably something like that of neophytes being inducted into a ritual cult with arcane ceremonial rites.

But we gained something that would not have emerged if our experience had been limited to the manipulation of the compass and ruler. In defiance of the transfer-of-training heresy, we learned to be methodical and persistent and to apply a rigorous logic to the solution of problems. Geometry disciplined our minds, specifically in providing us with a touchstone for detecting shoddy reasoning.

One mode of logical deduction, which I encountered for the first time in the geometry classroom, has remained a useful intellectual tool to this day. This is the method of reductio ad absurdum, that is, in demonstrating the truth of a theorem, you assume that the opposite theorem is true and then, following the consequences of this assumption, you show that it leads to an obvious contradiction. A second method of reasoning revealed in pure form in the study of geometry—and mathematics in general—is the dependence of logical thinking on clear definitions and premises, for example, that only one straight line can be drawn between two points, and, although less obvious, that parallel lines do meet at infinity, according to Euclid anyway. Public discussion and debate on capital punishment, abortion, energy conservation, and the like would be more rational if the conflicting premises held privately by the discussants were stated as explicitly as Euclid stated his. In a word, the study of geometry has values that are secured only through a structured course of study, values that would be lost if students learned only "for their own curiosity."

The fallacy of Holt's view of learning is his failure to recognize the importance of purposeful teaching in broadening the range of young people's natural interests. In the intermediate and secondary schools, especially, subject matter is often far removed from what is implied in the stricture: "what they want to learn when they want to learn it." What immediate interest do adolescents have in punctuating a nonrestrictive clause or solving a quadratic equation? The teacher's artistry consists in strengthening the links between subject matter and apperception that become visible to students only when their eyes have been opened to unsuspected issues and relationships. The teacher does not impose tasks arbitrarily; rather he elucidates the materials of his subject in ways that generate new insights and a broader range of interests.

Perhaps a formula might be worked out to represent in generalized form the accretion of interest and curiosity that grows out of the mastery of successive stages of adjustment to life. At the bottom of the scale is the infant exploring with every nerve end and muscle fibre the myriad faces of the world outside him. Trees and grass, dogs and cats and horses, rain and snow, toys, songs, shoelaces, and dentists—all of these must be assimilated into an orderly universe in which at first his consciousness was the only reality. Growing up requires that the outside world, the resistant reality of which is demonstrated to him by cuts and bruises as well as the benignant gifts of food and embraces, must be reduced to manageable dimensions by endless experimentation. Education, whether in the nursery or the street, consists in acquiring the techniques by which the individual can be successful in his interaction with the mysterious world that surrounds him.[3]

Schooling has a specialized task in this process of discovery and adjustment. Its task is to introduce aspects of the world that are beyond the range of the child's intensely eager but limited sensory grasp. The most potent tools for such exploration are literacy, mathematics, and scientific method, the intellectual levers that give a student the power and impetus to carry his vital exploration of the universe into the vanished eras of the past and the remotest regions of the earth. A unit in "Peoples of Other Lands" is nothing more than an expansion of the child's natural curiosity about the people in his neighborhood or the other children in the class. The justification of a syllabus in history, ancient or modern, is that it structures the student's private vision of time and man's existence— hitherto based on his own observations and surmises, random reading, and subliminal television influences—with supportive scholarship. The virtue of an organized curriculum and purposeful teaching is their service in fortifying the individual's efforts to gain self-reliance in the ordering of his life.

One might think of education as the mastery of skills and knowledge and concepts at increasing levels of complexity. Each stage generates and sustains an ever-growing capacity for further acquisition of knowledge. The growing child's curiosity remains the vital center of motivation, but it is sensitized during the formative years of experience and schooling to receive impulses from a wider and more finely differentiated spectrum of symbols.

A sequential and organized course of study awakens and develops interest in areas of perception that John Holt's faith in momentary curiosity would be unlikely to achieve.

2. Holt writes: "I believe that learning would be greatly improved if we could completely or at least largely abolish the fixed curriculum in its present sense."

Here, again, there is a certain ambiguity that gets in the way of comprehension. The pejorative expression "the fixed curriculum" implies that the schools teach the same old subjects in the same old ways as they did in the early part of the century, and ignores the fact that the schools' offerings are continually evolving and being adapted to changing conditions. Moreover, the looseness of the wording of the proposal to "completely or at least largely abolish" the present curriculum leaves too broad a margin for error. The intent of the statement is, however, clear enough—the standard curriculum must go.

Holt supports his disparagement of the fixed curriculum by pointing to the fact that the rate of new discoveries in every field of scholarship has made obsolete most of what his generation learned in school and at college. Most of whatever is being taught today will therefore soon become equally meaningless and useless. It is not necessary to teach arithmetic skills because, Holt tells us, computers will soon perform all the calculations we need. Scientists today talk a language that none of us who learned the rudiments of Newtonian physics and qualitative chemistry in school can begin to comprehend; in fact, specialization has narrowed to a point where one biologist does not understand what another biologist in a different special field is talking about. Holt cites the comment of a business executive who, when asked to suggest to vocational-school administrators what skills students would have to have seven years from now, replied, "I'm sorry. We can't tell you what our own employees are going to need to know seven months from now."[4] Holt's logic would suggest that even the ability to read and write need not be taught since these skills will soon be rendered obsolete by intensive television viewing and encounter sessions. The implication of Holt's argument is that no planned program of instruction should be attempted.

Such reasoning, wherever it is encountered in the vanguard of reformism, is far from convincing. Like Carl Rogers, Holt seems to be much too ready to accept a kind of science-fiction version of what the future will be. The fact is that the knowledge explosion that Holt refers to is the province of a relatively small group of specialists engaged in esoteric research and does not involve the overwhelming majority of scientists and scholars. The frontiers of scientific knowledge, in nuclear physics, microbiology, and genetics are extensions of, not departures from, the fundamental concepts that inform the science curriculum in schools and colleges. Moreover, the ability to absorb the new ideas as they came to light cannot be developed in a vacuum: the creative thinking necessary to appreciate them requires a solid grounding in basic scientific knowledge and an understanding of scientific method. These considerations should give us pause in assenting to a sweeping revision or indeed the complete rejection of a basic curriculum.

Ironically, the most glaring evidence of the superficiality of Holt's thinking can be seen in his suggestion of what should be substituted for the traditional courses of study. "The most important questions and problems of our time," he writes, "are not in the curriculum, not even in the hot-shot universities, let alone the schools. Check any university catalogue and see how many courses you can find in such questions as Peace, Poverty, Race, Environmental Pollution, and so on."[5] The common factor in these proposed courses is presumably that they are the burning problems of today and therefore close to the concerns of youth. Indeed they are. The issues of the present day and their bearing on future events are vitally important to all of us. It is precisely for this reason that this generation of students must be more than superficially equipped to face them.

Let us consider, for example, a course in a "hot-shot university" on "Environmental Pollution." Such a course, whether a seminar or a lecture course, would necessarily deal with industrial wastes polluting our rivers, exhaust emissions from automobiles and factory smokestacks polluting our atmosphere, and oil spills and atomic wastes destroying the ecology of our lakes and oceans. Students would be eager to listen, to do reading and research, and to seek for solutions. Somewhere in the course, however, they will run into a serious difficulty, namely, the need to know a considerable body of chemistry, physics, and biology. How otherwise will they be able to understand what biodegradable effluent or permafrost or radiation poisoning means? They will be unable to form enlightened opinions with an intellectual background devoid of basic science and sociology. Feelings, yes—but no valid opinions. Their legitimate anxiety about the destruction of our environment will be no more rationally founded than were the fears of medieval peasants of the demons and malign spirits that the peasants thought caused the Black Death.

By all means, let us involve students in questions of immediate importance and concern. But the way to do this is to strengthen the curriculum, not to dilute it or "largely abolish" it.

3. Holt writes: "I think that in more cases than not it is the act of instruction that impedes learning."

Let us try to picture for a moment the model of instruction Holt probably had in mind when he made this assertion. It would consist of daily assignments requiring study of a textbook, written exercises, memorization, and drill. There would be frequent testing of what was to have been learned. Students would be rated according to their performance in recitations and on homework and examinations. The teacher would be a martinet, a disciplinarian, governing his cowed classes through the ever-present threat of failing grades or referral to the dean. It is true that his students were likely to master subject matter and do well on College Boards, but this would be small consolation for all their joyless hours in the classroom. Every high-school graduate over thirty has traumatic memories of this kind of instruction. Such teachers, no doubt, were secure in their own self-esteem, and some even earned the grudging respect of their students that carried over to class reunions at which Mr. So-and-So was referred to affectionately: "He was a slave driver, all right, but in his class you learned your stuff." Today such drillmasters are a rare and obsolescent breed.

Holt confesses that in his early days as a teacher he knew no better than to direct his own classes in the manner of a drillmaster and that he gained a more enlightened conception of teaching only through bitter experience and much soul searching. His conversion was sudden and complete. One cannot help wondering whether, and, if so, to what extent, the original orthodoxy and the adopted heresy were both based on an emotional need rather than on reasoned conviction.

Good teaching is now and has always been a subtle amalgam of discipline and freedom. The fact that certain oppressive methods are the only ones used by a certain type of teacher does not negate their utility when they are applied intelligently in combination with more stimulating methods. Motivation, interesting presentation, thought-generating questions, imaginative assignments, seminar discussions—these methods can coexist with solid, directive teaching in which high standards of achievement are demanded and enforced.

If a virtue is carried to an extreme, as Aristotle reminds us, it becomes a vice, and this leaning toward some extreme is the mark of a fanatic. Holt's obsession with the virtue of spontaneity blinds him to the commonsense value of drill and testing as components of the learning process. We hardly need to be told that learning should not be all exercise and drill, but we should insist that knowledge and skills are likely to be shallow and impermanent without the neural and muscular reinforcement provided by exercise and drill. Whatever is learned fades from memory unless it is soon put to use, applied in diverse settings, and strengthened by repetition. Memorization of dates, formulas, declensions, definitions, and passages of noble prose and poetry is prerequisite to mastery of concepts and principles.

Homework assignments—useless drudgery, according to Holt—are an essential component of learning. In preparation for the class recitation, the student may be asked to read a textbook, take note of salient points, answer assigned questions, work out problems. Each day, when he enters the classroom, he will be aware of the broad outlines of the topic being studied, puzzled by some points, baffled by others, but at least prepared to some extent to understand and absorb the salient points of the lesson, whether it is on the causes of World War II, the nuclear structure of the atom, the use of the apostrophe, or the nature of a musical scale. As a follow-up to the lesson, questions and exercises as an assignment will reinforce his learning through a rereading of the textbook with new insight, or the reading of supplementary material for enrichment, or the answering of additional questions and the working out of more demanding problems. As he goes more and more deeply into the subject, he will begin to see correlations, cause-and-effect relationships, and underlying uniformities. The fallacy in Holt's derogation of the "act of instruction" lies in his assumption that the immature mind is capable of the untutored apprehension of difficult ideas.

These considerations apply with equal cogency to the compulsion applied in the formal testing of students' achievement. Holt's belief that testing and grading "do not perform a useful function in learning" is an index of his unrealistic appraisal of the learning process. Ideally, perhaps, self-direction and self-evaluation are desirable objectives that will carry over into adult life to shield the individual from the crushing impersonality of a mass culture. However, the limitations of Holt's design for teaching are most evident in two of its presuppositions. One, the theory assumes that the student in elementary and secondary schools has sufficient knowledge of the world around him to be able to seek for himself the information that will serve his expanding intellectual needs and to judge for himself the degree of his competence in his fields of interest. This assumption is patently false. Two, the theory assumes that directed instruction and periodic testing are inimical to the student's ability to develop powers of critical thinking and independent judgment. This, too, is questionable, for a major goal of instruction—including homework, class recitations, tests, grading—is to ensure a reasonably solid foundation of skills and concepts that will enable the student to function with increasing self-direction at college and in the adult world.

4. Holt writes: "I believe that compulsory attendance no longer serves a useful purpose."

I must confess that there were times when I wondered whether Johnny or Betty, who were floundering in my classes and were not unacquainted with the attendance office, would not be better off out of school. We were failing to reach them; maybe we had nothing to give them. Sooner or later they themselves solved the problem: they dropped out, transferred to a vocational school, or got jobs and attended evening school. There were marginal Johnnys and Bettys, too, who somehow struggled through the grades and eventually made their way to college. The majority of students—close to 80 percent today—went through the prescribed twelve years of schooling with minimal trauma and even a gratifying sense of achievement.

Whatever the case may be, I am convinced that a sound educational program must be based, for most pupils, on compulsory attendance. It must not be forgotten that society has a stake in the education of its youth that cannot lightly be brushed aside. Only by continuity of intellectual growth can the rising generation be prepared to assume the responsibilities of citizenship and adult life. Truancy is as much a socially harmful act as any of the more obviously antisocial patterns of behavior that the law deals with. Compulsion is approved in a wide variety of matters that affect the welfare of society, as seen in laws that require pasteurization of milk and vaccination against smallpox, and this kind of sanction is being recognized today as applicable to a growing range of social interests, consumer protection and antipollution measures among others. Education is committed to ensuring the continuity of cultural and moral values that sustain the health of our social institutions, and educators' support of compulsory attendance is an index of the seriousness of their concern. The cavalier attitude of those who would solve the problems of the maladjusted students by setting them adrift too soon and too readily— Holt goes almost as far as Ivan Illich in this respect—seems therefore to be little short of irresponsible.

The requirement of school attendance is in itself an educational value. It is almost a truism to say that adjustment to life, whether as a worker or professional or a member of a social group, hinges in large measure on individual self-discipline. A sense of responsibility to others is no less contributory to a good life than self-expression and creativeness. Translated into pragmatic terms, this means the impulsive drives of children must be guided toward a willing conformity to the code of sanctions that govern adult life. Education is the surrogate of pitiless nature and the admonitory arm of society in carrying out this task. The rewarding experiences that the school provides cannot be attained without the uninterrupted presence of the child in the classroom and his diligent performance of assignments. The two sides of the fabric are interwoven: poor teaching breeds truancy and truancy, even if sporadic, impedes learning. It is naïve to think that social controls will operate automatically, as the law of supply and demand supposedly does in Adam Smith's marketplace. Compulsion in itself makes possible the attainment of educational objectives.[6]

The school is—or should be—a model of all other social institutions. The matrix of work, whether in industry or civil service, in the conglomerate world of banks and corporations, law offices and hospitals, is conformity to rules. Collective enterprises do not flourish when every employee or manager or executive can decide for himself whether he should come to work on time or carry out his duties only when he is in the mood. This does not mean there is no room for individuality and enterprise, which are as essential to the success of a business or institution as efficiency of performance is.

There is much talk today of the obsolescence of the Protestant ethic of work and individual commitment and much experimentation in farm communes and East Village enclaves with alternative patterns of life. But all the romantic idealization of these tawdry utopias cannot hide the fact that members of communes or communal pads live at or pathetically below the subsistence level and must devote much of their time to providing or scrounging the necessities of life. The new primitivism ignores the fact that our highly organized industrial society is sinfully self-indulgent in its steady reduction of hours of labor together with its assurance of an abundance of facilities for enjoying leisure time. The paradoxical truth, often unacknowledged by the disciples of Thoreau and Illich, is that the technological resources made available to everyone in our "regimented" society are conducive to self-fulfillment in recreation and the arts never before attainable in the history of mankind. These considerations should give us perspective in weighing the shallow talk of oppression and depersonalization in schools and in the world of work.

It is psychologically healthful for the majority of students to attend school up to a reasonable statutory age limit. I am not thinking here of the benefits of schooling as such—the development of skills and concepts and attitudes that are essential to a good life. I am thinking of a less tangible aspect of the school experience—its nurture of self-esteem. Adolescents are troubled by a compulsive search for self-identity. They ask: Who am I? Why am I living? What is the purpose of life? The answers to these questions are elusive, even to adults. During the formative years, there is one reassuring answer: "I am a student. I am part of a meaningful venture. I am preparing to be a successful man or woman." This sustaining self-image, reinforced by family and the social milieu, is an important ingredient of mental health, whether held consciously or vaguely sensed. It underlines the awesome responsibility of educators to do everything possible to maintain excellence in every phase of school life.

Moreover, there is a very real sense in which the fact of compulsory attendance protects the interests of students. The right to an education as codified in the law imposes an obligation on the schools to think out policy decisions responsibly. It compels school administrators to devise programs that will serve the needs of exceptional and disadvantaged students to counteract the corrosive effects of alienation. In the American past— even today in other countries—the ruthless denial of higher education to intellectually handicapped students was the normal process by which admission to the professions and the administrative ranks of business and civil service was restricted to an elite segment of the population. But in the United States, we believe in equal opportunity and upward mobility as inherent rights, and our commitment to compulsory schooling is an institutional expression of our democratic faith.

The historical extension of compulsory school attendance up to the age of sixteen or seventeen is sometimes attributed to trade-union pressures for keeping children off the labor market as long as possible. What a cynical and distorted view this is! It is no less offensive than the imputation of a vested interest in the professional staff as the reason for their supoort of compulsory schooling. Both of these explanations are grounded on a theory of self-interest and economic determinism as the operative causes of social behavior. The countervailing theory—which is more congenial to most people—is that purposeful intervention, based on moral principles and a belief in human perfectibility (or at least improvability) can and will make a difference in the course of human events. Even granting self-interest as a dominant force, we must acknowledge the crucial role of education in sublimating the raw energies of youth into an enlightened concern for social values.

In general, John Holt's ideas seem to be characterized by a kind of perversity. His reasoning is dialectical: whatever exists must be replaced by its antithesis. What is the psychological source of this attitude? Let me offer, tentatively, the following hypothesis: One of the concepts of psychoanalysis is the neurotic reverie by which we compensate for our frustrations. It consists of the rejection or destruction of an offending object by wishing it out of existence. Children enraged by a parent's undeserved rebuke will fantasize a Shangri-la uncorrupted by authority, or they will wish a horrible punishment, as lurid as the wings of imagination can devise, inflicted on the offending parent. Adolescents under similar stress create a psychodrama in which their running away from home and falling under the wheels of a railroad train plays a retributive role. On the more sophisticated adult level, the reverie may take the form of utopianism, the poetic reconstruction of the world along lines closer to the heart's desire, without the sobering limitations of what is possible.

The basis of the negativism and "withdrawal" in the thinking of educational reformists like John Holt may be a deep-seated insecurity that masquerades under the guise of permissiveness.

7

ANYONE
CAN TEACH ENGLISH

The art of teaching follows the pattern of any of the music or theatre arts. A violinist, for example, who has acquired skill in exploiting the resources of his instrument is only at the threshold of musical expressiveness, but his musicianship rests on an assured mastery of technique. The teacher-trainee goes through the required courses at college and graduate school and may have some experience in practice teaching, but a long road lies ahead of him before theory and practice come together creatively in the classroom. The first three or four years of teaching is a period of apprenticeship marked by experimentation and self-criticism. But in most cases, there comes a point at which technique and imagination fuse into self-assurance and artistry.

The uniqueness of the art of teaching lies in three features not shared by the other performance arts: (1) the scenario must be recreated each day before a critical and often restive audience; (2) there is a continuity of interaction between the teacher and his classes, extending over many days and weeks; and (3) the teacher's effectiveness cannot be judged by his words or actions or by the students' responses at any given moment, but must await final evaluation until a proximate or distant future, and even then by criteria that are difficult to define and apply.

It is for this last reason that discussion of the teacher's art sometimes falters: the results of teaching are not easily measured. This is what Professor Grubman was concerned with when she wrote about the difficulty of devising a system of accountability for teachers." In the context of a given school and grade level," she writes,

> the focus of accountability must be on short term and intermediate aims that may be measured readily during the school year. But we are seriously constrained because we do not know how to measure attainment of many of the things we are concerned about in education. There is no compelling evidence, furthermore, that shows a sufficient correlation between goals that can be measured and those that cannot so that the former are an adequate indicator of the latter.[1]

By these criteria, English is probably the most difficult subject to teach well because its outcomes are less easily evaluated than those of most other subjects. The boundaries of the skills and concepts the English course seeks to achieve are not so readily defined as in mathematics, the sciences, or the social studies. There are no textbooks in English—there are only literary works and life experiences, with manuals of style and reference books somewhere within reach. The English syllabus eludes all efforts to reduce its content to a clear prose statement because the subject is more dependent on the teacher's initiative and imagination than anything else. A license to teach English should bear the inscription: "Abandon ease, all ye who enter here."

The very formlessness of the English course has led to the delusion that it can be taught successfully by anyone who is fairly intelligent, moderately well read, and sincere. As chairman of an English department, I was always irritated when a language teacher or a mathematics substitute had to be assigned to take over an English class because of an imbalance in the program. The principal's assurance that these were competent teachers was not usually borne out under the pressure of the daily grind. I am more deeply disturbed by the widespread notion that goodwill and permissive-ness are sufficient guidelines for the teaching of English. The purpose of this chapter is to examine the assumption that anyone can teach English if, like John Holt, he has literary taste and likes children.

A measure of John Holt's credentials is suggested by his admittedly limited experience as a teacher. He served as instructor at various private schools for a few years, gaining little or no experience facing children beyond the fifth grade or those from culturally deprived inner-city areas, or, for that matter, bright, academically oriented high-school students. He entered the profession with the idea that a teacher should be a drillmaster, and he conducted his classes accordingly.[2] But he discovered very soon, as he tells us, that teacher domination and strict disciplinary methods led to resentment and apathy. In self-defense, then, he tried an informal approach to his pupils and more permissive methods of teaching—and they seemed to work. Within a short period, he had gained enough assurance to crystallize his newly discovered conception of class management into a formula. He had come full circle—he was now con-vinced that children are repressed by the stifling pedantry that pervaded, as he believed, most classrooms in the nation's schools. The reasons for his conversion were set forth in an article entitled "Making Children Hate Reading," published in November 1967.[3]

In this article (and repeatedly elsewhere) Holt asserts that most teachers of English destroy children's love of reading by associating the study of literature with heavy homework assignments, laborious exercises, and oppressive tests. "From the very beginning of school," he writes, "we make books and reading a constant source of possible failure and humiliation." As an illustration, he draws a portrait of the martinet who requires children to copy down and check in the dictionary every unfamiliar word

in the book being studied—the example cited is the formidable text of
James Fenimore Cooper's *Deerslayer*—and then subjects them to oral and
written quizzes each day to ensure their diligent performance of the
assignments.

Holt confesses that he, too, before he saw the light, used to ask his pupils
"the kinds of questions that English teachers usually ask about reading
assignments—questions designed to bring out the points that I had decided they should know." We are not given examples of these questions,
but it can be presumed that they focused on textual minutiae: "What is the
setting of the story? Who is the main character? What did Peter say to the
stranger? What happened next?" The answers were, of course, dutiful
and monosyllabic. There were no questions that required reflection or
interpretation, and none on which there could be differences of opinion
leading to discussion and perhaps a rereading of the text—no questions
that might give insight into character or lead to esthetic appreciation.
Holt's self-portrait of his early apprenticeship in the classroom fits the
classic mold of the schoolmaster-pedant.

His revelatory change of mind came when he faced a class in which
there were "many children who had great trouble with schoolwork, particularly reading." Feeling intuitively that he must take a new tack, he
announced to the children that, in place of the usual assignments, they
would be permitted to read any books they wanted and would not be
required to report on them or answer any questions about them. Inured
to adult hypocrisy, the children were skeptical at first and had to be
reassured that he meant exactly what he said.

The effect of this free-reading program on one child in particular is
reported. This intelligent girl, until then a reluctant reader, flourished
under the new dispensation and began to read books widely and en-
thusiastically. At Holt's suggestion, offered when he learned of her love of
horses, she read *National Velvet* and, even though she found it difficult,
liked it very much. One day, to his gratification, Holt found her reading
Moby Dick at her desk—she thought it was "neat," explaining that she
coped with the more difficult passages by skipping them over. The new
approach was apparently right—the children were reading and enjoying
themselves.

Holt also discovered, as many generations of teachers had done before
him, that reading stories aloud to his classes could be a rewarding activity.[4]
He read, among others, Jack London's "To Build a Fire," and "spooky"
stories such as "The Monkey's Paw" by Saki (H.H. Munro) and Shirley
Jackson's "The Lottery." (I hesitate to make a captious correction of a
minor detail of scholarship: "The Monkey's Paw" was written by W.W.
Jacobs, not Saki). In any event, Holt and his pupils shared the pleasure of
reading together some of the most delightful stories in the repertory of
British and American literature.

John Holt's missionary zeal for imparting a love of good books is probably the most important trait an English teacher brings with him into the classroom. The purpose that led me to become an English teacher was, among other things, the hope of conveying something of the excitement kindled in me by the infinite riches contained within the covers of books. My projected goal would be to share with my as yet faceless classes my own enjoyment of Shakespeare and H.G. Wells and Eugene O'Neill and the host of other writers who were then (and are now) my untiring companions. But my first years of teaching, like those of John Holt, made me conscious of the need for self-examination and a thoroughgoing revision of my approach to my volatile and not always controllable classes. Enthusiasm was there aplenty, but it was not enough.

I had to learn the pragmatics of teaching by trial and all-too-frequent error. Like every other beginner, I experimented with whatever devices I could find in textbooks or could resurrect from notebooks saved from lectures at Teachers College or acquire from more experienced colleagues. A whole generation of graduates probably still bear the stigmata of my initial blundering efforts. Over the years, as I became convinced that the mastery of sound method is essential to good teaching, I have grown more and more distrustful of the negation of method inherent in Carl Rogers's and John Holt's permissive approach. Encouragement of free reading and a bold exploration of the world of books goes in the right direction, but it does not provide a sound basis for the teaching of literature. John Holt, I am now convinced, committed himself to the dogma of formlessness and spontaneity too soon, without ever having experienced the challenges and rewards of systematic teaching.

Let me confess that I am a secret admirer of John Holt's pupil, and others like her who discover literary masterpieces on their own and commune with them in the privacy of their own imaginations, undisturbed by the intrusions of well-meaning adults. We teachers sometimes lose sight of the intellectual potential of some of our pupils, the range of their interests, the intensity of their quest for knowledge. The appreciation of literature is a sensitive growth that may flower or run to seed under our husbandry, no matter how conscientious or well-intentioned we may be. But I do know this: the most precious content of a literary work, as John Ciardi showed so brilliantly in his essay "How to Read a Poem," lies somewhere beneath the surface. The comic-book version of a great classic is, for this reason, an infantile distortion of the original text.

Most literary works—novels, plays, poems, as well as other fugitive forms—do not reveal themselves readily to the uninitiated; like the Delphic Oracle, they require a sacrificial offering. The surface content of the book may be grasped by a young reader in a first hurried reading, but understanding of less obvious values cannot be obtained without a purposeful second and third reading under a teacher's wise direction. Certain aspects of form and structure are not transparent, and important thematic elements are not easily discovered—they are unlikely to be understood without analysis and study. The pleasure of reading a book (I bridle at the word *fun*) is enhanced when its themes and characters and style are presented in a way that brings to light unsuspected meanings and fresh insights.

All of us like to share our reactions to books we have read or plays and movies we have seen. But what do we say? Too often our conversation is limited to whether we liked the story or the performance of one actor or another. We are made speechless by our lack of awareness of certain technical elements of literary form and a vocabulary adequate to clothe our thoughts. The study of literature attunes us to what is beneath the surface of a book. This does not mean acquiring a pedantic knowledge of titles and authors and literary movements so much as becoming sensitive to a range of perceptions we could not otherwise have.

An analogy will make this point clearer. Everyone enjoys a walk in the woods or along the seashore: the exhilaration of exercise makes the air taste sweet, and the visual impact of foliage and sloping meadow and breaking waves is a source of unending inspiration. But a walk in the company of a knowledgeable guide, a biologist or a park ranger, is a different experience. We learn to perceive a tree not merely as a majestic form but rather as a mechanism for drawing water and nutrients through its tenacious root system and using the sun's energy to replenish the life-sustaining oxygen we breathe. We learn to see the ocean as the restive servant of massive air currents and the pull of the moon's gravitation. Thomas Huxley added a new dimension to man's perception of nature with his essay "On a Piece of Chalk," in which he traced the geologic chain of events that formed the rocks and the desert and the shore.

The study of literature is ideally a walk through the library or a visit to the theatre in the company of a wise and talkative mentor, enabling us to appreciate aspects of the literary experience that might otherwise be hidden from us. We can discover, for instance, that a story has structural elements that can be delineated in certain technical terms: exposition, conflict, foreshadowing, suspense, climax, resolution. A story has characters—are they three-dimensional or cardboard stereotypes? A story is told in a certain style or tone: is it objective, ironic, satiric, poetic? A story embodies a theme, that is, a reflection of life, a commentary on the meaning of our own experiences. And there is an author standing in the wings. Does he move his puppets on tight strings or allow them to act out their feelings at their own volition?

I can hear the chorus of disapproval: books are simply to be enjoyed, not dissected! I would answer that the unexamined enjoyment of a book, like that of an unexamined life, is not worth having. Or to put it more accurately, although a story *can* be enjoyed for its narrative interest alone, the reader who understands its thematic and structural values will find, as he becomes increasingly sensitive and discriminating, that he gains a very different kind of satisfaction from his literary experiences.

How does the English course contribute to this change? To answer the question, let us trace the pattern of children's relationships to what they read or listen to or watch on the television screen, as they grow toward maturity.

The young child is fascinated by the stories unfolding in "Jack and the Beanstalk," "Snow White and the Seven Dwarfs," *Treasure Island,* and their progeny in picture books and comic books. At this stage, the myth or legend or tale of adventure has a self-contained existence for the child: it is vicarious experience that needs no justification other than its quickening of imagination and wonder. Later, say at age ten or eleven, the growing child is able to relate to his reading at a different level—to begin to see myths and legends as parables of man's experience: the myth of Ceres as a primitive explanation of the seasons; Tom Sawyer and Tiny Tim as identifiable figures of childhood in a world dominated by grown-ups; Prometheus and Joan of Arc as free spirits rebelling against tyranny.

At the secondary level, the more mature student can be led to perceive fiction in its many forms as one of the psychological mediums by which we sustain and console ourselves on this darkling plain with illusions of free will and immortality, trust in the inevitability of retribution, faith in human existence. He can understand how, to keep our emotional wholeness, we gladly receive the contemporary myths of Superman and James Bond and pay obeisance to the heroic figures the advertising arts have immortalized—the virile denizens of Marlboro county, the goddesses with gleaming teeth, and the bumbling masochist who resolves his pain with Alka Seltzer.

Literature can be taught as an extension of the myth. The tale of Huckelberry Finn, rich in the folklore and local color of the river frontier, is a parable of the progress of an untutored and profane pilgrim toward self-understanding. Ethan Frome, in Edith Wharton's masterpiece, is a mythological figure, too, revealing the inner core of nobility in a man whose momentary glimpse of freedom is shattered by a malign fate. Students identify with Salinger's *Catcher in the Rye* because their own doubts and hostilities are objectified in the whimsical heresies of Holden Caulfield; and they are strengthened by Herman Hesse's *Siddhartha* because they, too, are in search of metaphysical truth. *Hamlet* and *Moby Dick* and *The Return of the Native* are great works of literature in that they tear aside the veils of illusion and proclaim the tragedy of human existence and the dignity of man.

The study of literature, seen in this light, transforms the child's naïve delight in fairy tale and legend into a mature vision of the human condition.

One of the stories John Holt read to his class was "The Monkey's Paw," a tale woven of elements of realism and fantasy. Like most fiction, as I have shown, it can be experienced at several levels of appreciation. It can be read as a well-knit, ingeniously contrived narrative in much the same way as one can enjoy a television dramatization of an Alfred Hitchcock mystery. For the time that it takes to read or listen to the story, the individual identifies with the characters and shares, at a safe distance, their anguish and terror. It may be felt that this vicarious experience is enough. After all, the story is escapist literature and soon enough the dream will be shattered by the abrasive commercial or the clamor of the passing bell. I cannot accept this view: the story has not disclosed its secret in this one fleeting encounter. The teacher's role goes beyond reading the story aloud to his class. He must do more. He must guide his pupils in appropriate class activities to analyze the mechanism of the narrative, explore its artistic blending of illusion and reality, and examine its implications for moral and metaphysical truth.

To demonstrate how this short story can be "taught," a brief synopsis of the plot of "The Monkey's Paw" is useful. The story is about a talisman, a dried monkey's paw, that is brought as a gift to the White family—father, mother, and a grown son—by an old friend, a sergeant major just returned from years of service in India. He had obtained the mummified paw from a fakir who had told him that the talisman had the magical power of granting its possessor three wishes, at the same time warning him of its fateful potency, for the last of the three wishes would invariably be a wish for death. Half jocularly, Mr. White, egged on by his family, makes a wish for two hundred pounds. The next day the son is mangled in the machinery at the factory where he was employed and the factory owners offer two hundred pounds as compensation for his death. After days of abject despair, Mrs. White suddenly remembers that they have the power to make a second wish, and she relentlessly pleads and argues with her husband until he consents to wish that their son be brought back from the grave. That night they lie awake waiting for the miracle to be fulfilled. Suddenly they hear a knocking at the front door of their cottage, faint at first but growing louder. Mrs. White rushes frantically to open the door, expecting to see her son alive again. Mr. White, obsessed with a sense of imminent evil, desperately tries to stop her. As she struggles to open the bolted door, he seizes the monkey's paw and makes his third wish.

The story ends with this passage:

> A perfect fusillade of knocks reverberated through the house and he heard the scraping of a chair as his wife put it down in the passage against the door. He heard the creaking of the bolt as it came slowly back, and at the same moment he found the monkey's paw and frantically breathed his third and last wish.

The knocking ceased suddenly, although the echoes of it were still in the house. He heard the chair drawn back and the door opened. A cold wind rushed up the staircase, and a loud wail of disappointment and misery from his wife gave him courage to run down to her side, and then to the gate beyond. The street lamp flickering opposite shone on a quiet and deserted street.

Now what can a teacher do with this story? Several things. First, he must make sure the class understands the crucial and somewhat enigmatic ending. What was the third wish? Why did Mr. White make the wish? Why did the knocking at the door suddenly cease? How can we explain the eerie stillness outside? These questions cannot be fully answered without considering the author's use of foreshadowing and suspense as narrative techniques. At what point in the story is suspense initiated? How does the author keep us in uncertainty as to what will happen next? When is suspense at its height?

Looking back at the story, we can now detect the first hints of strange events to follow the opening scene. The first few paragraphs, viewed in perspective, disclose the author's artistry in contrasting the pleasant family scene with the impending tragic events soon to come. Rereading of this and other sections of the story will also reveal the character traits in the father and mother that play a crucial role in the climactic scene at the end.

Finally, when the story has been understood in its broad outlines, the teacher can raise the fundamental question of whether the incidents in the story are best interpreted as supernatural events or as a series of natural coincidences. Is this a conventional mystery story or is the author satirizing the genre? The extent of the analysis will depend, of course, on the maturity of the class, but for most students the examination of the narrative in depth will be an exciting road of discovery. They will surely become more perceptive readers than they would be after simply hearing the story read aloud in class.

Shirley Jackson's "The Lottery," another of the "spooky" stories Holt read to his students, is even more in need of explication than "The Monkey's Paw" and thus requires the most resourceful teaching. The plot is uncomplicated. The residents of a small American town assemble one morning to take part in a ceremonial ritual that has been held each year for generations, like the Fourth of July. They are ordinary people, some pleasant and talkative, some openly impatient, others subdued and apathetic. Like members of every small community, they are all familiar with one another's affairs, inquire about mutual acquaintances, gossip and exchange small talk. The ritual, we discover gradually, is a lottery in which the head of every household must participate. We have no inkling of the purpose of the lottery, however, until almost the very last sentence, and only then, incredulously, do we realize the horrifying truth that the person who draws the marked ballot is to be stoned to death by the others.

The story ends thus:

> Tessie Hutchinson was in the center of the cleared space by now, and she held her hands out desperately as the villagers moved in on her. "It isn't fair," she said. A stone hit her in the side of the head.
> Old Man Warner was saying, "Come on, come on, everyone." Steve Adams was in the front of the crowd of villagers, with Mrs. Graves beside him.
> "It isn't fair, it isn't right," Mrs. Hutchinson screamed, and then they were upon her.

Most students are puzzled by the story, simple as it appears to be. The shock wave of the startling denouement has shattered their normal expectations of people's behavior, and this emotional conflict must be rationalized. The teacher's aim, then, is to clarify the relationship between the earlier scenes and the horror of the last scene. What makes this story so difficult to grasp is that it is almost incredible. The setting is a typical New England or midwestern village and the people are all so familiar and recognizable, like those in dozens of small-town movies or soap operas on television, yet they willingly, even gladly, take part in the stoning to death of one of their neighbors, without hesitation or moral compunction.

The first pivotal question should, then, deal with this anomaly. Why do these people consent to take part in the ritual of the lottery? Why doesn't even one person protest? The class will very likely reach the acceptable conclusion that the people were simply following a tradition, a custom, certainly more cruel than other customs but not different in its compulsive sanction. The teacher might then pursue the point: "What customs or traditions do we follow that are similarly without reason? What collective actions do we take part in that are equally mindless?" Perhaps students will cite lynch mobs, or our tendency to look for scapegoats for our own failures, or our conformity in dress, life-style, and political biases. Somewhere in the discussion, no doubt, racism and male chauvinism will be cited, and reference will be made to current resistance to the women's-liberation movement. Then, to make clear the persistence of tradition and the difficulty of changing customs, the teacher might ask: "What does Old Man Warner mean when, on being told that some neighboring villages have given up the lottery, he remarks: 'Pack of young fools! Nothing but trouble in that'?" Thus, "The Lottery" becomes a parable, suggesting a number of applications and interpretations that are very real in our lives. The story can now be viewed as a brilliant exposition of the way we sometimes institutionalize injustice and unreason in the guise of custom.

The impact of the story will be reinforced by an analysis of its technical elements. How does Shirley Jackson make her strange story credible? First, in seeking to find a foreshadowing of the climax in the earlier scenes of the story, students would discover subtleties in the unfolding narrative that they might not have noticed in their first reading: for example, the black box in which the lottery slips were kept, Billy Martin's pile of stones, the growing tension and restlessness as the lottery proceeded, Mrs. Hutchinson's repeated protests. Then, to develop appreciation of the author's technical skill, the teacher might ask students to rewrite the final understated scene. This exercise would lead to a critical evaluation of two kinds of endings found in short stories, one definitive and explicit and the other a springboard for surmise. It could be followed by a fresh reading of stories already studied, those with surprise endings like O. Henry's and those with logical endings growing inexorably out of the linkage of events like Jack London's and Nathaniel Hawthorne's.

A teacher who merely encourages his pupils to read on their own and somehow discover for themselves what is important in literature has abdicated his function.

Holt exhibits a similar shallowness in dealing with the problem of teaching the technical skills of English. He speaks of the deadening effect of requiring pupils to look up and record all the difficult vocabulary encountered in the assigned reading—a dreary task indeed for young, avid readers. At the same time, we cannot ignore that, for every student who can grasp the meaning of words intuitively, there are a hundred who are frustrated by the vocabulary problem and need to be taught in some systematic way to become proficient in adding to their store of words. When the mayor of a great city announces in a TV interview: "The Police Department will be appraised of my decision . . ."; and a well-known news commentator, referring to his visit to a prison, says, "I was abhorred by what I saw . . . ," we must conclude that Holt's confidence in instinctual learning of vocabulary is misplaced.

The teacher of English, together with all other teachers, has the responsibility of making the mastery of vocabulary skills interesting and functional. Skill in using the dictionary is an essential tool that must be developed continually, but it cannot be the student's only resource. For long-range efficiency, the skill that should be stressed initially is that of guessing at the meaning of words by using contextual clues. This is what Holt probably means when he says people acquire a useful vocabulary by "meeting words over and over again.[5] It is doubtful, however, whether this is sufficient precept for most students unless the skill is deliberately taught.

Any sentence in a newspaper or magazine or book can be used to teach the contextual approach. For example, take a sentence from one of Holt's essays: "Our so-called best schools are turning out students most of whom, in any important and real sense, are as *inarticulate* as the most deprived children in the ghettoes, as little able to speak and write simply about things of importance to them. . . ." There should be no difficulty in deriving the meaning of *inarticulate* from the context. Of course, the transparency of this illustration may not be present in other sentences chosen at random, but it is surprising how often the context of unfamiliar words provides significant clues to their meanings.

A more challenging exercise in informed guessing will show the possibilities of this technique for the English class. The following passage is the opening paragraph of O. Henry's story "The Third Ingredient."

> The so-called Vallambrosa Apartment House is not an apartment house. It is composed of two old-fashioned brownstone-fronted residences welded into one. The parlor floor of one side is gay with the wraps and headgear of a *modiste;* the other is *lugubrious* with the *sophistical* promises and *grisly* display of a painless dentist.

For most junior and senior high school students, this formidable passage would at first glance be virtually devoid of meaning. "Why should children understand everything they read?" asks Holt.[6] For one thing, the reader who does not understand this passage, which sets the framework of the story, will lose much of O. Henry's humor and something of the tenderness of his portrayal of the waifs and outcasts of the impersonal city. Besides, the contextual method of word discovery makes the description yield its meaning in a way that equips the student for independent application of the method on his own.

The teacher must first make sure the class is familiar with the appearance of the brownstone-fronted architecture of a bygone era. In cities whose history does not go back to that period, a photograph or drawing will have to do. Once this apperceptive background has been provided, the students are ready to plunge into the game of guessing at the meaning of the four underlined words.

Step 1: What is a *modiste?* Well, what do we see in her window? What do the wraps and headgear suggest? She has something to do with women's clothing, no doubt. What further clues do we have in the word itself? Model, mode. Yes, these confirm our guess. A modiste is a fashion designer or dressmaker.

Step 2: Lugubrious? How was the dressmaker's window described? It was gay, bright, cheerful. Is the other side of the building likely to be the same or different? Probably the latter, a contrast, or else why mention it? What is the opposite of gay? Dismal, dull, gloomy. Yes, indeed. Lugubrious—even in its sound—must mean dismal and gloomy.

Step 3: Sophistical? Well, we must have certain additional information here. A dentist in the early part of the century—O. Henry's time—displayed a huge gilded (gold) molar outside his office, serving the same guild purpose as the barber's striped pole. Also—those were the days when anesthetics were not yet in common use—the dentist announced his modernity on a plaque under his nameplate: Painless Dentist. Well, now, is dentistry absolutely painless, even today? Of course not. Then how can we characterize the promise of painless dentistry? It was undoubtedly exaggerated, false, misleading. Of course—sophistical does mean deceptive.

Step 4: Grisly? Remember what was displayed—a huge molar. How would a patient feel on seeing it? A passerby? Not very happy. Why? Well, it would vividly remind him of the discomfort and pain associated with a visit to the dentist. What feeling, then, would be aroused by the sight of the tooth? Fear, distress. If we see a frightening object, what words do we use to describe our reaction? Fearful, horrifying, gruesome. Yes, the grisly display was the gilded molar with all its gruesome associations.

A lesson such as this, apart from its immediate aim, has the peripheral value of pointing to the ironic tone that infuses O. Henry's style.

Word meanings apart from their connotations in a specific context are of limited value. Teachers who assign the memorization of lists of difficult words are pedestrian and unimaginative; on this point, I agree with Holt. But I deplore his dismissal of the values of teaching vocabulary skills and his virtual abandonment of students to their own devices in the name of permissiveness.

Teachers must use other approaches to vocabulary building. New insights into the meaning of words can come from a study of linguistics. The history of the English language throws light on the prehistoric migrations of man, on the patterns of dominance in rising and falling empires, and the variety of ingenious ways in which the peoples of the earth learned to communicate with one another. Students are fascinated to learn that all the European languages, including English, are offshoots of a common tongue and still retain semantic and syntactic traces of their cognate parentage. For example, the word *mother,* the word that draws all men together in a common bond of reverence, is found almost unchanged in ancient Sanskrit *(mat'r),* classic Greek *(matros),* Latin *(mater),* German *(mutter),* French *(mère),* and almost every other European tongue.

Of equal interest in this study of etymology is the fusion of the Norman-French and Saxon-Germanic languages that was one of the crucial influences in shaping modern English after the Norman conquest (1066 A.D.). An interesting clue to this development is found in the pages of Walter Scott's *Ivanhoe,* a classic now sadly relegated to the dusty shelves of departmental bookrooms, in a passage in which Scott digresses from his narrative to explain how the Norman conquest affected the vocabulary of the emerging English language. Most of our words that refer to domestic animals, Scott tells us, have their origin in the old Germanic dialect of the Saxon underlings: *cow, sheep, calf, hen*—because the serfs who tended the cattle retained their native speech and vocabulary. But the corresponding terms that refer to the edible meats derived from the cattle are all

Norman-French: *beef, mutton, pork, veal, fowl*—because only the tables of the conquerors bore these costly viands. Using such materials, the teacher of English can make the study of vocabulary an exciting experience.

Discovering the derivation of words can also add zest to vocabulary study. Students learn to see common words and names as messages linking the present to the dim past: the word *daisy* comes from the *day's eye,* that is, the sun; *martial law* echoes the name of the Greek god of war, Mars; the *gladiola* gets its name from the swordlike shape of its leaves: cf. *gladiator;* Philadelphia means literally the City of Brotherly Love. Words that have their origin in Greek mythology—*tantalize, psychology, jovial*—are a useful means of vitalizing the study of classic literature and ancient history. I think it was Herbert Kohl who won over his reluctant pupils by seizing on a colloquial challenge: "You're psyching us" to relate to the class the story of Cupid and Psyche and taking off from there to initiate a successful unit in mythology and linguistics.[7]

The study of the origin of words can be expanded by the dissection of words into their structural elements—prefix, root, suffix. This kind of instruction runs the danger of lapsing into routine and drill unless the teacher is resourceful enough to make it come to life. For example, take the Latin root *spir*—to breathe. The basic meaning survives in *respiration,* but how does the root persist in derivatives such as *inspire, spirit, conspiracy?* Here the teacher must don the persona of the actor and pantomimist in the good cause of releasing words from the bondage of print. Act I—When we stand at the brim of Niagara Falls or watch the sun set in splendor behind the Jersey palisades, we draw in our breath—we are *inspired.* Act II—The breath leaves the body at the moment of death—the *spirit* has departed. Act III—The relationship between conspiring and breathing can be demonstrated by having three or four students (preferably after a reading of *Julius Caesar*) put their heads close together and whisper secretively, thus showing that a secret plotting or *conspiracy* involves breathing together. A teacher of English can be inventive and innovative in every phase of his lesson planning.

The teacher's search for fresh approaches to word study should not be limited to textbooks or literary sources. Professor Abraham Bernstein of Brooklyn College has pioneered in extending the quest for new vocabulary to the lyrics of popular songs, Sears catalogs, travel brochures, comic strips—any source in which the students can come face to face with current usage. Maxwell Nurnberg, in *What's the Good Word?*, adds the spice of wit and humor to make the study of words as much fun as a sack race or a roller-coaster ride.[9]

Much can be done, in addition, with the neologisms—slang, argot, hip talk—that have enriched (or debased, some think) the language. The English class may study such terms as: "You're putting me on," "He's up tight," "She has a hangup," and so on, viewing them as substitutions for the conventional diction against which the now generation is rebelling. I suggest tentatively that *putting me on* is a substitution for the Latinesque "imposing on me"; *uptight* is cognate with "tense" and "hypertension"; and a *hangup* is the mucker pose equivalent of "obsession." There seems to be a law of entropy in language as well as in physics. Whereas the development of English vocabulary was marked in the historical past by the increased use of learned borrowings, from Latin and Greek especially, in which the origin of the word root in concrete objects seen and felt was muted (e.g., *calculate* from pebbles; *supercilious* from a raised eyebrow; *emancipate* from loosing the chained hand), it is possible to detect the reverse tendency in contemporary usage (e.g., *down* for *depressed; rap session* for *conversation; to flip* for *to be overwhelmed*). The study of language as an evolving organism adjusting to changing psychological needs and social trends opens limitless possibilities for the teaching of English.

The code of symbols and forms that we call "grammar" is, to say the least, far removed from the centers of student interest delineated by Holt and Postman in their curricular proposals. Nonetheless, grammar must be included as an important part of the English program. The intellectual tools developed by man as he struggled out of primal sloth—his crafts, his skills, his logic, his scientific techniques, and his modes of communication—must be painfully acquired anew by each successive generation. The ability to speak is learned by every child through imitation and the pressures of his early contact with things and people. His mastery of language does not, however, keep pace with the increasingly complex demands of his environment as he approaches maturity. The study of grammar is geared to meeting this need, that is, to strengthen his ability to function efficiently in linguistic situations. If guided by this principle, the teaching of grammar need not be as dull and routine as it is, unfortunately, in many classrooms. It can indeed be an intellectually rewarding activity.

Let me illustrate this point by showing what can be done in teaching an area of grammar that is generally regarded as a matter of rules and mechanics, namely, the skills of punctuation.

The setting is a ninth grade class in English in which there has been much writing done in the form of stories, essays, letters, and reports. The students express their thoughts freely and even creatively, but it is apparent to the teacher that they are deficient—and even wildly eccentric—in their use of punctuation marks, especially the comma. So far the teacher has refrained from much criticism of their writing for fear of inhibiting them. Yet he is aware of their shortcomings and, in good conscience, he cannot put off his responsibility for developing an understanding of this important element of the linguistic code. Presumably the students have some stirring of recognition that such a code exists—they have grappled

with its mysteries in earlier grades—but at best their awareness lies somewhere in the recesses of consciousness. The teacher must find ways of
bringing the rationale of punctuation into immediate focus.

Here are some things the teacher might do:

1. Boldly, without preface, the teacher writes at the board the sentence:
The birds is coming. The students react at once: they know the sentence is
ungrammatical. Then the teacher points out that this was an announce-
ment displayed on hundreds of billboards throughout the city a few years
before and it is not likely that advertisers would waste their money on
nonsense. After some puzzlement, one or two students discover delight-
edly that this must have been an advertisement for Alfred Hitchcock's
movie *The Birds.* The sentence can then be rewritten as: *The Birds* is
coming. The concept of punctuation and capitalization as elements of a
meaningful code carries over to the lessons that are to follow.

2. The teacher writes at the board (still the most useful of visual aids)
these two sentences, unpunctuated:

A. As he spoke his words were greeted by outbursts of applause.

B. Mr. Wilson the dean has called a special faculty meeting.

Students are asked to read the sentences aloud. They soon become
aware of the ambiguity in both statements. In speaking, we resolve the
ambiguity by the use of juncture and intonation, that is, we pause notice-
ably at certain points and we change the tone of our voices appropriately.
In item A we say: "As he spoke . . . his words were greeted. . . ." In item B
it is either: "Mr. Wilson . . . the dean has called. . . ," or: "Mr. Wilson . . .
the dean . . . has called. . . ."

The rising inflection of questions, the rhythm of the spoken utterance,
the stress on certain words—these can be shown to constitute the system of
oral signals by which we communicate in speech. The transference of
these signals to writing now becomes an interesting subject of study,
despite its forbidding exterior.

After a secure grasp of the functions of marks of punctuation has been
developed and applied, the students are ready to be taught one of the
more sophisticated uses of the comma, namely, in the punctuation of
nonrestrictive clauses. This provides a striking instance of the parallelism
of linguistic devices in speech and in writing.

The teacher writes at the board—or provides on mimeographed
sheets—two sentences seemingly alike in form.

1. Advertising which is misleading or fraudulent should be banned.

2. Advertising which is vital to our economy is a multibillion dollar
business.

The teaching procedure is as follows:

A. The sentences are read aloud. The distinct pause before *which* in the
second sentence is contrasted with the smooth juncture in the first. The

difference signals a variation in structure. This is an application of the phonological approach discussed above.

B. The relative clause is deleted from both sentences. The main clause in item 1—"Advertising should be banned"—is clearly not what the writer intended to say. On the other hand, the remainder in item 2—"Advertising is a multibillion dollar business"—is still a truthful statement. This distinction is based on the grammatical concept of surface structures and deep structures, a concept that can be explored more fully at a later time. It is clear, however, even without further analysis, that the two sentences have different structures despite their surface similarity.

C. The meaning of the key word *advertising* is now examined in each sentence separately. In the first, the mental image signaled by the word is modified, that is, narrowed and restricted, by the relative clause. It no longer means *"advertising in general,"* but is now limited to the kind of advertising that is designated as misleading or fraudulent. The clause, then, can be said to be *restrictive*. In the second sentence, however, the concept indicated by the word *advertising* is not at all limited or restricted by the relative clause—hence, it is called a *nonrestrictive* clause.

The three approaches to analysis of the sentences confirm the need for differentiation of the two functional modes of the relative clause by proper punctuational signals. Thus: (1) Advertising which is misleading or fraudulent should be banned; and (2) Advertising, which is vital to our economy, is a multibillion dollar business. There are *no commas* in the first sentence and a *pair of commas* in the second. But even more useful than learning the rule is the insight gained into the linguistic theory underlying the rule. Once again, interest in an important field of scholarship has been developed by purposeful teaching.

I am convinced that the teaching of grammar, although scorned by Neil Postman and neglected by John Holt, is a vital part of the curriculum. Within the ranks of English teachers there is, to be sure, considerable disagreement about what grammar is, how to teach it, and what standards of "correct" usage to apply. Traditional grammar has been challenged by several competing schools of linguists, among them the structuralists and the transformationalists. It is therefore important for English teachers to know what grammar is, to explore the proposed methods of teaching grammar, and above all to come to grips with the vital issue of whether grammar is to be taught directly or whether it should be taught incidentally as the need arises.

What, for instance, is to be done about developing and maintaining standards of acceptable usage in students who have been bombarded from childhood by ungrammatical, debased dialect forms at home and in the streets? Well, the first thing to do is to have a sensible attitude toward what is called correct usage in English. Linguists are in full agreement on one point: languages are constantly changing in their forms and structures. C.C. Fries's comprehensive study of American usage[10] showed that, in every social class, certain standard forms were losing ground to more comfortable substitute forms, for example: "It's me" for "It's I"; "None are" for "None is"; "everyone of us are" for "everyone of us is." Vulgarisms are another matter: "I ain't," "I seen," and "I don't have no change" are less easy to condone. The stubborn persistence of habits acquired in childhood cannot be overcome easily, and it is an area in which teachers must move warily and sensitively. Patience and tact are more effective than dogmatic imposition. The best procedure would be to present both the standard and substandard forms as alternative choices in different social settings, thus giving students a persuasive reason for making the right choice.

For most young people, there is a gradual adjustment to the standards of their peer groups, and as the neighborhood loses its primacy as the student moves into high school and college, the more infantile and abusive idioms usually wear away since they are less and less esteemed in the setting of the campus or business office. But some especially lively and colorful expressions embedded in dialect or street jargon may have vitality enough to survive and influence the pattern of standard usage.

Special thought must be given to the problems of non-English-speaking Hispanic and Chinese children and to black students who have brought to northern cities the deviant patterns of their regional dialects. As to the children of foreign background, the schools in New York City and most other large cities have faced the problem constructively. Bilingual instruction has been adopted to ease the transition of linguistically handicapped children into regular classes. The Chinese students, unlike those of Hispanic background, take readily to learning English in the traditional way; like the earlier waves of immigrant children from European countries, they devote themselves to the incredibly difficult task of learning a new language that is totally unlike their native tongue, never questioning the need of becoming proficient in the predominant language of the society in which they hope to establish themselves permanently. None of the immigrant groups, other than the Puerto Ricans, has had apologists who have advocated bilingualism as a lasting value. Leaders of the Puerto Rican community would be well advised to reconsider their sponsorship of bilingual education as anything more than a temporary expedient.

The problem of black dialect is another matter, if only for the reason that it is a regional pattern of speech differing only in degree from all other dialects. Moreover, the sensitive area of civil rights and racial integration are involved and, as a consequence, there has been a lot of disagreement and confusion of issues in discussions of black dialects. There are scholars who view southern dialect as a colorful variant from standard English that should not be tampered with in the schools, since it is a linguistic artifact with legitimate roots in the past and a cultural possession that contributes to self-esteem and racial pride. However, it is doubtful that such locutions as "You is wrong," "He be working," and "I axed him" will not hamper the black student in his search for upward mobility into the mainstream of American life, despite their historic roots in the past, for example: "I axed" is straight from Anglo-Saxon *acsian;* "You is" has as legitimate parentage as "you are"; and "he be" is good Elizabethan grammar. Here, too, avoiding dogmatic imposition, the schools must be cautiously optimistic in trusting to the influences of peer groups, media dialogue at its best, and mature self-awareness to narrow the gap between a stigmatic dialect and standard colloquial usage.

All English teachers agree—even John Holt agrees—that their most refractory problem is the teaching of written English, the effort to equip students with a "minimal grace of style," as Anthony Burgess puts it. At departmental conferences and area conventions, the question of composition is raised more frequently and insistently than any other. Of course, teachers know that writing skill is in a sense unteachable. It is based on something more than paragraph logic, correct grammar and spelling, and adequate diction; it draws on the inner life and deepest intellectual resources of the writer. Style is truly the man.

Nevertheless, the elements of written expression can be identified and reduced to teachable skills and concepts. The primary factor in time as well as importance is that of motivation, of developing an interest in ideas, in current issues, in interpersonal and ethical and philosophic problems that generate a readiness to communicate in more than a casual or fragmentary form. This is in itself half the battle. The second task is to guide students in the difficult processes of gathering material for writing through reflection, discussion, and research. Then the teacher must somehow—by textual analysis or examination of models—help students to structure their ideas in organic form, involving the organization of the whole, the firm linkage of one section to the next, and the ordering of details within each paragraph. Above all, the teacher must inculcate respect for truth, relevancy, and clarity of expression as the essential qualities of writing.

In Francis Bacon's essay "Of Studies" there is a meaty epigram that, with deceptive simplicity, delineates the rationale of a systematic program for teaching writing. It goes: "Reading maketh a full man, conference a ready man, and writing an exact man." Here, in synopsis, is a profound formulation of the elements of a sound program. First, we must have ideas that are important to us, ideas shaped by our experiences and our contact with great minds in books. These ideas must not remain private, for it is only by conference, that is, discussion with others, that they are quickened and clarified. Then, when we set our thoughts down on paper, we are compelled to be precise, logical, accurate. Writing exposes our intuitions to the pitiless laser beams of public scrutiny and exposes the flaws and gaps and the vague perceptions that were not seen earlier. Definitions, premises, factual data must be exact, not approximate or general, as they might well have been in our solitary reflections and informal conversations.

Occasions for self-expression are everywhere—in newspaper headlines, magazine articles, television programs, school events, personal experiences. Some topics lend themselves best to informal talks in class and others to organized panel discussions, but all can be fruitful subjects for one form of writing or another. The most available, and the most useful, occasions for writing grow out of the study of literature. Vicarious involvement in the experiences encountered in books and identification with some character met in a short story or novel extends the range of subject matter to every aspect of life—emotions, moral values, metaphysical problems. A class that has studied *Macbeth,* for example, will certainly be deeply moved by the tragic downfall of a man corrupted by uncontrolled forces within himself and outside himself. Studying the play will raise questions that clamor for expression—fate, good and evil, retribution, the self-deceptions that all of us practice. The supernatural and the occult are fascinating subjects—perhaps students would want to interpret the prophecies of the Three Weird Sisters as the subconscious wishes and fears of Macbeth. Certain passages reverberate in the mind: "Out, out, brief candle. Life . . . is a tale told by an idiot, full of sound and fury, signifying nothing." All works of literature provide similar opportunities for creative writing. If there are conflicting interpretations—as in "The Lady or the Tiger"—students will need little spur beyond the challenge to their ingenuity. Fantasy is a natural mode of expression for all ages—thus students are readily motivated to write, as if it were a missing page in a book, an imagined diary, a long-buried manuscript, a letter of Sidney Carton's or Hester Prynne's (resurrected from the Dead Letter Office), or a newspaper article or editorial from the Poker Flat press. With such stimulating assignments, students write like angels—perhaps—when their sensibilities and imaginations have been touched.

The underlying motivation for writing is, as I have said, that the writer must have something he wants to communicate to others. To make this point in my own classes, I occasionally used an anecdote I had come across somewhere in H.G. Wells's autobiography.[11] Wells was describing his apprenticeship as a writer, and among other things he recounted the way he had learned to structure and organize the materials of articles or essays he was working on. The first words he placed on his blank manuscript paper, whatever the subject might be, were these: "Dear Uncle George." Uncle George, Wells explained, was a rather opinionated member of the family, with whom, as a youngster, he had often discussed the issues of the day. Wells and his Uncle George rarely agreed on any subject, and as a result Wells found himself hard pressed to hold up his end of the conversation. He was stimulated by this adversary relationship to think hard and draw on all his intellectual resources. When he became a professional writer, Wells found it useful to summon the ghostly presence of his Uncle George to sit across the desk from him and thus provide a real target for his argumentative thrusts. I hope my own students found this suggestion helpful—at least, some of them told me they had gained a certain soul-satisfying pleasure in beginning their more abrasive essays with the erasable caption: "Dear Mr. Vogel."

I can fully sympathize with John Holt's frustration when he faced a bright class and found it "astonishingly hard for most of the children to express themselves in speech or writing." In desperation, he says, he hit on a device that he named the Composition Derby, a contest to see which of the students could write the greatest number of words in a given time, say, twenty minutes. They could write on anything they wanted—"true stories, descriptions of people or places or events, wishes, made-up stories, dreams—anything they liked." The plan struck a responsive chord, that is, there was much writing done—and there is probably no significance in the fact that there was an inordinately hearty response to the one topic Holt happened to assign: "The Day the School Burned Down."

I must confess I am irritated whenever teachers tell me they have followed some such method in their classes or when people I meet recall with rueful approbation its use in a college course in writing. Free self-expression can, of course, be rewarding on occasion as a supplement to or relief from more intensive writing exercises. I remember vividly the night in the fall of 1967 when the electric-power supply in the New York metropolitan region broke down completely—the night of the blackout. The following day students in my classes were still visibly shaken by an experience that, in an unforgettable way, had revealed to them, perhaps for the first time, the abyss on which our technological security rests so precariously. Go on with *Arrowsmith* or *The Canterbury Tales?* Unthinkable. The students were all obviously eager to tell what they and their families had undergone during the eventful night. After a few effusive accounts of hardship and altruism had poured out and hands were raised at every seat, I said, "Very well. Let's get it down on paper," and scrawled across the blackboard in bold capitals: "The Night the Lights Went Out." Everyone wrote furiously—never before had there been such enthusiastic performance of a writing assignment. When we read the narratives aloud the next day—for everyone needed time to finish at home—it was clear that the students' fluency, indeed their eloquence, was a response to their need to talk out and write out the traumas of a significant experience. On one or two other occasions—the end of World War II, the assassination of President Kennedy, the first moon walk—students were similarly keyed up to spontaneous expression. In the absence of such stimuli, however, the free-writing improvisations that Holt recommends are bound to degenerate into exhibitionism and frivolity.

The classroom provides a realistic setting for speech activities—the "conference that makes the ready man." But speech is evanescent; it is difficult for the speaker to go back and rephrase an awkward sentence or substitute a word, and therefore the teacher cannot do much, except incidentally, to improve spoken English. It is hoped that experience in public speaking, answering questions, contributing to discussions, making reports, together with conscious self-criticism, will eventually assure sufficient verbal resources for meeting social needs and the demands of formal occasions for oral communication. But written English is another matter: writing can be edited and revised. During the process of composition the writer can change a word here and there, can weigh alternative constructions, can redesign whole paragraphs. Writing is a process of making choices; that is, apart from the linguistic automatisms that the writer uses almost unconsciously, he must make decisions at almost every point. Shall he use two simple sentences or a compound sentence? Shall he write out a relative clause or extract from it the imbedded appositive? Where in the sentence shall he place a transitional or a parenthetical phrase? These are the choices facing the writer continually.

It is at this crucial point that the teacher provides his most valuable service: in guiding students to make their choices intelligently. This is the burden and reward of being a teacher of English, the chore of reading and commenting, reviewing and marking, editing and counselling, that sets the English teacher apart from all others. It is sometimes possible for the teacher to go over a paper individually with the student at his side, and sometimes the entire composition or a single paragraph or sentence can be written at the blackboard or mimeographed or displayed with the aid of an opaque projector to be reviewed and criticized by the class as a whole. Most often, however, the teacher must burn the midnight lamp as he marks his never completed sets of papers, the ghostly writers looking over his shoulders.

How shall he deal with this awesome responsibility? I would hope that he will discover for himself the boundaries of common sense beyond which the law of diminishing returns takes hold. Too often we clutter the paper or the blackboard with the correction of mechanical errors in spelling, grammar, and punctuation. Only when these types of error have been reduced to manageable proportions—or discreetly overlooked—can we get to the heart of the problem, namely, matters of diction, sentence structure, and style. The emphasis shifts from finding fault with what the student has written to reenacting the writer's dilemma in choosing among alternative forms. Any corrections or suggested improvements must not be imposed dogmatically. Rather, they should be presented as instances of important rhetorical standards—greater clarity, greater emphasis, more effective communication—that have at one time or another been considered in class.

Too often discouragement sets in: the burden is too great and evidences of growth in writing skills are not readily discernible. But the answer is not to abandon the task, as Holt and his followers do, or to resort to meaningless charades such as the Composition Derby, or to shirk the responsibility of ever correcting a student's compositions by derogating the importance of writing skills. Complacency and cynicism are corruptive attitudes, inimical to the body and the spirit of the teaching of English.

8

THE CULT
OF RELEVANCE

Ray Bradbury's *Fahrenheit 451* should be on the reading list of every school child in the country. It is unpretentious science fiction but it has the hallmark of greatness. It tells about a time, not unimaginable today, when the masters of an efficient system of thought control have decreed that all books must be destroyed by burning. In this novel, those who secretly treasure the relics of the proscribed culture are hunted down and punished. There are some, however, who will not be reduced to ignorance and servility, and they have found an ingenious way of thwarting the book burners forever. They steal away to an isolated region, each carrying with him a copy of one great book—Plato, the Book of Ecclesiastes, Confucius and Mr. Lincoln, Homer and Dickens—and each devotes himself day and night to memorizing the text of the book. Parents transmit their memorized treasure of deathless words to their children so the books cannot ever be lost. Thus, in Bradbury's ingenious fable, teachers find an affirmation of the importance of their vocation and, whether their specialization is English, history, or science, they can see themselves as guardians of the book.

Intellectuals, teachers among them, who see their role as that of mediator and interpreter of the ordered world of books, must be reminded, however, that books are only mirrors to life. For most people, human contacts and emotional experiences are more intense than their reflections in novels and plays. Immersion in reading can be an escape, a way of substituting vicarious experience for the triumphs and defeats sustained in the clamorous arena of real life, but an educational philosophy that uncritically places literature and scholarly texts higher on its scale of values than immediate experience is unlikely to enlist the assent of students.

There are two major factors that must be taken into account in facing this dilemma. First, educators must concede that education is not the function of the schools alone. Children's attitudes toward society, their appraisal of democratic institutions, their conception of ethical values— all these are affected by their everyday experiences in the street, the playground, and their homes. If their families have a secure economic base, if their housing is decent, if recreational facilities are abundantly available, if social agencies are responsive to their needs, children are likely to develop positive attitudes that will carry over to their behavior in school and their conduct in public places. Safe neighborhoods, unpolluted beaches, and well-stocked libraries are visible evidence to them of the viability of our social institutions and the health of the democratic ideal. Thus, a well-ordered society contributes to the educational objectives of the schools and serves as a bulwark against alienation.

At the same time, we must recognize the limitations of the child's and adolescent's unaided search for meaning in their lives. Perhaps a second look at the quality of experience in the home, the street, and the community might reveal that the young too often have little motivation and direction in their out-of-school lives. Their energies are sometimes frittered away in rootless and at times self-destructive outlets—the street gang, hoodlumism, the drug culture. Television, too, its incessant din bombarding their nerve ends, exposes them to a kaleidoscope of violence, sexuality, and sentimentality. The effects of low intelligence, a short attention span, underprivileged homes, and hostile feelings are as real in the street as they are in the classroom.

Second, educators must realize that what is worth knowing is one thing to the teacher and quite another to the student. There is a blurred focus in the student's perception of how school subjects relate to his own life experiences and goals. The adolescent student wants to make friends, develop physical skills, cope with sexual needs, assert himself within the family group, dress and make up appropriately, and seek out and identify with folk heroes in the world of popular music, sports, and the movies. As he matures—say, in his junior or senior year in high school—his urgent concerns may become less narrowly egocentric, embracing a conscious interest in preparing for a vocation, a concern for society and its problems, an intensified search for self-identity. The school experience, centered largely on abstract reflections of reality, may therefore seem to students of both sexes somewhat pallid and remote from their intense emotional life outside the school.

How can we reconcile the seemingly incompatible interests of adolescents and the educational establishment? How can we bridge the chasm between the scholastic "ivory tower" and the palpitating world outside? The answer is crucial to every policy decision of school administrators as well as to the teacher's everyday procedures in the classroom.

The generally accepted current view is that the student's "real" experiences and drives can be and should be the source of motivation for vitalized learning in school. There need be no invidious contradiction between school experiences and life experiences. William James suggested that the task of civilization is to harness the aggressive instincts of man in what he called the "moral equivalent" of war and predation. The schools base their programs on a similar transference, that is, on a strategy to humanize and socialize the inherent drives of youth in constructive ways. The schools serve this purpose by establishing curriculums that cater to students' physical, interpersonal, and vocational needs and, above all, to their equally insistent intellectual needs. To the degree that schools perform this task effectively, their programs are relevant to the genuine interests of youth.

At the end of the nineteenth century, in a time less beset by anxiety and ambivalence than our own, Matthew Arnold could express his conception of the aim of education in these eloquent terms: "The great men of culture," he wrote in *Culture and Anarchy,*

> are those who have a passion for diffusing, for making prevail, for carrying from one end of society to the other, the best knowledge, the best ideas of their times; who have labored to divest knowledge of all that was harsh, uncouth, abstract, professional, exclusive; to humanize it, to make it efficient outside the clique of the cultivated and the learned, yet still remaining the best knowledge and thought of the time, and a true source, therefore, of sweetness and light.[1]

Of course, Matthew Arnold was a teacher as well as a scholar, and the terms he used to define "the best knowledge, the best ideas" are to be understood in the context of teaching. How, then, does he delineate the teacher's task? First, the teacher must possess the best ideas, that is, he must be secure in his mastery of a certain area of scholarship. Second, the teacher must divest knowledge of all that is "difficult, abstract, exclusive," that is, he must be skillful in making clear to students the most abstruse concepts in his field—say, nuclear theory or Hamlet's soliloquies—adapting his presentation to the students' limited grasp of mathematics and language. Finally, the teacher must "humanize" the best ideas, that is, without compromising his standards of scholarship or his in-depth knowledge of Plato or Newton or Pasteur, he must present ideas so young people living in what is largely a parochial and contemporary world can see the applicability—or, to use a much abused term, "relevance"—of scholarship to their own concerns.

Matthew Arnold, of course, was not unaware of the obstacles standing in the way of his vision of universal education. It was he who saw Europe as "a darkling plain, where ignorant armies clash by night." It was he who diagnosed the illness of British society, its hostility to ideas: on the one hand the Barbarians, the elitist upper class distracted by its pursuit of sensory and physical gratification, and on the other hand the Philistines, the stolid middle class with its rigid moral code and its materialistic values—with neither class committed to a life of the mind. Nevertheless, Arnold had faith in the power of education to make the best ideas prevail against the forces of ignorance and darkness.

Today, however, educators cannot be confident in the values of schooling: the very foundations of their vocation are under attack. The Owl

Critics, as I have shown, charge that the schools, as now organized, cannot be relevant to youth's problems and that only a radical transformation of curriculum and teaching method can achieve this goal. Their proposals, as we have seen, range from Carl Rogers's relegation of the teacher to a secondary role to Neil Postman's substitution of an eccentric "questions curriculum" for the present standard curriculum. Their negativism is reenacted in John Holt's advocacy of a noncompulsory, nondirective, permissive program. The more politically minded reconstructionists, among them Jonathan Kozol and Ivan Illich (to be discussed in chapters 10 and 11), would turn the schools into propaganda centers for one radical theory or another, or abolish schools altogether. These reformists unite in condemning existing public-school programs as being irredeemably irrelevant to the needs of youth.

"Relevance" rather than the diffusion of knowledge has been enshrined as a slogan, as potent as those of Women's Liberation and Black Power, and slogans do not ordinarily include a clear definition of terms. In the view of the reformists, the one criterion of relevance is what is present at the moment in a consciousness nourished by newspaper headlines and television shows. Study of the mass media, the threatened biosphere, the drug culture, and the problems of racism and sexism is proposed as the focal center of the curriculum on the ground that these problems are recognized by everyone as important issues of the day. The "school without walls," described by Charles Silberman with little short of reverence, has the virtue of releasing students from the bookish confines of the classroom and putting them into the streets, the museums, the business offices, the courts and prisons, where they come into direct contact with reality. On the other hand, the study of Greek civilization, mathematics, foreign language, and Shakespeare is belittled as an academic—the negation of relevant—pursuit that should be offered only, and then grudgingly, to the few students who evince an elitist inclination for such learning.

What is the premise of this scale of priorities? It is that certain issues, in most cases political and social problems, seem most urgently in need of solution, and that the schools should concentrate on guiding students to deal with them competently. More generally, the theory is that the test of relevance is whether a question or topic or activity is one that students happen to be curious about or concerned about at the moment. If there emerges a momentary flurry of interest in astrology, extrasensory perception, or exorcism, these subjects would become proper fields of study in the schools. John Holt's principle of immediate curiosity is set forth as the justification of every aspect of classroom activities.

But it is highly questionable that this concept of relevance can provide a valid and comprehensive basis for curricular content. First, the curiosity that Holt talks about is transient and unsustained, unlike the intellectual curiosity that is the objective of an organized course of study. The urgency of a social problem fluctuates with shifting events, and the student's intense concern with the environment or the plight of Appalachia at a given moment is unlikely to be sustained without the apperceptive support of courses in earth science and social studies. Second, students have their own personal needs, as urgent as any of the issues affecting society at large; that is, vocational goals are very real to them, and neglect of the intellectual and technical skills essential to achieving these goals would be a disservice to them. Third, the ideal of building a society of enlightened, compassionate, and socially responsible men and women is not attainable if the arts and sciences and the humanities are merely peripheral concerns of the schools. A sound definition of relevance must take into account the broader interests of society as well as the immediate interests of the student.

Relevance is not an absolute term. No school subject or activity can be said to be relevant in itself; it gains significance only in relation to the purpose it serves. Schools deal with the social problems of today, not because they are of immediate interest to an assembled group but because it is imperative that the soon-to-be-voting young adults should be knowledgeable in supporting or opposing political candidates and proposed legislation. Schools teach the sciences, not simply to appease a flurry of excitement and curiosity about space exploration and environmental pollution, important as these are, but in the conviction that human beings cannot live healthy lives and the nation cannot maintain a technological civilization without a societal base of educated citizens. Good teaching is, in large measure, the task of convincing students of the significance of the subjects they are studying. In this sense, the study of the active and passive voices and the logic of paragraph development becomes relevant to the degree that the importance of these concepts for effective communication is persuasively demonstrated.

Some of those who talk of the irrelevance of school subjects seem to have a low opinion of the young people they want to protect from heavy-handed pedantry. They envisage a mindless youth interested in nothing but filling his belly and exercising his large muscles not so much by solid exercise and competitive athletics as by frantic exertion to the raucous beat of rock music. They picture him as being unwilling to stretch his mind far enough to dig into an essay by George Orwell or a poem by Carl Sandburg or to work out an algebraic equation or a chemistry formula all because these assignments are not as exciting to him as a football game. They treat him as if the object directly in front of his nose is the only reality he can perceive, assuming that because an event is contemporary it must be easy to comprehend. Thus, some of the "alternative" schools, those spun off as minischools away from the main building, fritter away the students' time with card games (said to develop mathematics skills), in doing word puzzles (a pathway to literacy), and in sporadic talk sessions without direction and continuity, in the hope that somehow these pleasant distractions will curb truancy and hostility.

A certain ambiguity is detectable, also, in the charge of irrelevance. It is sometimes unclear what aspect of the complex process of education is under attack. Nor is it clear what philosophic assumptions underlie the critic's viewpoint. What are we to make of Holt's statement that the "act of instruction impedes learning," or of Christopher Jencks's casual remark that "in the absence of empirical evidence, some educators simply assert the intrinsic value of knowing geography, reading Dickens, or mastering Newtonian physics"? Openness to external criticism is, of course, a source of strength to any institution, but we must not ignore the fact that certain modes of criticism can only undermine and confuse.

Irrational criticism can usually be traced to specific sources—misinformation, gullibility, faddism, political ideology, or an unworldly idealism. Many of the doctrines of the Owl Critics, as we have seen in earlier chapters, are based on inaccurate appraisal of existing school programs and offer impractical proposals for reform. But even when the area of criticism is technical, that is, when it concerns teaching methods, curriculum, or school administration, these failings can be discerned. To illustrate this point, let me refer to a number of critics who have been outspoken in their disparagement of the English program in the schools.

Charles E. Silberman's appraisal of the English course of study and English teaching is entirely derogatory. "It is difficult for people, even those close to the schools," he writes, "to appreciate the puerility of so much of the literature assigned students to read, or the banality with which it is usually handled."[2] To be sure, Silberman sees little to commend in any aspect of the high-school program, but his sweeping judgment of English is less qualified than are his comments on other subject areas. His basic charge is that the English program has been static and inept, notably in its failure to adapt its materials and teaching methods to present-day realities.

I suspect that Silberman uses the terms *puerility* and *banality* to enlist himself in the company of those who worship at the shrine of relevance as the touchstone of curricular worth. For it is obvious that he has little respect for the cultural values of English, and it is evident that his attitude is not based on adequate information and seasoned judgment. Apparently he was only too ready to take his cue from whatever pronouncement of the Postman–Holt coterie was in fashion at the moment.

Silberman's main exhibit in support of his condemnation of the English program is a survey that found George Eliot's *Silas Marner* in the reading program of "more than three-quarters of the high schools of the United States." No other evidence is presented to show the puerility of the literature syllabus than this one report. To Silberman, and to many other critics of the English program, *Silas Marner* (together, perhaps, with Dickens's *A Tale of Two Cities*) has become a convenient symbol of sterility, for whenever an advocate of curricular reform wants to make a telling point, he directs his most barbed invectives at that innocent target. I have heard the book denounced at dozens of English conventions.

I hold no special brief for *Silas Marner*, although I have found that teaching it in bright classes can be a rewarding experience. It is interesting to note that this novel was adopted as a standard literary text some sixty years ago, together with *Treasure Island, Ivanhoe, The Ancient Mariner, Idylls of the King, The Return of the Native,* and a sampling of Shakespeare and other classics, at the recommendation of a panel of scholars assigned to draw up a list of excellent literary works suitable for high school. George Eliot's story of the weaver of Raveloe is an interesting and significant novel; it is an early example of realism in British fiction and comes to grips with some of the perennial problems of life: religion and superstition, drug addiction, alienation, the generation gap, and sexual mores. George Eliot's style, however, like that of other Victorian writers, has gone out of favor; it is too tightly woven, too intricate in sentence structure, and probably too challenging in its level of vocabulary for most of this genera- tion of students. Obviously, *Silas Marner* must go.

Whatever our attitude toward the established classics may be, however, Silberman and others of like mind ought to know that the study of literature has expanded in the past several decades far beyond the tradi- tional list of classic texts. There has been an increasing stress on modern and contemporary works—enduring works such as Edith Wharton's *Ethan Frome,* Pearl Buck's *The Good Earth,* Somerset Maugham's *Of Human Bondage,* Sinclair Lewis's *Arrowsmith,* John Steinbeck's *Grapes of Wrath,* as well as ephemeral favorites such as J.D. Salinger's *Catcher in the Rye* and William Golding's *Lord of the Flies.* The availability of paperback editions has revolutionized the English course, bringing into the classroom cur- rent best-sellers as well as masterpieces of world literature and biog- raphies of charismatic figures of the day. Poetry, contemporary plays, and the writings of minorities, together with translations of foreign literary works, have immeasurably enriched the English experience. Beating the dead horse of *Silas Marner* will no longer serve to close discussion.

As to the alleged banality of English teaching, it is difficult to appraise so sweeping a judgment without knowing its evidential basis. As the chair- man of a large English department, I have observed my share of inept and unimaginative lessons in literature and have been appalled at times by the teacher's failure to ask the right questions or conduct a stimulating discus- sion. After each formal observation, the teacher and I, in conference, would go over the salient points of the lesson as frankly and searchingly as the temperaments of both individuals allowed. On the basis of such professional experience, I can say with assurance that most teachers are as concerned with acquiring expertise in their craft as any other professional group. English teachers are readers and scholars and specialists in the language arts, and they are single-minded in their purpose of transmitting their hard won knowledge and insights to their students. Teachers naturally want to be liked and respected by the very observant and critical young men and women in their classes—this, too, is a spur to sincere effort.

If Silberman's researchers found the lessons they observed to be generally dull and uninspiring—sufficiently so to justify the term *banal*—it in part may be due to the incompetence of the observers. Perhaps it was not the lessons, but the observers' perceptions, that were dry. There is a built-in disqualification that most note-taking visitors to classes suffer from, and that is their inability to grasp fully what is happening before their eyes. They have not done their homework. How can a visitor appreciate the impact of a teacher's question about some detail of a story or poem or essay without knowing its relationship to the long-range objectives of the unit, or how the concept being developed—symbolism, irony, satiric tone, metaphor—has been covered in earlier lessons? An experienced supervisor will take into account these factors of prior learning and long-range objectives. But the less sophisticated observer is handicaped by lack of perspective, like a theatergoer who takes his seat halfway through the play.

As a counterirritant to the abrasive tone of Silberman's diatribe, let me refer to a more judicious evaluation of the English program. It is provided in Anthony Burgess's gentle admonition to his students at City College (New York) in an open letter published in the *New York Times,* in which Burgess describes his impressions and observations as a visiting lecturer.[3] Among other things, the article deals with the goals of his course, concluding with these words: "I would ask you only to expand your vocabularies, develop a minimal grace of style, and learn who Helen of Troy and Nausicaa were. And for God's sake, stop talking about relevance. All we have is the past."

In his final sentence, Burgess is saying, among other things, that our intellectual life is necessarily rooted in the cultural soil of the historical past. The present is ephemeral; even as we think about it or try to reflect on it, the fleeting moment is inexorably merged into the vast continuum of the past. Whatever thoughts or intuitions or visions we have are fed instantly into the computer bank of sensory data that each of us carries within himself as the raw material of his autobiography. It is our education, taken in its broadest sense, that determines the worth of our "remembrance of things past."

Burgess means that the study of literature—and by implication the study of history and science and philosophy—is the best resource we have for enriching our minds. On the bread and butter level, it provides us with a vocabulary and referential framework in which Captain Ahab and Madame Bovary, together with Helen of Troy and Nausicaa, are more than shadowy figures. It gives us the pleasure of being at ease in the company of men and women who are attuned to the life of the mind: we catch more readily the allusion in a pointed epigram and delight in a neat turn of phrase or an incisive metaphor. We become more responsive to "the best knowledge, the best ideas" of our times. Even our everyday sensory awareness—when opening our eyes to each morning or walking along a street thronged by fellow pilgrims—is sensitized when we have been drugged by the elixir of poetry.

But because he is a classicist—that is, he values Homer above Vonnegut—Anthony Burgess is impatient with talk of relevance, for he fears that those who insist on relevance to present interests as the guiding principle of curricular worth are likely to exclude everything but the immediate and contemporary. To them relevance is Angela Davis, "Sticks and Bones," and the lyrics of Bob Dylan; and Burgess wants them to understand that all of our literary heritage is, in the deepest sense, relevant to our concerns as human beings. *Gulliver's Travels,* he would insist, may take us as far from the present troubled scene as the wings of imagination can soar, but what Jonathan Swift says in his scornful sermon on the folly of war, the corruptive abuse of power, and the vice of ignorance is more timely than yesterday's headlines. The bolder-than-life portraits that Dickens has given us—Scrooge, Oliver Twist, Sidney Carton, Uriah Heep—have become household gods that exorcise our moral ambivalences. The citizens of the world of letters—William Blake, Emily Bronte, Henry David Thoreau, Mark Twain—speak to our minds and hearts with a warmth and humor and consolation that clothe this naked ape in robes of dignity and heroism. If literature is not relevant to our lives, nothing is.

There is one implication of Burgess's statement that I would question. "All we have is the past," he says. If I interpret him correctly, his preference for the novels and plays and poems that have become established in the literary canon implies a disparagement of the literary output of the present day. Current literature, he seems to be saying, should not be stressed in the English curriculum because most of the books published today have, if anything, an ephemeral interest only. Burgess advises us to wait out the problem of "sifting the significantly contemporary from the ephermerally trendy," and in the meantime to concentrate our attention on the established classics. Yet it is doubtful that teachers of contemporary students can avoid the dilemma by refusing to include recently published materials in their courses, even at the risk of making some bad choices.

At a lecture before the New York Association of Teachers of English in 1972, Burgess spoke wittily of the faddism that prevails in some scholastic circles as evinced in the impassioned embrace of certain popular works for a brief moment and their equally sudden abandonment. He cited Herman Hesse's *Siddhartha* as an instance of unmerited acclaim: its pretentious mysticism and colorless prose should have been apparent to any discerning reader. Most in the audience—all teachers—recognized their own complicity in having placed Hesse on their reading lists in response to various pressures, just as they had done with Salinger's *Catcher in the Rye* and Tolkien's elaborate epics; but whatever guilt they felt was tempered by their reasoned conviction that even a flawed contemporary work might have value in the classroom as a stepping stone to the more formidable heights of literary greatness. Thus, they used *West Side Story* as a means of introducing *Romeo and Juliet* in their English classes and mimeographed the lyrics of the latest rock-'n'-roll album as a bridge to the study of poetry.

Whether or not those in the audience agreed with everything Burgess had to say, they respected his integrity—his judgments were clearly based on a personally felt system of values. There are other educators, however, whose opinions are more susceptible to being swayed by the winds of current fashion and are ready to follow any Pied Piper that plays an alluring tune. Their confidence in established curricular programs and teaching methods has been shaken by the schools' failure to reach increasing numbers of students—the disadvantaged, the alienated, the ethnic minorities—as seen in low reading grades, student apathy, and campus unrest. These teachers are therefore only too eager to listen to the voices of those reformists who are most iconoclastic.

Typical of these is Robert W. Blake, professor of English at Brockport State University and editor of *The English Record,* a professional journal, who envisions a revolutionary change in the substance of education that will be brought about by the "different kinds of media, especially television." In an article entitled "The New English is Cool,"[4] he hails the beginning of a new era in education to be founded on the dictum of Marshall McLuhan that "our educational system is an outdated and dying system founded on literate values and fragmented and classified data wholly unsuited to the needs of the first television generation." Blake offers to serve as mentor and guide in the unexplored territory of the New English. There is much of interest to be learned on this tour.

We have already noted that whenever critics of the traditional schools want to make a telling point, they characterize current teaching methods as stressing nothing but memorization, excessive drill, the imposition of dogma through the lecture or the teacher-dominated lesson, and the force-feeding of dry, bookish crumbs of information to be regurgitated on examinations. Baker establishes his credentials as one of these Owl Critics by echoing the charge that present-day school programs are, in his words, "innocuous remnants of a bygone era." The lecture, he asserts, has become an anchronism in an era when "information can be transmitted so much more effectively by other means." The "other means" are described at first rather loosely: they seem to be nothing more than an extension of the developmental methods prevalent in the schools, involving student dialogue and interaction in the exploration of subject matter. But it soon becomes clear that Blake's paean to the New English takes its inspiration from a specific source of epistemological doctrine, namely, the writings of Marshall McLuhan.

In his major work, *Understanding Media,* McLuhan says that the one causative factor in our social evolution from the tribal organizations of primitive man up to the supranational community of mankind coming into existence today has been the prevailing medium of communication: speech, writing, print, electronic devices such as the telegraph and telephone, and finally radio and television.[5] No other factors are recognized by McLuhan. Classical sociologists, Herbert Spencer for example, take a somewhat more limited position. They see the superb road system developed by the ancient Romans as an important factor in the stability of the Roman Empire, and the Gutenberg invention of printing with moveable type as a significant step in the secularization of learning and the spread of knowledge that led to the Enlightenment of the eighteenth century. However, they do not ignore other factors—the growth of population, technological advances, new discoveries in chemistry, physics, and astronomy, and religious conflicts. But McLuhan's postulate is that all political, social, economic, and intellectual movements in Western civilization are the result of *nothing but* the evolving media of communication.

McLuhan insists that the message conveyed in a medium of communication does not matter; it is the medium itself that is the whole message. The nature of the medium in itself "shapes and controls the scale and form of human association and action." The invention of printing would have had the same far-reaching effects whether published books were composed of reasoned exposition or nonsense syllables. Thus, McLuhan need not be constrained by historical evidence or the canons of logic when he utters such sweeping generalizations as: "The printed word with its specialist intensity burst the bonds of medieval corporate guilds and monasteries, creating extremely individualist patterns of enterprise and monopoly";[6] or "That Hitler came into political existence at all is owing to radio and public address systems. This is not to say that these media relayed his thoughts effectively to the German People. His thoughts were of very little consequence."[7] The medium is the message!

There are two corollary elements in McLuhan's philosophy that should be of concern to educators. The first is his analysis of the effects of the various media on man's way of viewing the world. Before the present electronic era, books and newspapers were the common means of dissemination of information and ideas, and the fact that printed materials are organized in a step-by-step temporal sequence resulted in man's becoming oriented to rationality, science, and technology. This means that the form of printed texts—sentence following sentence, paragraph linked to paragraph, chapters arranged in a certain pattern—implants its logic in the minds and actions of men. Thus, printing led to the questioning of the moral and spiritual sanctions that had remained intact since the Middle Ages when, McLuhan asserts, direct communication in speech had fostered a sense of unity. The advent of print destroyed man's sense of a common humanity and fragmented the global village into competing nationalisms. Today, however, television presents the full range of its sensory data instantaneously, as an immediately perceived whole rather than in a sequential pattern. As a result the rationalism of the Age of Print has been replaced by a mode of experience that, like the mystics's vision, reveals all truth in one blinding flash of insight. Therefore, McLuhan concludes, the printed textbook no longer has a place in the educational scheme.

The second of McLuhan's ideas that directly bear on education is his classification of media into two categories—"hot" media and "cool" media. "There is a basic principle," he writes,

> that distinguishes a hot medium like radio from a cool one like the telephone, or a hot medium like the movies from a cool one like TV. A hot medium is one that extends a single sense in high definition . . . the state of being well filled with data. . . . Hot media are, therefore, low in participation or completion by the audience, and cool media are high in participation. Naturally, therefore, a hot medium like radio has very different effects from a cool medium like the telephone.[8]

Books and lectures are classified as hot media, and television and class seminars are classified as cool media.

The most important cool medium, we are told by Robert Blake (in his interpretive role), is television since it "provides men with an instant depth involvement with other men throughout the world," whereas students are turned off by the hot media commonly used in schools and colleges, namely, books and lectures. The second most important cool medium is talk. "The new English classroom," says Blake, in elaborating this point, "should be a seminar or guided bull session, where students and teachers discuss, question, and analyze together, and in which knowledge, understandings and values are developed and deepened through interaction and communication."[9] This may be sound doctrine in itself, but it is tainted by its association with McLuhanism. For, by definition, the content of the seminar or guided bull session will not necessarily be related to literature or any other subject matter; in fact, it is likely that attention to psychological or ethical or esthetic concepts, the lifeblood of the study of literature, will be casual and sporadic. If it is the medium, that is, the cool medium of the seminar, that matters above everything else, the intellectual content of the discussion is immaterial and irrelevant.

A critique of McLuhan's ideas in depth is beyond the scope of this book. In my view, however, they cannot be taken seriously as a philosophy of history or as a guide to education. Although McLuhan leaves the reader breathless and bemused by his dexterity in discerning cause and effect relationships where angelic historians would fear to tread, even a cursory examination of his thesis shows it is essentially false. It cannot be true that the form of the media predominant in a given period of history is the cause of every concurrent political and social development. The invention of printing is not a sufficient explanation of the emergence of the modern world—a cause that would have operated whether or not Galileo and Bacon and Descartes elucidated the principles of scientific method by which the face of the Western world was changed. Nor, to come to the present day, is the medium of television, considered as an abstract force apart from the nature of the programs it carries, a sufficient explanation of the quality of life in this generation. McLuhan's doctrine of the single cause is as irrational as that which attributes all human events to the configuration of the stars in the astrological horoscope.

What can we make of the pseudological classification of the media into "hot" and "cool"? For one thing, the perversity of McLuhan's metaphors is as perplexing as the basis of his classification. One would think that *hot* would be associated with vital, stimulating experiences and that *cool* would refer to dull, uninspiring activities. But McLuhan never fails to surprise. Perhaps the first characteristic of the New English that Blake derives from McLuhan can be seen as the abuse of metaphor. Does Blake want us to believe that watching pictures on a screen is more stimulating and involving than reading books? Since when has television viewing, beyond a certain point, been anything but the most passive, mind-dulling pastime? By no stretch of the imagination or the commonsense meaning of words can it be said that looking at a television screen is a more valid educational activity than reading a book. Equating television viewing with participation in class discussion under the blanket rubric of "cool" media raises further the suspicion that McLuhan is talking nonsense and that Professor Blake is his dupe.

Blake's uncritical acceptance of McLuhan's thesis is as disturbing as Neil Postman's reliance on the doctrines of Korzybski. For McLuhan's prose is clouded with dizzying half-truths and surrealistic metaphors to the point that there is hardly a paragraph that does not leave the reader with more questions than it provides answers. It is hard to decide whether he is a genius whose thoughts are too profound for utterance or a mystic whose inspired oracles never quite correspond with the realities that men of limited vision can perceive.

Stripped of their relation with McLuhanism, Blake's proposals for strengthening the English program can be judged on their merits. Less lecturing and more involvement of students in discussions is certainly good pedagogy. Blake's sharp rebuke of the teacher who stifles imagination by "conducting a historical survey of American poets, which results in the activity of matching poets' names with the titles of their poems" is deserved—if the teacher did nothing else with the poets. His suggestion to include an intensive study of "the nature of human communication, extra-verbal signals of language, and regional, social, and functional differences" in the English course has great value. But in derogating the printed page, overstressing the values of the mass media, and turning the classroom into a loosely organized bull session Blake diminishes the status of English.

Television and the other mass media have their place in the curriculum as intrinsic objects of study and as aids in the exploration of the basic areas of scholarship. It is one thing, however, to point to the great potential value of the mass media and quite a different thing to enthrone them in some Promethean role as the bearers of arcane and ineffable virtue.

The drum beaters of relevance, whether they proclaim the here and now as the supreme good or whether they are charmed by esoteric doctrine into the circle of the book burners, have offered little reason to turn away from the established values of the basic curriculum.

9 THE VAGARIES OF CHRISTOPHER JENCKS & CO

The campaign to undermine confidence in the nation's schools has taken many forms. As we have seen, the vanguard of denigration selects its targets one by one: administrative practices, personnel, curriculums, teaching methods, examinations. The momentum gained by the success of each attack adds weight to every successive move until, finally, a full-scale assault on the very existence of the schools meets with only half-hearted resistance. We may refute some of the criticisms with rational argument and dismiss others by appealing to common sense, but when the challenge is buttressed by an awesome display of statistical tables and charts, we hesitate and are silenced.

One such formidable monument was unveiled in the public forum with the recent publication of Christopher Jencks's *Inequality: A Reassessment of the Effect of Family and Schooling in America* (1972). In this book, Jencks sets out to challenge the "recurrent fantasy" that education can contribute anything toward the solution of economic and societal problems, specifically those associated with the unequal distribution of wealth and income. The book is a statistically grounded study of factors that perpetuate the wide disparity in wealth and status in American society. Jencks postulates five controlling factors: genotype or heredity, family background, environment, schooling, and an inscrutable force called luck. In his assessment of their relative importance in the individual's attainment of economic success, the least important of these factors is schooling. The book concludes with the sweeping assertion that reliance on such "marginal institutions as the schools to attain anything approaching an egalitarian society in America is futile"; and that the only effective means of reshaping the image of America as a true democracy would be to establish "political control over the economic institutions that shape our society. This is what other countries call socialism."[1]

As Jencks draws together the threads of his argument in his final chapter ("What Can Be Done?"), the suspicion arises that his book is not really about education at all. The real subject is political forensics. Jencks is making his contribution to a debate that has been raging since the early days of the New Deal on whether our socioeconomic governmental programs—such as social security, antipoverty programs, tax reform, subsidies to low-income housing—have been of any lasting help in eradicating our social ills. One of the areas in which the debate has been most intense involved education, and the movement in the 1960s to liberate the schools from the straitjacket of conservatism had a political focus, that is, to provide equal educational opportunities for all students through integration, curricular reform, and a vast number of compensatory programs. Jencks's sobering conclusion is that the claims of all educational reformers, whether moderate or extreme, are without foundation and that the schools, no matter how transformed, have made and can make no contribution to the solution of social problems.

The study, carrying with it the imprimatur of the Center for Educational Policy Research, Harvard University, and of the Carnegie Foundation, is a prestigious document. The Jencks report will very likely take its place in the pantheon of germinal works—Plowden, Conant, Jensen, Coleman—that superintendents of schools consult in making policy decisions at the grass-roots level. They would be well advised to study it most critically, however, before making any hard commitments on the basis of its findings. For the Jencks thesis, seemingly the product of objective and searching investigation of available material, is in fact based on questionable premises, a fuzzy definition of terms, and an underlying bias that vitiates its conclusions.

"Americans have a recurrent fantasy," writes Jencks, "that schools can solve their problems. Thus it was inevitable, perhaps, that, after we discovered poverty and inequality in the early 1960s, we turned to the schools for solutions."[2] This, the opening sentence of an article in the *Saturday Review* in which Jencks synopsized his thesis, sets the disturbing tone. I would say that not one word in this faddishly cynical statement is true. The reference to our rediscovery of poverty in the 1960s is no doubt intended as a clever jibe at federal welfare programs that were initiated in that decade; but the disparaging innuendo reveals more about Jencks's political views than it does about our national policies. As to schooling, Americans have indeed had a firm conviction, hardly to be characterized as a "recurrent fantasy," that universal education is essential to the health of our democracy. This conviction, however, was not visionary and never went beyond the belief that an informed, literate, and socially concerned citizenry, the end product of our schools, was essential to maintaining our institutions and grappling with the nation's complex problems. By setting an unrealistic aim as the presumed goal of education, that is, the cure of our economic and social ills, Jencks has no trouble, of course, in demonstrating that education has failed.

This misconception is exposed further in Jencks's discussion of "equality" and "inequality." Our national goal, he says, should be to eliminate poverty, and to achieve this we must reduce the wide disparity in income between the rich and the poor. So far, so good. He then defines poverty as the condition of those who are lowest in a distributive scale of income, regardless of their actual standard of living. This means that if every family in America had a sufficient income to afford decent housing, ample food and clothing, a car and a television set, there would still be a problem of poverty so long as other families were relatively better off, with incomes that would enable them to afford two cars or a country vacation home. Jencks postulates this concept of "relative poverty" because, like all Marxists, he seems unable to accept or value the remarkable fact that the United States has already come close to achieving the abolition of "absolute" poverty. We have certainly been unremitting in our efforts to attain this goal in the past half century, ever since Franklin D. Roosevelt translated his vision of a nation free from want into practical legislation. That we have far to go in eliminating poverty is conceded by conservatives and liberals alike, and this realization is precisely the reason for our faith in education, not only as a means of upward mobility but even more importantly as an essential means of developing an enlightened and concerned electorate. Such considerations are shrugged off by Jencks, however, for his single and dogmatic test of a just society is its all-or-nothing realization of a Platonic egalitarianism; and since this ideal has not thus far been attained—and is probably unattainable—all efforts to improve the quality of life, to make continuous relative progress, can be written off as futile.

Jencks's treatment of the goals of education as if they were identical with the goals of economic policy leads him to take an indefensible position—and a most ironic one—with respect to educational reforms. If our objective is to ensure equality of opportunity for all students, the compensatory programs in the schools make sense in that they give the disadvantaged more school services in the form of remedial instruction, tutoring, and a saturation of materials adapted to their needs. But Jencks will have none of this. In his closed system, compensatory measures cannot achieve the goal of equality in social and economic status. Therefore, with sublime objectivity, Jencks proposes that the superior student might be given a diluted education to neutralize his presumed advantage in genetic intelligence and family background. This is posited as being equivalent to tax policies that effectively narrow the disparity in income between the wealthy and the marginally poor. "If those who started life with genetic disadvantages," he writes,

> were given a big enough environmental advantage, and if those who started with genetic advantages were given big enough environmental handicaps, we could produce relatively equal performance in many realms where inequality now prevails. A society committed to achieving full cognitive equality would, for example, probably have to exclude genetically advantaged children from school. It might also have to impose other handicaps on them, like denying them access to books and television.[3]

Jencks's egalitarian dogma leads him into strange bypaths.

Similarly, Jencks's self-imposed delimitation of the scope of his survey makes suspect everything he has to say about education. He bases his findings almost entirely on the result of standardized tests in what he calls the cognitive skills—verbal ability, nonverbal ability, reading comprehension, mathematics achievement, and general information. These are, in his judgment, the only measurable outcomes of schooling. Time and again, he speaks derogatively of any opinion not derived from these quantitative measures. "In the absence of evidence," he says, "theorists must rely on intuition and personal experience. These have proved a poor guide to understanding the one thing we can measure, namely, cognitive skills."[4] The insights of a John Dewey or a James B. Conant are apparently of no value. The implication is that one educator's guess is no better than another's, or for that matter anyone else's.

Moreover, since Jencks is narrowly concerned only with the effects of schooling on economic success and social status, and not with its effects on the quality of life as reflected in intelligent citizenship and a variety of intellectual interests, his study has an artificial, hothouse air. On curriculum, he has only this to say: "In the absence of empirical evidence, some educators simply assert the intrinsic value of knowing geography, reading Dickens, or mastering Newtonian physics."[5] This is a most revealing statement. Jencks apparently looks askance at any assertion that is not reducible to mathematical formulation by the crude instrument of tests of cognitive skills. Thus, he has literally nothing of value to say about curriculum, teaching method, learning materials, elective courses, experimental programs, or any other aspect of education beyond the rudiments.

Relying then on his narrow definition of the aims of education, Jencks reaches the smug conclusion that schooling has no bearing on success in one's vocation or on social status; heredity, family background, and "varieties of luck" are the important determinants. "Neither school resources or segregation," he writes, "has any appreciable effect on either test scores or educational attainment."[6] Reforms in curricular offerings or teaching method, segregation or nonsegregation, tracking or nontracking, have no measurable effects either. The most that educational innovation can achieve is to make school life more bearable. "Advocates of change," he states, "feel obliged to claim that these reforms will reduce the number of non-readers, increase racial understanding, or strengthen family life. A wise reformer ought to be more modest, claiming only that a particular reform will not harm adult society and that it will make life pleasanter for parents, teachers, and students in the short run."[7] In a word, educators are harmless fools for thinking their profession has any value (the sarcasm of the "can do no harm" remark is patent) other than to make things more agreeable. Nowhere in the professional literature will one find so blatant an expression of contempt for the schools.

Jencks anticipates, earns, indeed invites the incredulity and hostility with which educators will react to his thesis. But he stands firm on the solid ground of his charts and tables. "Our studies show" and "our findings tell us," repeated time and time again as evidence of objectivity, would suggest that a meticulous concern for scientific accuracy and inductive logic guided the Jencks's research team. In fact, the most offensive feature of the book is the disparity between the quasi-scientific tone of the greater part of the text and the arbitrary and almost capricious opinions expressed throughout. A typical example is this offhand remark about teachers: "We have not done any empirical research," Jencks writes, "on what school administrators and teachers are really trying to do. We suspect that their primary objective is to teach children to behave themselves in the way schools want them to behave."[8] Such cynical utterances, eminently quotable, are strewn everywhere thoughtout the book.

The most flagrant instance of departure from "empirical" method is seen in the final paragraph of *Inequality*. Here Jencks asserts that an aimless drift has been characteristic of American economic and social policy and that our political ills have remained insoluble because we have placed too much confidence in "marginal institutions like the schools.", Therefore, he concludes, "what we will need is . . . what other countries call socialism. Anything less will end in the same disappointments as the reforms of the 1960s."[9] Here are the wolf's claws suddenly bared. We can see now the motivation of Jencks's massive apparatus of research: it was all intended, in utter disregard of facts and logic, to support a political dogma that, whatever its merits, cannot be demonstrated by findings and studies and empirical evidence of any sort.

Despite its glaring fallacies, or perhaps because of them, Jencks's book may have value for educational research by its revelation of the limitations in statistical measurement of the outcomes of schooling. Jencks himself concedes that tests of cognitive skills and the conclusions drawn from them are unreliable beyond a certain point; in fact, he takes a "dim view" of their validity, but he justifies his reliance on test results with the dubious explanation that all other means of assessing the outcomes of school programs are even more unreliable. Perhaps this is so, but there is surely a growing conviction among educators that too much reliance on standardized tests is unwarranted. Reading tests, for example, are conducted under highly artificial conditions of time limitation, and the arbitrary sampling of test items does not take into account the interest factor that is present in all purposeful reading. As crude measures of comprehension and facility, such tests can serve administrative convenience in ability grouping and assignment to special classes and reading clinics. But when the results of these tests are given undue significance and are correlated with remotely related factors such as racial origin and family status for the

purpose of supporting a political ideology, the acceptability of the conclusions drawn from such tenuous data is minimal.

In this connection, one does well to recall a statement made by Lou La
Brant, somewhere in her otherwise valuable book *We Teach English*,[10] to
the effect that no individual teacher has the right to a personal opinion
that is not supported by research studies and codified in statistical charts.
When I first encountered this stricture I was incredulous to the point of
penciling an angry question mark in the margin, and my reaction has not
changed in the intervening years. The aspects of education that can be
measured and charted are *not* the most important concerns of the schools.
The self-recognition made possible by great books, the patterns of reasoning, the web of philosophy, the forms of esthetic experience, the pleasure
of discovering the beauty and grandeur of the world—all these elude the
clumsy grasp of probing census takers. It should be noted, in passing, that
Professor La Brant's assertion is itself an article of faith unsupported by
research.

As to the now-entrenched worship of statistics and mathematical
norms, it should not be overlooked that many of the studies relied on by
policy makers have a specious outer layer of mathematical exactness that
obscures their flimsy material basis. For example, a number of studies
have been published that conclude there is no correlation between the
teaching of formal grammar and the students' ability to write correct
English.[11] This unsettling thesis struck me when I first encountered it as
being undemonstrable. In fact, I do not accept it to this day. There are too
many undefined terms in these studies. Troublesome questions keep
coming up: what elements of grammar were taught, how well were they
taught, how well were they learned, to what extent were the principles and
rules applied? Moreover, one would want to know by what criteria the
written English was appraised: was it organization, expressiveness, or
simply correctness? At some point, we would find ourselves hopelessly
confused by the whole business. There are too many undefined premises,
too many variables, too many uncontrollable factors in these efforts to
measure the operations of the human mind.

A parallel instance of the misuse of scientific method in the behavioral
area is provided by Edgar Z. Friedenberg in his book *The Vanishing
Adolescent,* an important study of the attitudes of students in divergent
socioeconomic settings. At one point in his analysis of the failure of
educational institutions to strengthen the average student's sense of self-
esteem and purpose, Friedenberg sets out to demonstrate that teachers
are largely responsible for this failure because they do not and cannot
serve as admirable models of courage and enterprise. Friedenberg dis-
missively describes the typical teacher—that is, the statistically average
teacher—as a "timid and constrained" civil servant, not quite a profes-

sional, drawn to teaching largely by the security afforded by a license and tenure. In support of this characterization, Friedenberg cites with approval a survey of student teachers that investigated "the possibilities of the Rohrschach Test as a means of predicting the supervisory ratings these students would receive in their practice teaching."[12] It is the effrontery and condescension of the research project that exasperates me. It is patently and self-evidently absurd to rely on any personality test as a predictor of performance in so complex an act as teaching. Yet Friedenberg solemnly cites the conclusions of the study as affording significant insight into the personality traits of teachers as a class. I would say that the comic-strip stereotype of the teacher as a "timid and constrained" person was only too congenial to Friedenberg's private a priori intuition and that he welcomed the Rohrschach study as a confirmation of his bias. The "class" view that sees hundreds of thousands of individuals who entered the teaching profession for a wide variety of motives as a monolithic bloc betrays a mind as likely to do the same injustice to students.

A more flagrant example of the doctrinaire misuse of statistical data can be found in Colin Greer's revisionist appraisal of education in America. In his major work, *The Great School Legend,* Greer sets out to undermine the commonly accepted belief in the historic role of the public schools. "The legend," he writes, "is that the schools were an important factor in the creation of our economy, social mores, and functioning democracy." It is simply not true, he asserts, that the schools were successful to any meaningful extent in educating the successive waves of immigrants in the nineteenth and early twentieth centuries, and even more naïve to think the schools are doing anything useful to meet the needs of the more recent black and Hispanic migrants to urban centers.[13]

The reality, as Greer sees it, is that the public schools were established primarily to "support and transmit the values and practices of the society intact"—that is, to strengthen "a restrictive, exclusionary, exploitative capitalist system and its institutions."[14] Greer's "great school legend" is comparable to Jencks's "recurrent fantasy"—both phrases designed to bolster the tired shibboleths of Marxian ideology.

In support of his thesis, Greer cites statistical evidence—which is abundantly available—to show that in the past the children of immigrants received minimal educational services, dropped out of school at an early age, and were largely excluded from secondary schools and colleges. He lists a number of surveys that show the attrition of school registers from the early elementary grades to the twelfth year. Studies in the 1930s and 1940s indicate that about half of the entering high-school students remained in school for the full four years. In some cases, the dropout rate was even greater: the Philadelphia high schools "lost 65 percent of incoming students at the end of the first year, lost another 32 percent of those remaining at the end of the fourth, and were down to 19 percent of the total in the final semester." These and other surveys lead to the conclusion that "a monumental proportion of school pupils do not experience school as the stepladder to achievement and mobility characterized in the 'Legend.' "[15]

Greer acknowledges that the number of students graduating from high school "dramatically increased around and after World War II." But even when confronted with the obvious fact that educational opportunities have expanded in recent decades for all types of students (the U.S. Office of Education reported that, in 1973, 3,060,000 out of a total seventeen-year-old population of 4,054,000 graduated from the high schools),[16] Greer does not modify his position. Indeed, he argues that an increase in the years of schooling merely delays the entry of the disadvantaged ethnic groups into the employment market and does nothing to improve the chances "of the people traditionally victimized in the lowest ranges of the economic ladder." Moreover, even among the students who remain in school a large percentage—Greer says 40 percent—"are permitted to fail." Therefore, he concludes, the great school legend is a fraud and a hoax.

Educators, of course, are equally disturbed by the depressing consensus of numerous studies of pupil achievement—the stubborn persistence of low reading grades and the decline in college entrance examination scores. The problems of truancy and alienation are recognized as serious concerns by school administrators and teachers. Their professional response, however, has always been to try to identify the causes of specific problems and take steps to improve educational services. This construc-tive attitude has been crucial in sustaining massive budgetary allotments by city, state, and federal agencies for innovative and remedial educa-tional programs.

Greer, however, dismisses this pragmatic approach as hardly worth the effort, since any improvement in the schools is deliberately designed by the dominant class to perpetuate the class structure of our soeciety, condemning definable ethnic and socioeconomic groups to social immo-bility and continuing exploitation. Even if the retention rate approached 100 percent and all students earned the maximum score on achievement tests, it is not likely that Greer would be shaken in his negative attitude. For his allegiance to a narrow ideology—running through every chapter of the book—compels him to conclude that the American system is inher-ently unjust and oppressive. Any evidence of progress in the public schools is illusory—"new phrases for old deceptions," as Jonathan Kozol put it. The criteria of success are identical with those of failure: in either case, education perpetuates the evils of the capitalist system. Efforts to improve the quality of education are suspect to Greer, as they are to Christopher Jencks and Jonathan Kozol. "What if the schools are success-ful," he asks superciliously, "only to the extent that maintaining economic and social deprivation on a massive scale is, as H. Rap Brown called violence, 'as American as apple pie'?"[17] This is what Greer really thinks.

Christopher Jencks is no less guilty of misusing statistical projections in arriving at his untenable position, that is, his derogation of the value of schooling. I suggest that he began his project with a set of hypotheses drawn from a political bias, namely, that the existence of equal opportunity in America must be a myth. He then went through the motions of sophisticated statistical manipulation to confirm rather than to test his hypothesis. Even his postulation that genotype, environment, and luck are inexorable facts, not to be modified or counterbalanced by education or individual effort, is arbitrary. His inclusion of the factor of "luck," assertedly the most influential factor in an individual's success, is itself a recognition of the flimsiness of his reasoning, for positing luck as a causative factor is another way of saying that the things that happen just happen—that they are unpredictable.

But even granting Jencks's listed hierarchy of influences on success and status as meaningful, luck among them, it still must be noted that the one factor among those cited that can be influenced by voluntary and purposeful action is schooling. Therefore, whatever else can be said, society must work to improve its educational services since they constitute the only determinative factor over which we have any control at all. Even if we accept the dismaying negativism of Jencks's study, we must not be fatalistic or discouraged.

If belief in the value of education is a myth, it is the best myth we have come up with thus far. Until we have abolished all formal schooling and its attendant ills and seen the results, we would do well not to abandon our faith in education.

10 IVAN ILLICH AND THE DESCHOOLED SOCIETY

The proposal to do away with all schools is not without its serious and vocal exponents. It follows with frightening logic from the assumption that formal education destroys the innate creativeness of children and impedes their intellectual growth.

The prophet who proclaims this iconoclastic dogma is the charismatic priest Ivan Illich, whose book *Deschooling Society* argues that schools should be virtually abandoned and their educational function transferred to other agencies. Illich's philosophy has influenced much reformist doctrine and, even when not accepted in full, is reflected in any number of articles and books and even in the reports of prestigious commissions. The Center for Intercultural Research in Cuernavaca, Mexico, Illich's base of operations, has been for many years the intellectual source of much of the radical ideology of the reformists.

What Illich says is fascinating, even though his opinions are so surrealistic as to verge on the absurd. His thesis is that our faith in institutionalized education is unwarranted because schools as such are incapable of educating the young. Professional educators, he believes, are exponents of a pseudoscientific discipline verging on quackery. The process of assembling the young in school buildings and classrooms for the purpose of instruction is inherently wrong. "The restraint on healthy, productive, and potentially independent human beings," he writes, "is performed by schools with an economy that only labor camps can rival."[1] Moreover, it is ridiculous to suppose that universal schooling is necessary in our time to sustain a healthy democratic society.

One might suspect at first that Illich pronounced his anathema with intentional irony, as Jonathan Swift did when he offered his modest proposal to solve the Irish question by utilizing the flesh of Irish children as a marketable commodity. But Illich is quite serious. His convictions are solidly imbedded in a firm logical and philosophic framework.

Ivan Illich is half priest, half revolutionary. Like the Berrigan brothers, Daniel and Philip, Illich interprets Catholic doctrine as a moral imperative to succor the poor and downtrodden of the earth and to unseat (or exterminate) their oppressors. Much of his writing consists of an eloquent plea for social justice. His distrust of the established order has led him to accept uncritically the misconceptions of the New Left with regard to the

nature of democratic institutions. He sees the United States as an oligar-
chic society, no different from the feudal regimes of Latin America, that
masks its predatory nature under a façade of democracy and benevo-
lence. The American people have been deluded about the true nature of
their political institutions by a massive and subtle conspiracy of deception
carried out primarily by the schools and reinforced through the mass
media. This indoctrination has blinded the people to the truth. The
schools are programmed to train the technicians and bureaucrats who are
essential to the operation of the huge industrial machine, and education is
designed to implant in the young the ethics of patriotism, subservience,
and conformity to repress any questioning of the morality of the system.[2]
Illich's proposal to emasculate the schools is, therefore, a function of his
political ideology.

It is not institutionalized education alone that Illich denounces—he
condemns all social institutions that "confuse process and substance." He
sees the mechanisms we have developed to perform social services—
hospitals, roads, government, industry, as well as the schools—as necessarily destructive and inhumane. Like Thoreau, he views the indus-
trialized society that has grown to maturity in the United States and
Western Europe and that is now emerging in the Third World as a
juggernaut crushing mankind beneath its wheels. The technology that
provides us with clothing, automobiles, refrigerators, and the like makes
men so dependent on the marketplace and smothers them under such
dustheaps of needless gadgetry and obsolescent hardware that, like the
masters of the robots in Molnar's vision, we have become impotent.
Hospitals, in Illich's cosmology, do not alleviate pain or restore health so
much as they retard the development of preventive medicine and lead us
to view "doctoring one's self as irresponsible." Even birth and death have
been institutionalized—and thus diminished in dignity. "Ten years ago in
Mexico," he writes, "it was the normal thing to be born and die in one's
own home and to be buried by one's friends. Only the soul's needs were
taken care of by the institutional church. Now to begin and end life at
home have become signs of poverty or of special privilege. Dying and
death have come under the institutional management of doctors and
undertakers."[3] A nostalgic delusion—a flight from the realities of today
into an imagined idyllic past—underlies Illich's thinking in a critical sense.

All dogmatists, whether their dogmas are religious or political or philosophic, see the world in a distorted focus. They see only what they want to
see or what their closed system of thought enables them to see. To Illich, a
policeman directing traffic is the agent of a bureaucracy that restricts
individual freedom and autonomy; and a surgeon performing an appen-
dectomy in a well-equipped hospital is intruding on the patient's privacy.
So positive is he in his conviction that social institutions are oppressive that
he can utter the most blatant falsehoods about them without seeing the

need for substantiation. For instance, he says at one point: "Preventive concentration camps for predelinquents would be a logical improvement over the school system."[4] Perhaps one might think this airy pronouncement was intended as a rhetorical use of hyperbole, not to be taken literally. On the contrary, it is typical of Illich's mode of expression. His ideas rest on a closed system of thought.

Illich therefore has an advantage over empiricists like Christopher Jencks and Colin Greer. He states his premises clearly and openly and leaves no doubt about the theoretical framework of his dogmas. It is one thing to offer statistical evidence purporting to show that the schools have failed in certain respects (which Illich does not have to do), and quite another to say the schools have failed because *all* social institutions must *necessarily* fail. The latter represents Illich's position. Thus, everything he says about education is predictable, with no further investigation or empirical support, from his major premise. In short, his proposal to "deschool" society is part of his broader program to "deinstitutionalize" society.

There is one additional point to be considered in evaluating Illich's thesis. A certain ambiguity in his point of view must be resolved. The fact is often overlooked by his followers and critics alike that Illich based much of his analysis of educational programs on conditions he observed in Mexico and other Latin American countries. Much of his thinking reflects conditions that are indigenous to the undeveloped countries of the world. In an early essay, "The Futility of Schooling," Illich makes the point that the expansion of schooling in Latin America has built "a narrow bridge across a widening social gap," that is, it has strengthened a privileged elite and condemned the masses to virtual enslavement.[5] The schools lure the young into the deceptive belief that the knowledge and technical skills they acquire in pursuing an education will enable them to attain social and economic status. But the demand for professional expertise and intellectual skills in the undeveloped economies of these countries is minimal. The result is disillusionment and discontent.

In the text of his book *Deschooling Society*, Illich contrasts the resources available for schools in advanced industrial societies such as the United States with the meager resources of the "have-not" nations. It is never clear whether Illich would take the same stand with respect to the problem if budgetary resources in Mexico or Bolivia were sufficient to support universal schooling and absorb its graduates into the mainstream of economic and political life. He probably would, in view of his philosophic position.

Within this framework, then, let us examine Illich's plan for establishing a new kind of educational design.[6] He would abolish schools as such and replace them (above the lower elementary grades) with a network of resource centers for self-directed learning activities. Young people would form voluntary associations with peers who shared common interests. These groups would seek guidance and instruction from adults in the community who advertised their expertise in one field or another. To facilitate the plan, a directory would be published listing the names and addresses of these educators-at-large, who would presumably need no accreditation but their self-styled competence.

The peer groups would be autonomous in their choice of learning activities under the tutelage of the educators-at-large. They would be free to study whatever they wished. Their choices might be drawn from conventional areas of scholarship—such as a foreign language, mathematics, or a vocational field—but might also provide outlets for individual interests such as playing the guitar, developing skill in photography, or exploring the frontiers of parapsychology. The length of any given "course of study" and the number of hours of group meetings would be decided by mutual agreement. Meetings would take place in any convenient location—private homes, community centers, museums, parks, and possibly in the no-longer-used public school buildings. Any large city, as Philadelphia and New York discovered in their city-as-school programs, should be able to accommodate the large numbers of itinerant youngsters who would now be released from confinement in the conventional schools from 9:00 A.M. to 3:00 P.M. As to the content of courses and methods of instruction, there would be no prescribed or imposed standards. It can be assumed, however, that each educator and his disciples would discover modes of communication that were most congenial to their diverse temperaments and the nature of their studies. Being highly motivated, the groups would need a minimum of supervision or administrative control.

Undoubtedly—although Illich does not dwell on this point—some kind of administrative apparatus would have to be set up, but it would be certainly far less extensive and cumbersome than the old bureaucracy. A voucher system would have to be established to provide for tuition payments, the rental of meeting places, and the purchase of educational materials. A central office would be necessary to publish the directory of educators-at-large and keep the listings up to date. Possibly, too, an auditing bureau would be needed to keep records of the activities and achievements of students. These problems of logistics, however, would be peripheral to the operation of the system as a whole. Whatever measures of control were finally adopted would be geared to the one objective of freeing students from the restrictions of formal schooling.

Is it conceivable that the system proposed by Illich would work? Under special conditions, it might. It is conceivable that a selected group of boys and girls, living in a sheltered community, might be able to get together in informal peer groups by advertising their individual interests and needs—on a bulletin board, perhaps—in hopes of finding partners in one project or another. It is also conceivable that they would be able to select qualified teachers from a directory listing the names and special competencies of a dozen or so consultants in the neighborhood. Such an educational community does exist in some small progressive schools, in summer camps, or even—if one stretches the concept a little—in well-managed classrooms in the public schools.

But in our vast urban complexes, where the majority of students reside, the Illich plan would undoubtedly end in chaos. There are, for example, more than a million students and sixty thousand accredited teachers in New York City, and another sixty thousand who would assume the title of educator-at-large. The problem of communication, the scheduling of meetings among students and educators, and the logistics of keeping track of students' progress would be insurmountable. To the extent that this intricate network of relationships became organized, that is, workable to a minimal extent, it would come to resemble the least efficient school system now in existence.

Apart from this practical flaw in Illich's proposal, the theoretical fallacies inherent in his blueprint for a deschooled society should be pointed out. For one thing, the goals that society entrusts to its organized educational system are too important to be left to chance. The knowledge and skills that equip the nation's youth for constructive roles in adult life are not likely to be attained in the absence of a planned educational program. Knowing how hard won are even the rudiments of learning, can we share Illich's confidence in the ability of children and adolescents to find their way through the maze of factual and conceptual knowledge that is essential to self-understanding and social adjustment? Can society approve an education that will at best give students a fragmentary and shallow grasp of history, the sciences, literature, and the arts, and will do little to ensure that they develop the ability to read with comprehension and to write effectively? We can assent to Illich's reiteration of a truth that the schools have perhaps slighted at times, namely, that, to be meaningful, academic learning must be interwoven with experience and that active participation in the learning process is sound pedagogy. But his fatuous blindness to the need for an organized program of instruction in the basic curricular areas, which is inseparable from the institution we call the school, discredits his fantasy of a society without schools.

Moreover, Illich suffers from the Owl Critics' fundamental misconception of what schools actually are like. His derogation of accredited teachers is a case in point. For example, he asserts that the teaching of skills—typing, languages, watchmaking—can be carried out by persons skilled in the craft with greater economy of time and cost than it can be done in the schools. He cites as an illustration the enlistment of Harlem teenagers by the New York Archdiocese to teach Puerto Rican Spanish to priests serving or training to serve in the ghetto, a project that was carried out in small groups and successfully completed in less than six months.

"No school program," he states, "could have matched these results."[7] Perhaps not. The point of his story, which cannot be disputed, is that strong motivation and a high degree of intelligence and self-discipline are major factors in the learning process. But Illich must go further if his disparagement of the schools is to be sustained. He asserts that certified teachers in the schools could not have done as well. "Most high school teachers of Spanish or French," he says with assurance, "do not speak the language as correctly as their pupils might after half a year of competent drills." This kind of invidious comparison is made repeatedly in his discussion of the teaching of skills.

Illich's impression of the competence of teachers is totally at variance with the facts. The problem of securing qualified teachers for the public schools is a continuing problem that is not easily solved. Communities differ widely in their methods of recruiting and selecting teaching personnel. Over the years, academic requirements everywhere have been raised and methods of certification have been geared to higher and higher standards. Wherever practicable, some form of pupil-teacher experience or internship has become prerequisite for a license. Once on the job, in-service courses and workshops keep teachers abreast of current trends in their field, and sound supervisory programs help teachers improve their classroom techniques. These measures do not, of course, ensure that every teacher will be successful, but they do maintain a professional level of competence. Certainly, Illich's confidence in the miraculous ability of his educators-at-large is as little justified as his condemnation of the professional staff.

An equally glaring misconception clouds Illich's discussion of conceptual learning. "Schools," he writes, "are even less efficient in the arrangement of circumstances which encourage the open-ended, exploratory use of acquired skills, for which I will reserve the term 'liberal education.' "[8] The most fruitful exploration of ideas, concepts, and values occurs, he believes, when people with common interests come together voluntarily to discuss a problem "chosen and defined by their own initiative." The assembling of peer groups with mutual interests is, as we have seen, the fundamental feature of his educational program, and he is confident that this voluntary system would work out far better in providing a liberal education than the class groupings in conventional schools that are based on compulsory membership.

Illich does not, however, seem to be aware that the voluntary peer group does exist in the schools—it takes the form of clubs, dramatics societies, orchestras and glee clubs, leaders' groups, the Arista, and so forth. Voluntary peer groups are formed when schools organize drives for the Red Cross or Korean relief, hold book fairs, publish literary magazines, or give art exhibits. Elective courses in the high schools are designed to bring together students with common interests in creative writing, contemporary social problems, black or Chinese culture, the mass media, or calculus. A well-managed school gives ample scope for student initiative. One illustration comes to mind. At a time when debate over the war in Vietnam was at a crucial stage, a group of students at Seward Park High School requested that the administration set aside a full day for discussion of the issues raised by the Peace movement. A series of assembly programs and panels was organized by a committee of students and faculty and carried out successfully, all regular classes being suspended for the day. The point is that the "rigid" structure of the schools does not, as Illich charges, preclude voluntary activities.

Even in the conventional classes in American history or English or biology, the imaginative teacher makes room for open discussion and exploration of important issues. The teacher and his class are, indeed, thrown together by the mechanics of a program committee's random distribution of cards. There is a degree of selectivity, however, in the fact that all the students in the class have gained a more or less common background of knowledge in earlier prerequisite courses. Thus there are shared interests and apperceptions that unify the class group naturally. Most important, however, is the teacher's skill in transforming the class group into a cooperative learning community. Whatever the subject may be, the alchemy of contact with a body of ideas infused with meaning by the teacher's artistry can work a miracle. The class is transformed into a peer group that participates willingly in "the open-ended, exploratory use of acquired skills" in the best sense of Illich's definition. The compulsion that is said to turn students away from whole-hearted involvement in learning ceases to be a deterrent *when there is a good teacher*.

Illich is, of course, right in saying that educational experiences are not limited to the schools—or to the school age. The urban scene is replete with stimulating sights and sounds that quicken the senses and the mind. Thousands of groupings—social, fraternal, political, athletic—form spontaneously in the city to leaven the impersonality of megalopolis. Most adults are able to find friends and form social sets and organize clubs for card playing, poetry reading, chamber music, bowling—all educational activities in the best sense. Extension courses at colleges and evening classes at the high-school level offer all kinds of opportunities for personal enrichment or vocational advancement. The network of resource centers that Illich proposes might be more applicable to the needs of adults than to students of school age. The elementary and secondary schools serve needs that are unlikely to be fulfilled in the network of informal peer groups.

Even before the publication of *The Deschooled Society* the Illich cult was gaining adherents and was referred to with respect in intellectual journals such as *The New York Review of Books*. Today it is apparent that the cult's dogmas have permeated the attitudes of educational reformists. Those who echo his contempt for the established school system seem not to be aware of the doctrinaire basis of his program (that is, his disenchantment with all institutional structures) and the myopic inaccuracy of his observations of what the schools are like. They borrow from his writing the specific aphorisms that are consonant with their own patterns of thought. Illich's judgment that certified teachers are less competent than untrained laymen to direct learning is paralleled in Charles Silberman's characterization of teachers as "mindless" and reflected in practice by downgrading the accreditation process in New York and elsewhere. Illich's assumption that organized syllabuses in school subjects are incompatible with the vividness and immediacy of direct experience has led to John Holt's advocacy of "free" and "unstructured" learning that ignores the value of continuity in the mastery of subject matter. His derogation of teacher-directed lessons in classrooms has encouraged the vagaries of planless teaching and courses without content, as articulated by Carl Rogers and his coterie.

The denigration of formal schooling did not begin with Illich. The kind of thinking that underlies his master plan for deschooling society has been evident in the vanguard of reformism for a long time. Wherever it appears, however, it must be recognized for what it is—a form of extremism that is, in essence, subversive. Its appeal is to those who are impatient with the slower pace of constructive reform. The Illich mind-set is typical of the idealist's tendency to equate a verbal formulation with pragmatic truth. This tendency is seen, for instance, in Thoreau's vision of a society in which political government will no longer be necessary and man's innate goodness and enlightened self-interest will be sufficient guarantors of stability and peace.[9] It is seen in the airy architecture of utopians who construct an ideal society without taking into account the realities of greed, hunger, and traffic congestion. But we must not be deluded: the doctrines of the Illich cult are inimical to progressive change and will not be appeased with anything less than the total dissolution of our culture and democratic values.

11 EDUCATION AND THE
SOCIAL FABRIC

Man is a political animal. With every action, from the time he takes a hot shower in the morning to the time he watches the Late Show on television at night, he is deeply enmeshed in a sociopolitical system in which his well-being and indeed his survival are predicated on a social order and a body of laws devised and administered by men acting in cooperation. His water supply and the fuel that heats it are a function of collective planning and foresight. The transportation he uses going to work, whether by an air-polluting and highway-consuming automobile or by a railroad or bus operating under complex governmental regulations, would be unavailable without the concerted efforts of thousands of his fellowmen. Run through the day, and the close interdependence of individual citizens and their governments becomes more pervasive with every passing hour. Life would be chaotic, if indeed it could be maintained, without the intricate network of controls, the willing acceptance of rules and customs, and the collective determination to deal constructively with problems that are the hallmarks of a democratic society.

It is significant that Charles E. Silberman, in *Crisis in the Classroom*, devotes his first chapter to an exposition of the shortcomings of our economic system, our cultural institutions, and the mass media, implying that the archaic schools must somehow bear full responsibility for all these conditions. Paul Goodman's *Growing Up Absurd* is not so much an indictment of our schools as it is a cry of indignation at a debased system of values in a society that adolescents cannot respect and for which they express their contempt by dropping out. More pointedly, Edgar Z. Friedenberg, in his *Coming of Age in America*, supports the political thesis that a dominant ruling class perpetuates its control of the masses by brainwashing the passive recipients of its hypocrisies and lies through twelve years of compulsory school attendance. Jonathan Kozol, appalled by the substandard conditions in Boston's ghetto schools, detects racial discrimination and deliberate segregation in the official policies of the school system as well as in the attitudes of teachers toward their alienated pupils. The political orientation of these writers is patent.

Within this framework, the "crisis" in the schools can no longer be viewed as an academic panel discussion on problems of curriculum or methodology, but must be understood as a reflection of the political and social cleavages that exist, like geologic faults, within the foundations of our society. John Dewey, in *School and Society,* had delineated the responsibility of the schools for effecting changes in social institutions. The aim of education, as he formulated it, was to develop in students the intellectual skills and moral imperatives for dealing intelligently with social problems. Among Dewey's colleagues at Columbia University, however, the social reconstructionists, among them George S. Counts and Harold Rugg, were more explicit in defining the goal of education: it was to lay the groundwork for the transformation of our present political structure into some form of collectivism. Elements of their political radicalism are clearly operative in the thinking of a number of today's reformists. The innovative drive of these critics may indeed stem from a genuine concern for making the school experience more interesting to children and more relevant to their lives (although this is precisely what the schools have been attempting to do), but the controlling factor in their thinking is essentially a political ideology.

Those who see the conventional teacher-pupil relationship as oppressive and charge the public schools with imposing the values of a dehumanized society have every right to plead their cause within the system or to set up so-called free schools in protest against the system. But every set of values, whether it upholds tradition or rejects it, must submit its credentials to public scrutiny. If those who place critical thinking high on their list of priorities do so to develop an attitude of objectivity in the appraisal of political and social issues, they are standing squarely in the mainstream of American tradition. If, on the other hand, their goal is to indoctrinate impressionable adolescents with a system of values that is antithetical to democratic ideals and is designed to implant the ideologies of Karl Marx or Mao Tse-tung, we must be vigilant to expose them.

Political issues cannot be discussed intelligently without taking into account their ideological premises. In certain historical crises—as when the League Against War and Fascism, a Communist front organization, supported Hitler's invasion of Poland in 1939, and when the New Left coalition in 1969 called for immediate withdrawal from the war in Southeast Asia and demanded an end to our support of Israel in the Near East—the political premises underlying these demands were transparent. In current issues—the ongoing debate on racial integration, law and order, censorship of the mass media, abortion, and capital punishment—the underlying assumptions of a William F. Buckley or a Martin Agronsky may be less explicitly stated but are therefore no less real. When Paul Goodman and others assert that our democratic society is unjust and inhumane and that education should be geared to exposing its inequities, they are engaged in political forensics. When Jonathan Kozol sees greater value in the teaching of Langston Hughes's "Ballad of the Landlord" in place of, say, Henry Wadsworth Longfellow's "Ship of State," and would focus attention on the evils of our society rather than make an objective study of its ideals and institutions, he is the sponsor of a political program that should be judged clear-sightedly.[1] There is no greater virtue in doctrinaire opposition to the established order than there is in unthinking conformity.

Even so private a trait as individualism, sanctified as an admirable quality in the American ethos, must be judged in terms of the moral principles it challenges. Ralph Waldo Emerson's famous dictum: "Whoso would be a man must be a non-conformist" (in his essay "Self-Reliance,") can be cited to rationalize the most antisocial behavior—mind-destroying indulgence in drugs, the worship of anti-intellectualism, a retreat to mysticism and the occult. Emerson himself unwittingly illustrated the pitfalls of self-reliance as opposed to reliance on reason when he denounced "your miscellaneous popular charities; the education at college of fools; alms to sots; and the thousandfold Relief Societies (to which) I confess with shame that I sometimes succumb and give the dollar." Even more revealing is his statement: "If an angry bigot assume the bountiful cause of Abolition, and comes to me with his latest news from Barbadoes, why should I not say to him, 'Go love thy neighbor, love thy woodchopper, be good natured and modest; have that grace, and never varnish your hard, uncharitable ambition with this incredible tenderness for black folk a thousand miles off. Thy love afar is spite at home.' " We can admire Emerson's impatience with hypocrisy and blind conformity, but can we overlook his ambivalence toward the "black folk a thousand miles off" or his strange characterization of the cause of abolition as "bountiful," with its connotation of advantage to oneself, the conferring of grace on its supporters?[2] Nonconformity is a virtue only to the degree that its impact is not socially destructive.

Nonconformists sometimes reveal an inverted dogmatism of their own. One of these, for example, exposes his own strong biases, both political and philosophic, in the program he would introduce to jolt the complacency he sees in school programs everywhere. "The schools," he writes in a euphoric mood,

> have never been places for the stimulation of young minds. If all through school the young were provoked to question the Ten Commandments, the sanctity of revealed religion, the foundations of patriotism, the profit motive, the two party system, monogamy, the laws of incest, and so on, we would have more creativity than we could handle. . . . In teaching our children to accept fundamentals of social relationships and religious beliefs without question, we follow the ancient highways of the human race.[3]

This interesting proposal assumes that teachers in the public schools impose orthodox beliefs on students and prevent them from forming independent opinions. It is more likely that the nonconformist would encourage his students to subscribe to his own enlightened heresies. He himself seems to be unwilling to concede that there may be some value in following the ancient highways, and that option would be closed to his students. Thought control, even when it derives from the most "liberating" doctrines of the radical Left, is inimical to the spirit of democracy.

Most educators have always accepted their responsibility for making democracy a viable concept, and today more than ever they realize that the imposition of dogma and the stifling of free thought would be a perversion of this commitment. The syllabus of every subject area is designed in part to encourage open-mindedness and a critical attitude, both of which are viewed as essential to intelligent participation in a democratic society. The social studies are directly concerned with fostering a critical approach to political issues. Courses in literature reflect a wide spectrum of social philosophies, and the value judgments implicit in literary works support or challenge established mores and codes of ethics. The study of foreign languages serves in part to promote intercultural and international understanding. In the sciences, the need for suspended judgment and critical analysis of all possible hypotheses is emphasized in the classroom and the laboratory. The aim of these and all other programs in the schools is to provide the tools of self-realization and social adjustment in a democratic society.

The question at issue is whether such stated goals and policies of the educational establshment are consistent with social and political realities. The reformists' answer is unequivocal: the schools' programs are not relevant to the needs of today's students. Curriculums and instructional methods are out of date. Administrative policies are dysfunctional and indeed destructive of democratic values. These charges are raised by all the Owl Critics in one way or another, but are expressed most definitively in the writings of Paul Goodman and Jonathan Kozol. The views of these critics are worth examining in depth.

The prophetic outcries of Paul Goodman, in his major works *Growing Up Absurd* and *Compulsory Miseducation,* may best be understood as the reflection of his political philosophy. It is true that Goodman's dissatisfaction with the schools was based partly on his observation of conditions that all educators are troubled by: the problem of the dropout, the alienation of ethnic-minority students, the persistence of low reading scores, the dilution of standards, and in general the failure of education to sustain John Dewey's high purpose. But these are only marginal reflections of Goodman's despair with the declining quality of our national life. "Fundamentally," he writes, "there is no right education except growing up in a worthwhile world." The inference is that education cannot achieve any worthwhile goals in a social setting that does not correspond with his ethical standards.[4]

Goodman's political philosophy was the dominant factor in his views on education. He saw the United States as the vestige of "the missed revolutions we have inherited."[5] The social imbalances that have resulted from our failure to perfect our institutions in the service of liberty and justice for all have disaffected our youth. Our technological substructure has become dehumanized and offers little outlet for talent and creativity. The consumer psychology implanted by the omnipresent drumbeat of commercial advertising demands ever increasing increments of shoddy and useless gadgetry with minimal standards of quality. Our freedom of thought and of speech has been perverted by corporative control of the media so voices of dissent have no way of reaching the people since the "powerful interests have the big presses." Democratic controls still exist in the pro forma right to vote for candidates for public office, but the common man has no voice in selecting candidates and no role in decision making where it counts. The hope that the technological revolution would release man from bondage and enable him to use his increased leisure creatively has vanished under the impact of commercialized sports and entertainment and the subliminal poisons injected by the Madison Avenue hucksters.

Goodman inveighs against the "dangers of a highly technological and automated future in which we might become a brainwashed society of idle and frivolous consumers . . . and continue in a rat race of highly competitive, unnecessary busywork, with a meaninglessly expanding Gross National Product.[6] It is this prophecy of doom that colors Goodman's ideas on education and those of the other reformists who share his dismay with the tarnished image of the American dream.

It would take volumes of data and endless pages of exposition to establish the truth or falsity of such sweeping judgments, and it is not easy to withhold assent to so resonant a phrase as "a meaninglessly expanding Gross National Product." Nevertheless, it is a specious phrase. I for one do not accept this description of the American scene as either accurate or persuasive despite its appeal to some of the more vocal philosophers of today, such as Alvin Toffler and Charles A. Reich. Perhaps it was our national sense of guilt in having enjoyed for years a high standard of living in the midst of a worldwide condition of want and hopelessness that fostered our acceptance of the negativism so pervasive in current literature. It was not until Ben J. Wattenberg published his "surprising examination of the state of the union"—*The Real America* (1973)—that a well-documented refutation of this dismal image of the United States became available.[7]

The portrait of the America that Wattenberg paints enables us to read Goodman's jeremiads in a new light. We can now view the gross national product as a measure of the increasing capacity of our technology and economic structures to satisfy human needs. It is certainly not "meaningless," except perhaps to a utopian, that now, for the first time in history, we have an economy of abundance that is able to combat hunger and disease, release men and women from backbreaking drudgery in factories and homes, and make possible the enjoyment of leisure in its myriad forms. The frictions inherent in the functioning of any machine demand constant servicing, and it is only through the vigilance of government and civic agencies and people that the social machinery can be made to work efficiently. We are living in an "age of anxiety" but, as Margaret Mead points out, anxiety is a healthy, energy-lifting emotion that is unlike both the fear that primitive man lived with and the despair that seemingly afflicts many of our social prophets. We must learn to understand the technological foundation of our lives and to master technology for humane goals. This is precisely what education is all about.

Moreover, even if Goodman's grim projection of a decadent society is partly true, it is not clear what inferences should be drawn with respect to educational policy. Certainly it is not self-evident that all the failings of society can be attributed to deficiencies in education. Nor, for that matter, can it be shown that reform in education, no matter how far-reaching, will eradicate or even alleviate the destructive impact of our highly technological and automated mass culture. The belief of the reconstructionists, from George Counts to Paul Goodman, that the changes they advocate in the schools will somehow reverse the growth of big government, big business, commercialized mass media, and other "evils" is a delusion. What the schools can do is to equip the young with the skills and understandings that will enable them to deal effectively with the demands of adult living and to act responsibly as citizens of a democracy. If the schools succeed in this purpose, we can face the challenges of the future with confidence.

It is, of course, obvious that the educational programs of those who view the American scene in different perspectives will vary widely. Consider, for example, Goodman's disparagement of the structure of the educational establishment as he saw it. "The top-down dictated national plans and educational methods that are now the fad," he wrote, "are quite irrelevant."[8] He argued for less regimentation and greater encouragement of student initiative, not only in learning activities but also in administration of schools and curriculum construction. Goodman's assumption—and that of other reformists—is that students are qualified to devise and manage sound educational programs. They are not. It is one thing to involve students in planning specific projects and undertaking independent researches, and quite another thing to give students a responsible role in policy-making.

Goodman, I am sure, would agree that students of high-school age can hardly be expected to have the scholarship and judgment of experienced educators. This is evidenced by his strong support—somewhat inconsistent with his other statements on the subject—of the comprehensive science program mapped out by the National Science Foundation. Moreover, Goodman demonstrated by his own example that it needs an adult mind, nurtured by wide reading and experience and seasoned by much reflection, to make sound judgments on so complex an issue as educational policy. What misled Goodman in his derogation of "dictated national plans" is the halo effect of his nostalgia for a way of life that has all but vanished in mature industrial societies. The administrative apparatus of our school systems is distasteful to him because he sees it as an analogue of the superstructure of big government.

Goodman's opposition to testing and grading is similarly related to his political ideology. He asserts that the anxiety bred by the schools' testing programs is emotionally destructive, and he charges that "the galloping increase in national tests guarantees that classwork will become nothing but preparation for these tests,"[9] Goodman equates the testing of students with the intense competitive pressures of business and politics that must be eliminated if we are to build a cooperative society. This mode of thinking colors his judgment on what is really a technical issue in pedagogy. Most educators see definite values in periodic class tests and final examinations as well as in the more comprehensive College Entrance Board examinations designed to measure scholastic achievement. In addition to their motivational force, tests provide teachers with some indication of the effectiveness of their instruction and serve as directional signals to students as well. Moreover, what goes on in most classrooms cannot be described as "nothing but" preparation for tests but is more accurately viewed as the effort to attain intellectual objectives that can be measured in part by well-designed tests. Although some hypersensitive children are indeed affected emotionally by the ordeal of taking tests, most students are not. Of course, not all educators agree on these matters, but the important point to be weighed in this context is that Goodman's opposition to testing is linked to his belief that a competitive society is immoral.

It is noteworthy that the vanguard reformists are in accord with Goodman in opposing any kind of meaningful testing programs and any systematic grading of students' achievement. Administrators and teachers who hold to the belief that students should be held accountable for mastery of subject matter are castigated as die-hard traditionalists. Such testing programs as the New York State Regents examinations have been under attack for many years on the ground that they stress memorization and drill and inhibit creative teaching. A related trend in "progressive" school administration is the abolition of final grades and the substitution of broad categories such as "pass" and "fail," thus blurring the distinction between barely satisfactory work and excellence. In some schools the imposition of a failing grade is regarded as a traumatic experience for students, and some such euphemism as "not satisfactory" or "incomplete" or "needs further work" is substituted. Schools without walls and class-rooms without doors must now be joined by courses without tests or grades.

An extension of the same mode of thinking is seen in Goodman's proposal that compulsory attendance laws should be relaxed or perhaps even abandoned.[10] This point is crucial. Accepting Goodman's vision of a just society as the goal of education and social legislation, it is hard to reconcile his vision of a reconstructed society with his readiness to place school attendance in the same category of optional obligations as giving money to charities or attending religious services. If he believes that a sound education can be devised "to foster independent thought and expression, rather than conformity,"[11] there is all the more reason for a serious and persistent effort to ensure that students should have the fullest opportunity to experience these values. Those who support compulsory attendance are committed to the development of intellect and responsible citizenship, and view the maintenance of standards as essential to these goals. Goodman's willingness to relax standards of achievement and attendance would surely be inimical to the realization of his own stated objectives.

There is abundant evidence in Goodman's essays on the anguish of growing up absurd in America to show that he was a humanist—sensitive, compassionate, intellectually oriented. One would have expected him, therefore, to ally himself with Robert Hutchins, James B. Conant, James D. Koerner, and others who believe in the values of education in the best traditional sense, rather than to strike out against the legitimacy of the establishment. His awareness of the unresolved problems and contradictions of our society should lead him to fight for the intensification, not the dilution, of educational processes so that coming generations will be as well informed and as deeply resolved to correct inequities as he was in his own generation.

More single-minded and far more extreme in his application of reconstructionist doctrine is Jonathan Kozol, whose first published book, *Death at an Early Age,* described in harrowing detail his experience as a beginning teacher in a Boston elementary school. The school building was dilapidated and rat infested, and textbooks and other school supplies were scandalously inadequate. The student body was largely black, exhibiting all the scars and emotional stigmata that are the by-products of growing up in the unwholesome atmosphere of urban slums. The teachers, as Kozol saw them, were not only unsympathetic to the children but were in most cases openly hostile. Whatever benefits the children might have derived from schooling were neutralized by the administration's adherence to an outdated and irrelevant curriculum that stressed ideals of conformity and moral rectitude that were totally incomprehensible to children bred in the slums, where they had learned that survival required strength and cunning.

It was inevitable that Kozol's outspoken criticism of the failings of the school would result in his dismissal. The overt cause was an innocent act: his bringing into the class some poems by Langston Hughes, among them a simplistic cry of protest called "Ballad of the Landlord."[12] The children readily identified with the poet's indignation at the exploitation of the black poor by the white ruling class. Kozol was charged with insubordination because he did not restrict his teaching to the prescribed literature syllabus. There were other alleged incriminating acts—such as his absenting himself from school to take part in a civil-rights demonstration and his speaking out abrasively against school policies. Kozol had become a thorn in the side of the educational hierarchy and had to be removed.

After his dismissal, Kozol taught for a time in a a suburban school far removed from the inner city. But here, too, although the ethnic incubus was not in the foreground, there was a more insidious evil—the administration-dominated system left little room for teacher initiative or creativity, at least in Kozol's eyes. School was no less regimented here, and any deviation from the prescribed code of middle-class morality was frowned upon. Accordingly, Kozol broke away and established an experimental "free" school in which he could conduct the kind of liberating educational program he believed in, unhampered by the restrictions and punitive atmosphere of the public schools. In breaking with the establishment, he showed the strength of his convictions, much as Leo Tolstoy had done in organizing his pioneer school at Yasnaya Polyana or as A.S. Neill had done in throwing all convention to the winds at Summerhill. Kozol's was to be a crusade of liberation.

The controlling motivation of Kozol's actions did not come to light until the appearance of an article of his in the *New York Times* on April 1, 1971.[13] The article, entitled "Look, This System Isn't Working," is a forthright enunciation of a political creed that made inevitable his alienation from the educational establishment; indeed, it is the missing chapter in *Death at an Early Age* that would have resolved some of its ambiguities.

In the article, Kozol sets forth a tightly argued syllogism. (1) America is an unjust society. (2) The public schools are designed and administered to produce citizens who will conform to and perpetuate that society. (3) Therefore, the public schools must be radically changed if we want a just society. In the next breath, however, Kozol tells us that he has become completely disillusioned with educational reform and laments his earlier naïveté in hoping that effective change was possible within the existing political framework. He no longer has patience with "phantasies of open schools within closed buildings, new phrases for old deceptions." Like Ivan Illich and other extremists, he sees all efforts to improve our institutions, among them the schools, as a devious strategy for placating and

deluding the people. The establishment is the villain, having programmed the schools and the educational system to turn out robotlike
men and women who will be incapable of thinking for themselves or even
of asking questions. This Orwellian concept of society as a closed system of
Big Brotherism and thought control is implicit in every word of Kozol's
pronouncement.

Kozol goes on to deride the schools for their failure to nurture idealists
such as Gandhi and Thoreau and for producing men "like Richard Nixon
and, even more, a population like the one that elected him."[14] In Kozol's
demonology, saintliness and evil are easily distinguished from one
another because there are no gray areas between them. Whether a society
composed of unworldly visionaries would be able to enhance our
earthbound lives is a question that might trouble other philosophers—but
not Kozol. For he has a secret source of reassurance: his faith in Marxism
as the road to salvation. The name of Richard Nixon has a connotation of
clear and present evil for Kozol, as it does for his fellow travelers: in the
lexicon of the New Left, the mention of Nixon—like that of the Pentagon,
Wall Street, middle-class values, and so on—is a signal for a tribal chorus
of ecstatic loathing. The possibility that his symbols may not automatically
trigger the appropriate conditioned reflex in his readers does not occur to
him.

Kozol's alienation emerges most blatantly in his statement: "A school
that flies the flag and serves the interests of that flag cannot serve those of
justice." The flag as a symbol of injustice is not merely a rhetorical image
for Kozol. It objectifies his deep-seated aversion to everything he thinks
the flag stands for: chauvinism, imperialism, oppression of ethnic
minorities, exploitation. It is something of an anomaly that Kozol fails to
acknowledge that his being able freely to express his dissent is grounded
in Constitutional principles symbolized by the flag. It is a distortion of
truth—not uncommon in the diatribes of the New Left—to charge that
our democracy does not and cannot serve the interests of justice. Our
freedom of thought and speech ensures the right of open discussion of
political issues. Our ability to adapt our institutions to changing patterns
of human need in an evolving society is one of the valuable end products
of these freedoms. Democracy means, among other things, an unyielding
search for justice.

In his book *The Free Schools* (1972) Kozol makes it clear that his opinions
on education and politics have not been modified but have rather hard-
ened.[16] The free-school movement, which had grown extensively in the
past few years, did not live up to his expectation that small school units
with an untrammeled curriculum, student involvement in decision making, and informal methods of instruction, would become instruments for
the transformation of society, or would at least produce more sensitive
and compassionate students in the image of Gandhi and Thoreau. What

Kozol observed in his pastoral visits to the free schools around the country dismayed him.[17]

Most of the schools he visited had abnegated their mission. Their students had indeed been freed from the "public school system of indoctrination," but they had opted for shallow activities, games and crafts and trivial diversions, instead of pursuing the truth of "the way they live and the way the nation lives, and about the way in which it serves or does not serve the cause of justice," Kozol exhorts the directors of these schools to mend their ways. Children, he declares, must be made aware of the poverty, crime, and racism that are the concomitants of our inhumane economic system. They must be introduced to the literature of dissent—to, among other things, the official publications of the Castro and Mao regimes and the revolutionary movements in Latin America and the Third World.[18] This confrontation with revolutionary ideas would open their eyes and minds to *reality!* Children are denied the impetus to develop toward healthy maturity when they are sheltered from knowledge of the radical ferment abroad and kept in the dark about the debasement of the American dream in Appalachia and the black ghettoes.

How such indoctrination can be reconciled with the free schools' philosophy of student autonomy and freedom of choice is not discussed by Kozol, and it is painfully obvious that he is far more interested in assuring the spread of his political dogmas than he is in developing inquiring minds. His disillusionment with the free schools stems from their literal interpretation of their charter, that is, their free exercise of the right of self-determination.

Kozol's scorn for the established schools as he sees them had become more deeply rooted than ever. In *The Free Schools,* he contrasts the small free school, with all its limitations, with the "grim, archaic, racist, and at times dysfunctional character of the public high school on the opposite corner." He marshalls all the clichés of opprobrium to attack the public schools, for he no longer believes even in the possibility of their atoning for their failures by adopting cosmetic innovative programs. In his mood of disillusionment with the free schools, however, he is willing to concede one virtue to the public schools: their lack of pretense. "A child in a rigorous, old-fashioned public high school would be more fortunate in several respects," he writes. "At least he would not be deceived into believing that his choices were his own and consequently would be able to react with secret rage and silent skepticism to the undisguised mendacity around him."

Kozol does not elaborate this point. It is self-evident to him that the public schools perform an assigned political role through indoctrination and "undisguised mendacity." I think he would find it difficult to substantiate the charge.

Any fair-minded survey of the public schools would show the very opposite to be true, namely, that instructional programs encourage the critical examination of divergent viewpoints on controversial issues in every area of the curriculum. It is not indoctrination to teach the concept of democracy in terms of the Constitution and the Bill of Rights, the legal safeguards protecting the individual, and the open channels of communication that ensure the accountability of elected officials. It is not indoctrination to teach the elements of our economic system—part capitalist, part socialist, part open-ended and unpredictable—so students will have a realistic basis for making decisions as producers and consumers and will have good reason to commit themselves to productive work and social service. It is a concept totally inconsistent with indoctrination that governs the teaching of scientific method, critical thinking, semantic analysis, and the skills of interaction among students in the classroom. Moreover, the presentation in literature of the ethical ideals and the humanitarian goals of our Judaeo-Christian heritage pays homage to diversity of thought as well as conformity, to the breakers of new ground as well as the upholders of tradition, to the voices of protest as well as the defenders of established values. There is literally no opportunity in the day-by-day functioning of teachers for the indoctrination and mendacity Kozol attributes to them.

In a word, then, Kozol's present thinking boils down to this: the free schools deceive their students through misdirected good intentions, and the public schools deceive their students with deliberate lies. Apparently he is disillusioned with every kind of educational structure—the conventional school, the innovative school, the free school. He cannot feel otherwise, for his political ideology compels him to reject every idea that does not fit into the narrow categories of Marxian dialectics. This is, in a very real sense, death at an early age.

But the influence of Goodman's and Kozol's criticisms of the schools continues to be felt. More and more it is evident that the public schools have become the pressure centers of conflicting ideologies. The tone of the debate has changed: voices are more abrasive and there is less and less evidence of mutual respect. The advocates of reform within the system vitiate their cause by grossly misrepresenting the actualities of school programs, thus reinforcing the image of a stagnant and unresponsive school system. Others mask their revolutionary objectives behind proposals that give the appearance of sincere concern, while in fact they carry on a strategy of subversion. Political militants and community pressure groups, impatient with the democratic dialogue, disrupt the schools with all the catalogued tactics of revolutionary movements—boycotts, sit-ins, staged interruptions of school-board meetings, and physical violence.

The crisis these forces have generated is, or should be, a matter of deep concern for every citizen and presents a clear and present danger to the men and women who "sit or stand in front of their classes." Their mission, as they have always seen it, is to search tirelessly for better ways to touch the minds and hearts of youth. They know that the schools and the nation they serve will continually need renewal and redirection, but they will not be deluded by faddists or discouraged by false prophets.

12 THE PENDULUM SWING

The tendency to think in slogans and labels is inimical to discussion in the field of education, as it is elsewhere. Programs are classified as either conservative or progressive, a book-centered or experience centered, academic or vocational—but never both. Thus, the forensic give-and-take in educational literature is frequently pictured as a pendulum swinging from one extreme to another. Within the frame of this convenient image, classification of school programs is readily adapted to preconceived patterns of thought.

One illustration of this mode of "pendulum" thinking is seen in a recent series of letters to the editor of the *New York Times*—very likely paralleled in newspapers throughout the nation—in response to a report of the United States Department of Health, Education, and Welfare showing that test results in every field of scholarship had declined in the early seventies as compared with the decade of the sixties.[1] The first letter made an impassioned plea for a return to the "basics" of learning. A few days later, a rebuttal letter asserted dogmatically that the "standard curriculum" (whatever that might mean) had alienated a large segment of the student body and that new programs—innovative courses, stress on experiential learning, unstructured and open classrooms, and the like—should be adopted. Shortly thereafter, a correspondent declared that "the pendulum cannot swing back far enough to eradicate and replace the slovenly, worthless, and ineffective teaching procedures of the so-called progressive, open classroom approach to education." Finally, as a kind of authoritative summing up, the issue was reduced to its logical components in a series of admonitory propositions: "If traditionalists conceive of education as force-feeding information under the constant threat of failure through testing . . .," and "if the only way to get people to be educated—be it in school or in life—is through fear and narrow institutional guidelines . . . ," then new ways must be explored. These are the terms in which the either/or modes of thinking are codified in the public forum.

A second illustration may be cited as a more sophisticated version of "slogan" thinking. In the 1960s the Ford Foundation, through its Comprehensive School Improvement Program, spent some $30 million in grants for experimental projects in many communities to encourage reform of curriculum and teaching methods. These grants were to be used to set up working models of innovative programs in selected schools, with the expectation that the success of these pilot programs would encourage their acceptance on a wide scale. Among the funded programs were: team teaching, flexible scheduling, programmed instruction largely with teaching machines, the use of paraprofessionals as classroom aides, nongraded course offerings, unstructured teaching, independent study, and a variety of curricular projects.

A report issued by the foundation in 1973, entitled "A Foundation Goes to School," concluded that the impact of the reform movement had been minimal. In the judgment of Fred Hechinger, education editor of the *New York Times,* the failure could be readily accounted for. "The major roadblock to reform," he wrote, "was conservatism—in the profession and among the public. Communities and teachers often reacted to any form of openness, lack of structure, and independent student activities as a threat to discipline. The result, though by no means always, was a return to traditional operations."[2]

The phrase "a return to traditional operations" may be deplored by some educators as signaling a retreat to the rigid and stifling practices alleged by the Owl Critics. On the other hand, it may be interpreted as a "restoration of learning," long overdue. Yet neither assessment is entirely valid, since the terms used in the Hechinger statement and in the various reactions to it are semantically diffuse.

The meaning of a term varies with the time frame in which it is located. The term *traditional* has a clear denotation only at a given moment in a historical continuum. Today a return to fundamentals does not mean the adoption of a narrow curriculum, stripping the schools' offerings of the courses developed in the past several decades in the sciences, the social studies, and the arts. We cannot recreate the curricula of the nineteenth century any more than we can go back to the horse and buggy or the kerosene lamp. The educational pendulum cannot swing back beyond a certain point, thus suggesting that the physical laws of inertia and entropy are not fully applicable to human affairs.

The alternative to the unstructured learning designs sponsored by the Owl Critics is not necessarily a system in which schoolmasters impose a regimen of dry academic subjects on reluctant pupils such as prevailed, we are told, in the schools of the benighted past. The fact is, as I have shown repeatedly, that traditional schooling in the United States, in the framework of the twentieth century, has been characterized by the continuous adaptation of curriculum and methodology to the needs of youth as these needs came to be recognized. The academic curriculum has always been flexible in adopting vocational and life-centered courses as extensions of the standard subjects. The expansion of subject areas and the development of new teaching strategies have been pragmatic and experimental as a matter of policy.

In short, education in the past five or six decades has undergone change in much the same way that government, industry, and social ethics have. It is unthinkable that a preindustrial way of life will ever be restored, except in a few small and scattered communes organized here and there as refuges from the impact of the pervasive mass culture. Every administration in Washington since the 1930's, "liberal" or "conservative," has been under an inescapable mandate to implement and expand the concepts of social justice initiated by Franklin D. Roosevelt. The enforcement of civil rights, the maintenance of humane social-security programs, the protection of our threatened ecology, the beginnings at least of a national health program—these have become an inherent and irreversible part of our recent political tradition.

The forces that have brought about educational progress in the United States in this century remain as strong today as ever. New programs are adopted in response to problems that come into the foreground of attention and demand solution. This is seen, as I have shown, in the concepts that have been translated into school realities during the past few decades: the Headstart Project, the More Effective Schools Program, Higher Horizons, College Discovery, workshops and clinics, minischools, specialized schools, comprehensive high schools—these are the imaginative designs of public education in the seventies and eighties. Their roots are embedded in the pragmatic philosophy that has shaped all American institutions, a philosophy that is not hospitable to doctrinaire extremism.

Another factor that narrows the range of the pendulum swing is that today, more than ever, the community is concerned with what the schools are doing. In an earlier age, when formal education was accessible to an elite few, judgment of curriculums and teaching methods was the province of philosophers and sages. Francis Bacon, for example, summed up the attitude of Elizabethan men of affairs in the neatly balanced aphorisms of his essay "Of Studies." "Crafty men," he wrote, "condemn studies; simple men admire them; and wise men use them; for they teach not their own use, but that is a wisdom without them and above them, won by observation." Again: "To spend too much time in studies is sloth; to use them too much for ornament is affection; to make judgment wholly by their rules is the humor of the scholar." Bacon's voice, like that of Montaigne and others, was raised in criticism and counsel as a corrective to the schoolmen's misdirected zeal for abstract and bookish learning.

Today, of course, we have a full complement of counselors, ranging from men of vision such as John Dewey and James B. Conant, to the sciolists and visionaries I have called the Owl Critics. Their words filter down to the public through all the current media of communication, often distorted in transmission. The schools have become fair game for every theorist, crafty or wise, with an axe to grind. The situation is complicated by the fact that political and ideological factions see advantage for their interests in their advocacy of educational reforms.

In our time, also, a more sophisticated and demanding public, conditioned by their edifying or traumatic experiences as students in classrooms, are ready to express their opinions about education with more assurance than might have been forthcoming a generation ago. More and more vocally, parents and community groups articulate their concern with the objectives and practices of the public schools.

Social pressure for change and redirection in the schools is, of course, a healthy part of the democratic process. Generally it is applied with a minimum of strain, since boards of education usually reflect the interests and aspirations of the community and naturally provide the kind of education that will satisfy public demand. Bitter disagreements do occur, however, and must be resolved. At times, confrontation erupts into open conflict—the indictment of a teacher for defying a law restricting academic freedom, as in the *Scopes* case; the dismissal of a school administrator for implementing a "progressive" educational philosophy, as in the case of *Superintendent Willard Goslin* in Pasadena in 1950; or the boycott of schools over the issue of "godless" and "dirty" textbooks, as in Charleston, West Virginia, in 1974. The deep-seated tensions between ethnic groups in our cities have led to school sit-ins, violence in the streets, and the open defiance of court-ordered plans for desegregation of schools. The insulation of the schools from the tidal currents of social conflict is illusory.

Educators are understandably swayed by outside social pressures. Such pressures are usually exerted by the most vocal and well-organized segments of the community. The result is that policies are sometimes adopted hastily, with insufficient research or experimental controls. The headlines announcing the Soviet launching of Sputnik in 1957 initiated a crash program in the sciences and foreign languages that seems to have lost its momentum today, perhaps because it was adopted for the wrong reasons. The schools responded to the demands of minority ethnic groups by establishing separatist Black Studies programs and bilingual instruction for students of Hispanic background that have proved to be, at best, of marginal value, creating, in Bayard Rustin's words, "a new tribalism." This kind of overresponsiveness to external pressures has led to the adoption of policies based on contradictory and inconsistent principles— so the pendulum swings nervously between avant garde innovation and a return to Spartan rigidity.

Society's concern about the goals of schooling has been reflected in the increasing demands in the late 1970's for more rigorous systems of teacher accountability. It was not enough that more open channels of communication between the schools and the community were developed through parents associations, open school-day visits, school performances, and the like. Nor were the conventional supervisory programs of principals and chairmen of departments regarded as sufficiently tough and persistent to ensure high standards of performance. The burgeoning cost of education, too, intensified the demand for a valid method of auditing the operations of the schools.

An interesting concept, "accountability." It is a term more appropriate to the lexicons of industry and banking than to those of social institutions. To appraise the schools' productivity by objective measurement implies an omniscient monitor tuning in on the dialogue of the recitation, surreptitiously inspecting the classroom scene through one-way mirrors, computerizing test scores and deviations from the norm. Such measures may succeed in placing teachers and administrators—as well as children—in neat categories: superior, average, marginal, substandard. But one obvious limitation of the attempt to develop a comprehensive system of accountability is the fact that the statistical tools currently available are unequal to the task.

Standardized tests may be useful in measuring cognitive skills—reading comprehension, computation skills, language automatisms—but it is questionable whether they are appropriate for assessing the less tangible but more significant outcomes of schooling: communication skills, esthetic sensibility, interpersonal relations. Performance objectives that can be measured do not include the broader tests of education—attitudes, awakened interests, aspirations—that elude measurement at the moment but are more important in the long run.

Similarly, no system of accountability can do justice to teachers if it takes into account only those evidences of performance that can be observed and recorded, namely, courses taken or degrees earned, diligence in making reports, conformity to administrative directives. These are important data, but less valuable than the qualities of mind and personality the teacher reveals in his relationship with pupils, the insights and sensitivities that infuse his everyday lessons with humor, delight, and a sense of adventure. The teacher is not properly to be judged as an accountable agent but rather as a self-directing, responsible professional. The distinction is not, of course, absolute; it is better perceived as a spectrum of variables shading into one another. It does, however, expose the limited reach of any "objective" system of accountability.

In this ongoing interaction between the school and the community, the vulnerability of the professional staff became increasingly apparent. Whatever autonomy teachers and other professionals had enjoyed over the years was eroded. They could no longer be sure of their ground when they insisted that they should have a controlling voice in decisions on controversial issues. A proposition that had seemed self-evident, namely, that teachers and supervisors should have a major role in determining educational policy, was no longer tenable.

One of the reasons for this decline has been the success of the Owl Critics and their sycophants in sowing confusion. Among other things, they confirmed the commonly accepted stereotypes of teachers. The timid and constrained teacher, the martinet, the drillmaster—these became all the more firmly fixed in the public mind. The mass media and published books repeated the cliché that the virtue most highly regarded in the schools was conformity, its imperatives geared to servility: follow the syllabus rigidly, impose regimented discipline, do not question authority, do not rock the boat, and so on.

At the same time, the Owl Critics convinced too many board members and citizens that innovative concepts demanded a different kind of teacher. Intellectual vices were clothed in the guise of virtues. The quality most to be prized would be a tolerance verging on irresponsibility. Whim, in the Emersonian sense, would be sufficient as a guide to classroom procedures. Lacking any positive convictions of what it was important to teach, the vanguard teacher would be expected to bend with the wind of whatever fad happened to be in vogue at the moment. Amorphous ideas about the goals of education would nurture a kind of eclecticism that moved in every direction at once.

Two decades of broadside attacks by the Owl Critics on the foundations of American education have indeed brought about a "crisis in the classroom." The incessant clamor about "irrelevance" and "dysfunction" deepened conflicts that already cut across every segment of the professional staff, the student body, and the community.

I think of the inner doubts of teachers as they carry out their daily tasks. Their self-esteem has been subtly eroded by the barrage of unconstructive criticism of every aspect of the curriculum. Do students really profit in the long run from mathematics or history or grammar? Maybe there is some truth in John Holt's derogation of standard courses of study and standard teaching methods. Maybe Christopher Jencks is on the right track in his disparagement of the importance of schooling. Maybe there is something to the charge that teacher domination, rules and regulations, testing and grading, all repress students' individuality and creativeness.

Their confidence shaken, teachers have become increasingly defensive, and the result has been either a defeatist conformity or the too-ready embrace of any innovative proposal. The "mindless" teacher is driven to behave as if the epithet was deserved.

Those teachers who are least secure in their conception of their role take refuge in routines and mechanical programmed devices as substitutes for the creative teaching they might otherwise be capable of. The caged bank teller in the story goes to pieces when he is released from his safe enclosure by promotion to an executive desk. The teacher who resorts to incessant drill and daily quizzes is as much a victim of his own insecurity as the teacher who regards drill and testing as forms of oppression. The weaker teacher finds solace in an undeviating weekly schedule: literature on Monday and Tuesday, grammar on Wednesday, speech activities on Thursday, composition on Friday. The teacher who has been led to distrust his own resources becomes obsessed with teaching machines, programmed instructional materials, drill books and the like. A college teacher I know spends the two-hour art history period lecturing uninterruptedly, rejecting the suggestion that some kind of student participation might be of value on the ground that "students do not pay their fees to hear the uninformed opinions of classmates."

Insecurity is evidenced, too, in the trend toward "off-beat" courses. As if the central core of disciplines in the standard curriculum were not enough to stimulate the minds of students and release their energies, these courses are dredged up to appeal to the momentary curiosity of those who are turned off by conventional course titles. Family Living, accepted widely as a useful life-centered area, is now beefed up by units in Divorce and Thanatology. Study of contemporary society is trivialized in a synthetic venture in Pop Culture under the aegis of a "professor of pop culture," a title that sends a slight shudder along the spine.

The imprint of Carl Rogers is seen in the hundreds of encounter groups that have spread on and off campus everywhere. Formalized in courses with enticing titles and credits, pseudoscience flourishes under the guise of psychology and sociology. For example, a course entitled "The Space of Intimacy" is offered at a prestigious college, registration limited to couples "living together" on campus and thus presumed to have a certain expertise in the field. The metaphoric title of the course suggests that somehow the students' horizons will be expanded infinitely. This promise is bound to be illusory. If the course deals with the economics and logistics of keeping a household (a very unlikely possibility), it will perhaps have some utilitarian value. If it attempts to probe the area of psychological and emotional adjustment—that is, provide some insight into the tensions that arise in any human relationship—it may founder on the rocks of exhibitionism and ego-gratifying self-exposure no less murky than articles in true confessions magazines. In such a course, too, the instructor may play an ambivalent role, torn between his attested scholarship in psychology or philosophy and his own sexual hangups.

The image of the public school—its aims, its programs, its achievements—can best be protected from misrepresentation through open discussion in the public forum. The fictional portrait of the teacher, deeply ingrained as it is, cannot persist in the face of public awareness of the not easily discovered truth. Already there are indications that the tabloid distortions of reality at both extremes of the pendulum swing are being critically examined in the news media and in professional literature.

Newspaper articles, editorials, columns, book reviews, articles in scholarly journals—all of these have carried the debate into the public arena. True, much of the discussion that has made headlines centered around issues that only indirectly bear on the essential nature of education. The voucher system advocated by Christopher Jencks as a means of giving parents more flexibility in the choice of schools; the growth of community and, indeed, student participation in policy making; the complex logistics of programs to achieve racial integration—these are important matters, but they are peripheral to the basic problem of providing sound education.

I cannot cite surveys of lay or professional opinion in support of my conviction that the tide is turning. Opinion polls are of questionable value when the issues are too complex to be formulated in intelligible questions. General questions such as "Do you think the schools are doing a good job?" or "Do you think the schools need fundamental changes?" are pointless. More meaningful questions, for example, "Do you agree with John Holt's disparagement of directive teaching?," are too technical to be answered by any but specialists in methodology. The present situation, moreover, is too fluid to be codified in percentiles.

There is another factor, too, that blurs perception. In the past decade or two, discussion of educational issues was dominated by the charismatic personalities of the reformists. The moderate and reasoned statements of the professional staff were less colorful and were therefore less likely to gain attention. Somehow the everyday problems of the classroom do not lend themselves to empathetic comment in the media. What is seized on by reporters is the occurrence that is exceptional and off the beaten path, the *man bites dog* syndrome. Deviations from the norm make good headlines and caricatures of classroom teachers on TV are good for a laugh. Faculty meetings, in-service workshops, regional and national conventions, supervisory practices, syllabus revision—these ongoing, down-to-earth efforts to ensure the highest possible level of educational services go unnoticed.

Yet signs and portents are everywhere. After the stunned silence that followed the publication of Silberman's *Crisis in the Classroom,* educators who were appalled by his attitude toward the professional staff and his disparagement of the standard curriculum and developmental teaching found their voices again. George A. Antonelli (referred to earlier) placed the current reformist movement in historical perspective by pointing out that "many current innovations can be defined as revivals or reinventions," and urged administrators to weigh carefully the validity of some of the extreme proposals. Seymour Lachman, president of the New York

City Board of Education, at a time when the cry for innovation was most strident, struck a note of caution by advocating a policy of "moderate incremental reform—one that weaves together continuity and change."[3]

One thing became clear in the early 1970s, namely, that the most dramatic of the Owl Critics' proposals—the open classroom, unstructured lessons, invertebrate curriculums—had lost something of their initial attractiveness. Dissension in the ranks of the radical reformists became visible. Jonathan Kozol, disillusioned by the lack of direction in the free schools he observed, referred to the "phantasies of open schools within closed buildings, new phrases for old deceptions." Herbert Kohl, who remained generally sympathetic to the free-school movement, conceded that "free schools are notorious for their divisiveness, for their high mortality rates, for their utopian dreams and rhetoric."[4] The erosion of the high hopes of the vanguard reformists was matched by the downward trend in the vogue of innovative programs such as team teaching, programmed textbooks, teaching machines, and so on, as Fred M. Hechinger reported, somewhat ruefully, in an article entitled "Where Have All the Innovations Gone?"[5] It was evident that the pendulum had swung too far, and that the need for countervailing efforts to restore equilibrium was more urgent than ever before.

In this resurgence of enlightened opposition to the doctrines of the reformists, the definitive statement of principles embodied in the Council for Basic Education's publications, notably *The Case for Basic Education (1959)* (referred to in chapter 3), and in Arthur A. Bestor's *Restoration of Learning* (1955) was germinal. In the past few years, an increasing number of intellectual leaders have taken up the cause of a return to fundamentals. Among these are three outstanding scholars who have, despite their different approaches to the subject, concurred in their conviction that the schools are imperiled by uncritical assent to the doctrines of the Owl Critics.

Professor Sidney Hook, of New York University, long a protagonist of rigorous scholarship, rejected the ideas of the reformists because of his concern for logic and truth. A liberal education, he maintained, provides the intellectual skills without which students cannot lead productive lives in our society. These are the outcome of the standard curriculum in the social sciences, the physical sciences, literature, and the arts. Hook consistently argued that "the acquisition of knowledge and the mastery of skills requires a grasp of sequential order in subject matter; that teachers can be helpful in the process of learning until the students are in a position intelligently to choose their own patterns of growth."[6] In a review of Ivan Illich's *Deschooling Society* (in *Encounter,* January 1972), Hook refuted the assumptions "explicitly made by Illich but also widely held by other romantic critics of the school system who draw back from his extremist remedies."[7] In numerous articles and speeches, Professor Hook has affirmed his thesis that the debasement of standards implicit in the proposals of the extreme reformists is inimical to the health of our civilization.

Donald Barr, formerly headmaster of the Dalton School in New York City, was no less disturbed by the loose premises and shoddy thinking of the new radicalism burgeoning in the 1960s and early 1970s. In a collection of his articles, book reviews, and public addresses, all bearing the imprint of his abrasive wit (even in the book's title, *Who Pushed Humpty Dumpty?*), Barr excoriated some of the less defensible trends in current education, namely, the impersonality of programmed instructional materials, the fostering of passivity through the overuse of teaching machines, and the overreliance on the short-answer catechism in standardized tests. Like Professor Hook, Barr saw a relationship between the neglect of scholarship and the growth of flamboyant subcultures among youth—drugs, mysticism, hippy cults. In a review of John Holt's writings, Barr pinpointed the fallacy of Holt's reliance on a shallow conception of learning—"an unstable faith," as he called it, "because it despises stability."[8] A genuine radicialism, as Barr sees it, finds its proper mode of expression in an organized curriculum and imaginative and resourceful teaching.

Perhaps the most searching critique of radical reformism was enunciated by Professor Harry Broudy, of the University of Illinois, in a book refreshingly entitled *The Real World of the Public Schools*. In this book, one of the most valuable contemporary works in education, Broudy discusses with clarity and insight the labyrinthine complexities of every aspect of schooling—curriculum, teachers and teaching, materials, accountability, and budgeting. Broudy does not gloss over the dilemmas that confront teachers and administrators and school boards at every step of the way. He offers no easy solutions, but his analysis of fundamental issues contains the indispensable data for whatever solutions are possible.

Broudy's rejection of the "new humanists"—as he labels the Holt-Illich-Kozol coterie—is based on their failure to come to grips with the fact that we live in a technological society whose imperatives pervade every facet of our lives. Within the nexus of this society—in the United States it is both technological and democratic—the ultimate goal of education must be to prepare men and women to take their places as responsible adults who will contribute to the social organism as workers and citizens and be able to find satisfying outlets for their emotional and esthetic needs. Education must therefore guide students toward responsible participation in society, not coddle them with nostrums of self-indulgence. This important function cannot be accomplished in classrooms that enthrone "self-expression" and incidental learning as guidelines of the educational process.[9]

There are two points, however, on which Broudy concedes too much to the critics. Take, first, his judgment that the schools have been unresponsive to demands for change. "Why are the schools unresponsive?," he asks in a chapter title,[10] thereby foreclosing an objective consideration of the issue. Like Charles Silberman, Broudy seems to take for granted the validity of the indictment, implying that the schools are—and have been—insensitive to the needs of contemporary youth. I deny that this is so. I must differ, also, with Broudy's portrayal of the typical teacher, presented in the chapter entitled "The Professional Teacher—a Mischievous Illusion." He accepts (too readily, I think), the Friedenberg stereotype of the timid and constrained teacher. "The single outstanding fact about teachers," Broudy writes, "especially in American public schools, has been their docility."[11] Perhaps it was true at one time that teachers did not question the decisions of their supervisors and principals. It is certainly not true today, however, with teachers organized in unions and associations and insistent on having a voice in school policies. I prefer to think that the seeming docility of teachers was, even in the past, a self-protective device to conserve their constructive energies for the task they felt was most useful, that is, guiding the young toward intellectual and emotional maturity.

On all the important issues, however, Broudy's contribution to the current debate on the aims and content of education is invaluable. The "real world" of the public schools is delineated on a vast canvas by Broudy, as an enterprise in social engineering unprecedented in design and scope, self-critical and pragmatic in facing its problems, and dedicated, in the deepest sense, to fulfilling a trust that is vital to the survival of our democratic institutions.

Throughout the seventies, the admonitions of Hook, Barr, and Broudy (and countless other observers) were increasingly confirmed by events. Local and state boards of education, alarmed by the decline in basic skills and in scholarship, moved to establish minimum standards of competence in reading, writing, and mathematics as qualification of high school diplomas. The concept of "back to basics" became a rallying cry at educational conferences and in professional journals, although it did not have the same meaning for everyone. Certainly, innovative programs that had flourished in the past decades were now more and more subjected to close scrutiny before being adopted.

This trend was definitively analyzed in Paul Copperman's book *The Literacy Hoax,* published in 1978. In this well-researched study, Copperman, director of the Institute of Reading Development based in California, traces the insidious effects of the Owl Critics' doctrines on school policies. His thesis is that the decline in every measurable outcome of schooling can be attributed to the adoption of their unproven and, in fact, fallacious concepts. The decline set in during the sixties when, as he demonstrates, "the primary goals of elementary education were replaced with a combination of psychological goals and restructured intellectual goals."[12] Copperman urges a return to traditional values in much the same sense that James D. Koerner did in *The Case for Basic Education*. Copperman foresees a continued disintegration of the public schools unless parents and educators reestablish authority and discipline in every area of education.

Returning to traditional values is easier said than done. Restoring the schools to health will be a long-range challenge. There can be no panacea for the deep-seated ills of so complex an organism as the schools. Every segment of society must become involved, for education does not take place in a vacuum: it is enmeshed in all the complexities of the enveloping society. There is much insight in Paul Goodman's dictum, "there is no right education except growing up in a worthwhile world." This interdependence is perhaps the most cogent reason for whatever efforts are necessary to undo the corruptive trends of the past few decades.

EPILOGUE—*A PARABLE*

"It's the visitor from Outer Thailand," said the principal's secretary over the intercom.

"Show him in," said the principal.

Through the doorway came a smiling, round-faced figure clad in a somber black suit. At the principal's gesture he seated himself at the conference table.

"As you know from my letter," said the visitor," I am undertaking a survey of the schools of the United States at the the behest of our minister of education. It is the minister's intention to model our educational system on that of the most advanced nation in the world, the United States. Like Peter the Great, we believe that direct observation is likely to be more fruitful than the perusal of books and reports."

"Who is Peter the Great?" asked the principal. "The name sounds familiar, but I can't quite place it."

The visitor's expression was impassive. "Peter the Great," he said, "was the czar of Russia, circa 1750, whose aim was to westernize his backward empire. Following the example of Haroun al Raschid, he went in disguise among the common people, worked in Holland as a ship's carpenter, and thus was able to bring back to his people some of the technical knowledge of Western Europe. In a similar way, I would like to get information about your objectives, curriculums, methods of instruction, and teaching materials. Later, I hope to have the privilege of visiting some of your classes."

"Good show," said the principal. "Fire away."

The visitor placed a cassette tape recorder on the desk, flipped the "Record" switch, and leaned forward.

"First, sir," the visitor began, "what are your curricular requirements for a high school diploma?"

"I'm glad you asked that question," said the principal. "There was a time when a rigorous system of course credits made it extremely difficult for students to obtain a diploma. They had to secure passing grades in prescribed areas of study—English, Social Studies, Mathematics, Science, Languages, Art, Music, and Physical Education. Many students—about 50 percent of the entering class—found these requirements too difficult and dropped out of school. Now all of this has changed."

"In what way?" interjected the visitor.

"Well, let's take a concrete case," said the principal, extracting a folder from his desk drawer. "This is the permanent record of one Joseph Marlin, at present a senior. In his tenth year, he made a splendid record in several fields—he won the handball championship of the grade, listened to all the recordings of Engelbert Humperdinck, and had several prolonged interviews with his guidance counsellor. In the eleventh grade, Joseph was given the opportunity to develop his self-initiated interest in our system of criminal justice by spending sixty days in jail for committing the impulsive act of mugging a fellow student. While in detention, he carried out an intensive study of certain sociological aspects of penology—for which, of course, he received scholastic credit. In this, his senior year, where our elective program is concentrated, Joseph chose elective courses in—let me see—Monsters and Ghouls in Contemporary Literature, A Survey of the Eutrophication of Lake Erie, Kant's Categorical Imperative and the Pentagon, and Remedial Reading. He has already attained a reading grade of 6.3 and is, therefore, qualified for a diploma."

"Very interesting," said the visitor. "I am curious, however, about the fact that no courses in history appear in Joseph's record. Surely you wish to develop a reverence for the great men and women who exemplify the high ideal of selfless service to their country. We in Southeast Asia have had a deep affection for your great President Abraham Lincoln ever since Margaret Landon visited our country in 1860 to tutor the children of our emperor. Her charming book *Anna and the King of Siam* has become a minor classic in our land."

"I have so little time for reading," said the principal. "As for Abraham Lincoln, we honor his memory by making his birthday a school holiday. But, in general, we do not believe in history as fitting subject matter for study. We have long since abandoned the pursuit of archaic, irrelevant subjects such as history and classic literature. After all, it is only the problems of the present day that matter to our students in any real sense."

"Indeed, that is true," said the visitor, nodding benignly. "I have read with intense interest your educational sages Neil Postman and John Holt and find much substance in their philosophies. However, you must remember that we in Indochina are a backward people and face the problem of developing political and social institutions. Without an understanding of the past, how can you prepare your young people to take their places in the mainstream of American life and build a healthy society?"

"That is a fundamental point," said the principal. "We have given much thought to the matter under the guidance of Paul Goodman and Jonathan Kozol. Ours is a sick society. The industrial and political achievements of the United States, which impress you and others throughout the world, are founded on injustice, racism, poverty, pollution, militarism, political corruption, subway graffiti, and male chauvinism. Therefore, an educational system that supports such a debased society is evil. Our purpose is to weaken the foundations of the establishment, and, if I may say so, we are highly gratified by our achievement to date."

"I fully understand your position," said the visitor. "Yet I cannot help thinking of the difficulties your students will encounter when they apply for college admission without a background of scholarship in the basic fields of learning."

"We have solved that problem satisfactorily," said the principal. "The colleges in our conference area have adopted a policy of what is called 'open admissions.' This means, in effect, that every student who receives a high-school diploma is automatically accepted for admission by the college. We have discarded the stuffy college-entrance examinations that once were used as instruments of selection. As you well know, these tests were of doubtful validity in predicting social adjustment and athletic success on campus. With open admissions, we have removed the effeteness and inbreeding that were observed in our colleges by Alan Toffler."

"I am pleased to hear that," said the visitor. "It leads to my next question. To attain your educational objectives, such as they are, what methods of instruction do your teachers follow? Do they favor the methodology advocated by John Dewey and William Kilpatrick or that championed by Hyman Rickover and Max Rafferty?"

"Sir," said the principal, exhibiting a trace of irritation, "name dropping is a mark of egocentricity. We do not feel the need of bolstering our individual perceptions by referring to parallels in the dim past. We believe with Alfred Korzybski that no one individual's thoughts can be communicated to another across the insurmountable semantic barrier. We have detached ourselves from Aristotelean logic. In brief, we believe that nothing can be taught. This is the essence of our philosophy of education."

"How is this philosophy implemented in the classroom?" asked the visitor.

"Well, our methodology, delineated so admirably by Carl Rogers, is essentially improvisational. There is only one rule—under no circumstances must the teacher plan his or her lessons. The teacher must enter the classroom each day as if the world had been newly created that morning. The best possible procedure is to announce at the beginning of each class meeting, 'Well, kids, let's get it on the road. Anyone got anything to say?' From then on, the teacher is enjoined from expressing any thought except when he is asked by the students to do so or, of course, in case of a fire drill. There are some teachers who have consistently achieved a fine record of taciturnity throughout many years of service. Good teaching is more honored in the breach than the observance, as Shakespeare said."

"But," the visitor interposed, "how do you determine whether a student has grown intellectually as a result of his school experiences? What methods of evaluation do teachers use? What records do they keep?"

"We *trust* our students," said the principal firmly. "They alone are capable of determining whether they have learned anything and to what extent they have matured. As our Edgar Z. Friedenberg has noted, teachers in traditional schools would base their evaluation of students on distrust and hositility. By giving tests and holding the threat of failing grades over the heads of students, they made them feel threatened and therefore insecure. We believe in self-evaluation."

"What evidence do you have of your success in attaining your educational goals?" asked the visitor.

"Well," said the principal, opening a glassined loose-leaf folder, "take the matter of attendance. As you know, we do not require regular attendance, since we feel that any compulsion is emotionally destructive or, as Charles Silberman puts it, demeaning. Now, if you will look at these charts, you will note that our average percentage of attendance has been declining steadily. In fact, this school —I say this in all modesty—has achieved the enviable record of having come close to perfect nonattendance for two weeks in a row. Unfortunately, the bad weather last week was a serious setback—a number of students reported to school. But we are certain this will be a temporary condition."

"I sympathize fully with your anxiety," said the visitor. "In our country, we have yet to learn the importance of school nonattendance."

"We have the word of Christoper Jencks that schooling, of all the factors that contribute to success in life, is the least important. His statistical studies prove that the most important factors are one's genetic makeup, one's early environment, and luck. It is obvious that we schoolmen cannot control any of these things, so why bother?"

"Mr. Jencks is undoubtedly right," said the visitor. "As you well know, we Orientals have much in common with Mr. Jencks. We too value intuition above understanding, mysticism above science, and emotional wholeness above a sterile intellectualism."

"Beautifully put," said the principal.

"Now," said the visitor, "I have but one final question to ask. To carry out your educational plans, obviously the quality of school personnel— teachers and supervisors—is a matter of crucial importance. How do you select your staffs?"

"There was a time," said the principal, "when a clumsy examination procedure was used to select teachers, and especially supervisors. But, as Judge Walter Mansfield pointed out in his landmark decision in 1971 abolishing the examination system in New York City, any competitive test discriminates against the less competent candidates, many of whom are very nice people. Therefore, tests were eliminated. Instead, we have developed a screening procedure under which selection of supervisors is made by committees of local politicians, parents who happen to drop in, and the most vocal faculty members. As a result, we have developed a nice family feeling among our teachers and principals. The important thing, to use a colloquialism, is to be one of the boys—or girls."

"Indeed, it is," said the visitor, gathering up his material. "I must go now. I am most grateful for your enlightening responses. I do not have time to visit your classes as I had hoped to do, but perhaps that would be superfluous. As our philosopher Tau Leung said, experience can only reveal to us what we already know. Good day, sir."

As the door closed behind the visitor, the principal, with a sigh of satisfaction, went back to his crossword puzzle.

NOTES

Chapter 1. THE OWL CRITICS

1. Jonathan Kozol, *Death at an Early Age* (Boston: Houghton Mifflin, 1972), p. 190. As a matter of fact, literary anthologies in widespread use in the schools included the writings of Robert Frost, Carl Sandburg, Edna St. Vincent Millay, W.H. Auden, Langston Hughes, and other contemporary poets.

2. Charles E. Silberman, *Crisis in the Classroom* (New York: Random House, 1970), pp. 349 ff. In a letter to the *New York Times* (September 20, 1970), I wrote: "Silberman makes sweeping generalizations that are based on second-hand reports, observations from a comfortable distance, and idealistic illusions." His judgment of the value of innovative programs, as will be shown later, is hardly to be trusted.

3. P.A. Graham, "The Progressive Education Movement," in the *Encyclopedia of Education,* vol. 7, pp. 249–55.

4. James Waterman Wise, *The Springfield Plan* (New York: The Viking Press, 1945). This is a graphic account of the experiment in child-centered and community-oriented education developed by Superintendent John Granrud.

5. Silberman, *Crisis,* p. 283.

6. Silberman, *Crisis,* chapter 4: "Education for Docility."

7. Kozol, *Death,* p. 6, and elsewhere.

8. Edgar Z. Friedenberg, *Coming of Age in America* (New York: Random House, 1963), p. 194. Friedenberg's study of adolescent attitudes and values is a fairly well-documented analysis of the subject. The analysis is flawed, however, by tangential comments that are not based on relevant data.

9. Silberman, *Crisis,* p. 133. This clumsy witticism, as I characterize it, is an instance of a tendency among the Owl Critics to leaven their abrasive criticism of teachers with "humor." This tendency is pronounced in the writing of Christopher Jencks, John Holt, and especially Neil Postman.

10. Silberman, *Crisis,* p. 148.

11. Neil Postman and Charles Weingartner, *Teaching as a Subversive Activity* (New York: Delacorte Press, 1969), p.22. ff. Time and again, in Postman and Weingartner's books, a thinly disguised contempt for the schools and for teachers surfaces.

12. Silberman, *Crisis,* p. 148.

13. Kozol, *Death,* chapter 1.

14. John Holt, *The Underachieving School* (New York: The Pitman Publishing Co., 1969). Holt's encouragement of free reading in his class, which teachers of English approve as a supplementary source of enrichment, became a fetish with Holt. He codified this program in a doctrinaire prescription of free reading without teacher guidance.

15. Silberman, *Crisis,* p. 125.

16. Ibid., p. 126.

17. Ibid., p. 92.

18. Ibid., p. 336.

Chapter 2. AND GLADLY TEACH

1. John Holt, *The Underachieving School* (New York: The Pitman Publishing Co., 1969), p. 204. Epigrams of this kind—"It is the act of instruction that impedes learning"—are often used by the Owl Critics for their shock value. They are usually modified in the next breath by some qualifying phrase, in this case: "in more cases than not". The crucial term is: "the act of instruction," and Holt's weakness, as will be shown in Chapters 6 and 7, lies in his failure to understand the teacher's directive role.

2. Francis Bacon described the schoolmaster as being dedicated to his vocation. In his essay "The Good Schoolmaster," Bacon wrote: "God mouldeth some for the schoolmaster's life, undertaking it with desire and delight, and discharging it with dexterity and happy success." Not all teachers, of course, fit this mold, but in my many years of teaching and supervision, I have rarely met a professional colleague who did not to some degree fit Bacon's definition.

3. Edgar Z. Friedenberg, *The Vanishing Adolescent* (Boston: Beacon Press, 1964), p. 82. The recruitment and selection of teachers is a major problem for school boards. If prospective teachers rank below prospective lawyers and doctors in academic achievement, as some studies have shown, it is more than likely that the differences in measurable qualities are less significant than the differences in attitude and purpose. In any case, teacher-training programs at college and in graduate schools should be upgraded and teacher selection and certification should be held to more rigorous standards. The negativism of Friedenberg's assessment of teachers cannot provide guidelines for recruitment and training.

4. This is a composite portrait of the teachers who are likely to be approved by the Owl Critics. It is based on models provided by Carl Rogers, John Holt, Neil Postman, and Jonathan Kozol, among others, in their writings and public statements.

Chapter 3. THE DEAD HAND OF CONSERVATISM.

1. Charles Silberman, *Crisis in the Classroom* (New York: Random House, 1970), p. 10.

2. George A. Antonelli, "Questions for the Innovator," *NAASP Bulletin* (February 1973). To say that a proposed change has been tried out in the past is not necessarily to reject it. The initial implementation of the plan might have been faulty, and therefore it may be worth trying once again. Antonelli's point is that innovations proposed today should be weighed in this historical setting.

3. Roy L. Woolridge, "Cooperative Education," *The Encyclopedia of Education*, vol. 2, pp. 438–44.

4. P.A. Graham, "The Progressive Education Movement," *The Encyclopedia of Education*, vol. 7, pp. 249–55.

5. National Council of Teachers of English, *The English Language Arts* (New York: Appleton-Century-Crofts, 1952), p. 7.

6. James D. Koerner, *The Case for Basic Education* (Boston: Little Brown and Company, 1959). The quotation comes from the Statement of Purpose of the Council for Basic Education, organized in 1956. It is noteworthy that this state-

ment defines basic education in terms that are very different from those used by proponents of a return to the basic skills. As a response to steadily declining scores on college aptitude tests and standardized reading and arithmetic tests, there has been a widespread clamor for a Spartan curriculum consisting of little more than the three R's and other skills. The Council for Basic Education advocates a more extensive program of scholarship in the arts and sciences.

7. Clifton Fadiman, in Koerner's *The Case for Basic Education,* p. 7.

8. The three major developments analyzed in this chapter are patently only a small part of the total picture. I have selected these as typical illustrations of the adaptability of the schools to recognized needs. Later, at the end of the chapter, I mention a number of other emerging programs that reflect the pragmatic and experimental direction of the nation's schools.

9. *Intelligence quotient:* a measure of mental ability, now largely abandoned because of its alleged bias toward certain ethnic groups. Arthur R. Jensen's article "How Much Can We Boost I.Q. and Scholastic Achievement?," in the *Harvard Educational Review* (Winter 1969), opened up a Pandora's box of bitter controversy over the validity of intelligence tests, the issue being, as usual, whether they measure genetically inherited abilities or environmental conditioning.

10. Christopher Jencks, *Inequality: A Reassessment of the Effect of Family and Schooling in America* (New York: Basic Books, 1971). Jencks's ideas on this problem and on the futility of schooling as a useful instrument for strengthening our democratic society are analyzed at length in Chapter 9, "The Vagaries of Christopher Jencks & Co."

11. George Norvell, *The Reading Interests of Young People* (East Lansing: Michigan State University Press, 1973).

12. All standarized reading tests are to some degree culturally biased. The subject matter of reading passages will vary in apperceptive impact, that is, it will be more readily grasped by those familiar with the subject than by others. One passage in a widely used test, for example, deals with the habits of penguins, a species that is known to few urban children. The New York State English Regents examinations did not always avoid this cultural bias: some vocabulary items— *mulch, cruse, silo*—put a strain on students whose environment was the asphalt jungle.

13. Neil Postman and Charles Weingartner, *Teaching as a Subversive Activity* (New York: Delacorte Press, 1969), pp. 39–58.

14. Ibid., pp. 47–50. The authors express contempt for all academic subjects. This passage is typical: "The children know that none of these questions has anything to do with them." It is my purpose in this section to show that the unit on ancient Greece *can* be presented to students through well-planned developmental teaching so they will recognize, little by little, that learning history is not a "game of Let's Pretend" but an exciting intellectual experience.

Chapter 4. CURRICULUM—THE HEART OF THE MATTER

1. Alvin Toffler, *Future Shock* (New York: Random House, 1970), p. 363. Toffler too readily leaps on the bandwagon of disparagement of the standard curriculum. In support of his statement he can point to similar charges made

repeatedly by the Owl Critics. His readers, having no special reason to distrust Toffler's judgment, mistake his debatable assertion for an established fact.

2. Charles E. Silberman, *Crisis in the Classroom* (New York: Random House, 1970), p. 173.

3. Jerome Bruner, *The Process of Education* (Cambridge: Harvard University Press, 1960); and, more succinctly, in an article: "Needed: a Theory of Education," in *Educational Leadership*.

4. An account of competency-based learning is presented in an article in the *New York Times*, April 1, 1975.

5. Neil Postman and Charles Weingartner, *Teaching as a Subversive Activity* (New York: Delacorte Press, 1969), p. 57.

6. Ibid., p. 55. Postman attacks English grammar as a useless subject of instruction, arguing that it is more important for students to study contemporary social and political problems. Even granting this premise, however, it does not follow that the study of linguistics, including grammar, is of no importance whatever.

7. Ibid., p. 57. Postman falls into his own trap here. An educated person will readily identify the dates 1776 and 1861 with social upheaval and civil war. But how will the student who has not been required to study history in an organized course of study be able to grasp the significance of the dates?

8. Ibid., p. 42. Strangely enough, John Holt and Christopher Jencks both cite the same triad of "irrelevant" school subjects as instances of the irrationality of the conventional curriculum.

9. Ibid., p. 47.

10. Ibid., p. 60. Here, at last, Postman offers *his* curricular program, one that would meet the test of relevance and immediacy. It turns out to be a miscellaneous list of questions assembled seemingly at random, a thing of shreds and patches.

11. Ibid., p. 62.

12. Ibid., p. 92.

13. Ibid., pp. 104–09. Postman bolsters his esoteric proposals by providing them with a theoretical framework. Semantics is an important field of scholarship and should be part of the study of linguistics in the schools. Korzybski's thesis, however, has little credibility among scholars.

14. Thomas Henry Huxley, "A Liberal Education—and Where to Find It," in *Lay Sermons, Addresses, and Reviews* (New York: D. Appleton Company, 1910). Although Huxley emphasized the importance of science and technology above the humanities, his respect for literature and the arts as well as the social sciences was apparent. "Education," he said, "is the instruction of the intellect in the laws of Nature, under which I include not merely things and their forces, but men and their ways; and the fashioning of the affections and will into an earnest and loving desire to move in harmony with those laws."

15. Postman and Weingartner, *Teaching as a Subversive Activity*, pp. 70–72. Transcription of actual classroom lessons is very useful as a training device. In New York City and elsewhere, experiments in televising lessons have been carried out with success. The most fruitful project in this area has been the series of live demonstration lessons conducted before audiences of teachers, with opportunity for discussion of various aspects of content and teaching method.

16. Ibid., pp. 137–40.

Chapter 5. PERMISSIVENESS AND THE HAPLESS STUDENT

1. Carl Rogers, *Freedom to Learn* (Columbus, Ohio: Merrill, 1969).

2. James Fenner, *Principles of Student Centered High School English Teaching* (Doctoral Dissertation, New York University, 1971).

3. Earl C. Kelley, *The Workshop Way of Learning* (New York: Harper, 1951), p. 6.

4. Ibid., p. 17. Over the years, I have taken part in a number of workshop sessions at professional conventions and special conferences, such as those conducted for staff involved in the College Discovery Program. At some sessions the chairman would divide the participants into groups of five or six to explore more fully the issues raised in the general session. Although I enjoyed being part of this "interactive process," I usually had the feeling that much time was wasted in small talk in the groups, in the required summation by each group's chairman, and in the repetitious and inconclusive comments by the session chairman.

5. Rogers, *Freedom to Learn*, p. 103.

6. Ibid., p. 106.

7. Ibid., p. 106.

8. Sylvia Ashton-Warner's first autobiographical work, entitled *Teacher*, brought to light a too-seldom-recognized quality in the person who sits or stands in front of the room, namely, a courageous individualism that does not hesitate to challenge bureaucratic rigidity.

9. Ibid., p. 109.

10. "The Cardinal Principles of Secondary Education" have been revised again and again, but the philosophy underlying their statement of goals has remained firmly imbedded in the policies and programs of most of the nation's schools.

11. Rogers, *Freedom to Learn*, p. 58 ff.

12. Ibid., p. 59.

13. Perry London, *Behavior Control* (New York: Harper & Row, 1969), p. 66. Professor London is one of any number of authorities in current psychological theory who have become skeptical of the claims of psychoanalysis and the mystique of group encounters as forms of therapy.

Chapter 6. JOHN HOLT, ROMANTIC

1. John Holt, *The Underachieving School* (New York: Pitman Publishing Company, 1969), p. 204–05. In this statement of guiding principles, Holt places himself squarely in the ranks of those reformists I call the Owl Critics. As an apprentice teacher, he was, he tells us, a strict disciplinarian and a schoolmaster in the narrow traditional sense. His conversion to a philosophy of permissiveness was sudden and impulsive. He apparently did not explore the middle ground of curriculum and methodology, prevalent in most schools, that met the needs of children and adolescents without crushing their individuality or abandoning them to grope in the dark.

2. Ibid., p. 99.

3. This paragraph is in substance a paraphrase of Thomas Henry Huxley's definition of education, developed in his essay "A Liberal Education." Nature and

society, in his view, are severe taskmasters and hold all of us strictly accountable for our actions.

4. Ibid., p. 170.

5. Ibid., p. 33.

6. When a practice is based on unsound theory, it leads to predictable failure. And when the practitioner of unsound teaching method comes up against the inevitable consequences of his error, he is sometimes shaken into undertaking a healthy self-examination.

An instructive example of such a corrective change of practice in midstream can be seen in the experience of an instructor in social psychology at a prestigious university. Professor D, we are told (*The New York Times,* June 2, 1973) was given a grant of $30,000 to study the effectiveness of an innovative teaching method he had devised. For years he had conducted his courses in a benign, permissive way, trusting his students to have done the assigned reading for each week in preparation for the weekly seminar on the curricular unit. He discovered, however, that many students did not do the assigned reading and that their contributions to the discussions were, to say the least, uninformed.

Accordingly, Professor D. devised a new system of control: before being admitted to the discussion group, students would be required to answer a few questions to test their mastery of or at least their familiarity with the week's reading. In a word, their homework assignments would be checked!

The grant of $30,000 will be a small price to pay if it reaffirms the validity of a practice that most teachers adhere to despite the blandishments of John Holt and his coterie.

Chapter 7. ANYONE CAN TEACH ENGLISH

1. Hilda Grubman, "Accountability for What?," *The Nation's Schools* (May 1972).

2. John Holt, *The Underachieving School* (New York: Pitman Publishing Co., 1969), p. 80 ff.

3. Ibid., pp. 80–95.

4. Ibid., p. 87.

5. Ibid., p. 82.

6. Ibid., p. 82.

7. Herbert Kohl, *36 Children* (New York: New American Library, 1967), pp. 23–26. This is good teaching. "One must learn," Kohl says in his book (in another context), "to respond to what happens spontaneously in the classroom, and to put aside one's other plans." Unfortunately, this useful idea is carried by Holt and, to a lesser extent, by Kohl to the absurd conclusion that lessons need *never* be planned.

8. Abraham Bernstein, in a series of monthly bulletins distributed to high schools entitled "Letters on English and Reading," published by the Department of Education, Brooklyn College, beginning in March 1971.

9. Maxwell Nurnberg, *What's the Good Word?* (New York: Simon & Shuster, 1942). This textbook illustrates how a teacher's imagination and humor can make the most pedestrian of subjects, English grammar, most appealing.

For example, to teach the difference between words that are often confused, Nurnberg uses this device:

    1. I *spilled* some tea into my saucer.

    2. I *poured* some tea into my saucer.

       (Which is worse table manners?)

Along these lines, I have developed devices for teaching pronouns:

    1. After the game, everyone returned to *their* class,

    2. After the game, everyone returned to *his* class.

       (Is there a difference in meaning?)

    10. Charles Carpenter Fries, *American English Grammar* (New York: D. Apple-
ton Century Co., 1948). Fries surveyed the speech and writing of Americans of
different social levels and concluded that standard grammatical forms are being
modified or abandoned under social pressures.

    11. H.G. Wells, *Experiment in Autobiography* (Philadelphia: J.B. Lippincott and
Co., 1934). Much concerned with the problem of establishing a sound educational
system in England, Wells had this to say on one of the issues that have been
debated in our generation: "There are many valid objections to a system of
education controlled by written examinations; it may tend very easily toward a
ready superficiality; but I am convinced that it has at any rate the great merit of
imposing method and order in learning. It prevents the formation of those great
cavities of vagueness, those preferential obsessions, those disproportions between
detail and generalization which are characteristic of gifted people who have never
been 'examinees' " (p. 110).

Chapter 8. The Cult of Relevance

    1. Matthew Arnold in his brilliant essay on British culture, in *Culture and
Anarchy* (New York: D. Appleton and Co., ed. 1924), pp. 38–39.

    2. Charles E. Silberman, *Crisis in the Classroom* (New York: Random House,
1970), p. 175–79.

    3. Anthony Burgess, "An Open Letter," in the *New York Times* (November 22,
1972).

    4. Robert W. Blake, "The New English is Cool," *The English Review* (April 1970).
Like Holt and Postman, Professor Blake throws out the baby with the bath. Uneasy
about some obvious shortcomings in the English program, he seizes on a faddish
straw proffered by a transiently acclaimed sciolist—in this instance Marshall
McLuhan—and advocates a complete revision of the English course. I try to show
in this section that the values Blake evidently wishes to conserve can be, and in fact
are being, realized in conventional teaching procedures and, conversely, that they
cannot be attained by the adoption of McLuhanesque ideas.

    5. Marshall McLuhan, *Understanding Media* (New York: McGraw-Hill, 1965),
chapter 1.

    6. Ibid., p. 23.

    7. Ibid., p. 300.

    8. Ibid., p. 22.

    9. Ibid., p. 54.

Chapter 9. The Vagaries of Christopher Jencks & Co.

    1. Christopher Jencks, *Inequality: a Reassessment of the Effect of Family and School-
ing in America* (New York: Basic Books, 1971), p. 265. The offhand, sly intrusion of

Jencks's political creed in the very last sentence of his book is very significant. The phrasing ("This is what other countries call socialism") suggests that the concept of socialism has not yet come to the attention of people in *this* country. It implies that the theory of socialism is something we might want to look at when we have the time, like a new shop that everyone is talking about. What is most irritating in the statement is that Jencks has led us to believe throughout the book that his conclusions are based on rigorous statistical data. Yet he presents the dogma that socialism will remedy the ills of our inegalitarian society with no factual or logical support whatever.

2. Christopher Jencks and Mary Jo Bane, "The Schools and Equal Opportunity," *The Saturday Review* (September 6, 1972).

3. Jencks, *Inequality*, p. 75.

4. Ibid., p.12.

5. Ibid., p. 54. This triad of "useless" subjects is held up to scorn in Neil Postman and John Holt, as well. The Owl Critics seem to draw sustenance from one another in the details of their texts as well as in their broad concepts.

6. Ibid., p. 8.

7. Ibid., p. 42.

8. Ibid., p. 95.

9. Ibid., p. 265.

10. Lou LaBrant, *We Teach English* (New York: Greenwood Press, 1951). This is in general a valuable pedagogical work. My reference to the author's snide comment on ideas not supported by statistical studies stems from my conviction that many, perhaps the most important, operative principles in the social studies and the humanities are not susceptible of exact measurement. Overreliance on statistical measurement was what Richard Hofstadter probably had in mind when he wrote: "The American mind seems extremely vulnerable to the belief that any alleged knowledge that can be expressed in figures is as final and exact as the figures in which it is expressed." *Anti-Intellectualism in American Life* (New York: Alfred A. Knopf, 1963), p. 339.

11. If a grammatical rule or principle is well taught, it will be applied in exercises and drills and illustrative sentences. Thus application of the rule or principle will become automatic in the writing of students. The problems of the run-on sentence, the placement of adverbial modifiers, parallel structure of coordinate elements—as well as the formal rules governing tense, number, and case—are dealt with similarly through drill and application. It is inconceivable that students who have been taught how to use these syntactic and rhetorical tools will abandon them when called on to write a composition.

12. Edgar Z. Friedenberg, *The Vanishing Adolescent* (Boston: Beacon Press, 1964), p. 82. The study referred to in Friedenberg's text is self-evidently incompetent to reach any rational conclusion with respect to the personality of teachers.

13. Colin Greer, *The Great School Legend* (New York: Basic Books, 1972), chapter 1. The substance of the book is a massive assemblage of statistics in support of an untenable thesis. Greer does indeed show that public education in the United States faltered and stumbled during its formative years. It faced unprecedented difficulties, for nothing like it had ever been attempted in the history of mankind—that is, providing education for *all* the people. The "legend" exists only

in the minds of those who demand that the real world correspond with their idealistic prescription—starting now.

14. Ibid., p. 44.

15. Ibid., p. 114.

16. *Associated Press Almanac* (1974), p. 735.

17. Greer, *The Great School Legend*, p. 25.

Chapter 10. IVAN ILLICH AND THE DESCHOOLED SOCIETY

1. Ivan Illich, *Celebration of Awareness, A Call for Institutional Revolution* (Garden City, N.Y.: Doubleday, 1970), p. 111.

2. Ivan Illich, "The Futility of Schooling," in ibid., p. 119.

3. Ivan Illich, *Deschooling Society* (New York: Random House, 1971), p. 3.

4. Ibid., p. 10. There is something disarming in even the most irreverent heresy expressed by Ivan Illich. The reason for this is that he is utterly sincere and single-minded in his conviction that our technological civilization has destroyed more than it has fulfilled human values, and that we must return to a simpler mode of life. Illich thus takes his place in that small group of bold spirits who quicken our souls by daring to defend hopeless causes.

5. Illich, *Celebration of Awareness*, p. 109.

6. Illich, *Deschooling Society*, pp. 19 ff. and 72 ff. Illich's educational design is obviously impractical in the populous, complex urban setting that is the norm in Western societies. Yet, as I show in this chapter, most of the goals sought by Illich are already being implemented or striven for by the teachers in our nation's schools.

7. Ibid., p. 15.

8. Ibid., p. 17.

9. Henry David Thoreau, "On the Duty of Civil Disobedience." The parallels in Illich's and Thoreau's philosophic outlooks are noteworthy. When Illich speaks of institutionalized health care—in childbirth, treatment of diseases, sanitation—and institutionalized burial services for the dead as offensive to human dignity, he apparently presupposes a time in the past when, as he believes, the individual or the family did not depend on resources beyond the village community for their needs. Thoreau, in much the same way, visualized a "free and enlightened State . . . which at last can afford to be just to all men, and to treat the individual with respect as a neighbor; which even would not think it inconsistent with its own repose, if a few were to live aloof from it, nor embraced by it. . . ." This common element in the philosophies of both men touches a sensitive chord in all of us, but can it provide a model for practical decisions?

Chapter 11. EDUCATION AND THE SOCIAL FABRIC

1. Jonathan Kozol, *Death at an Early Age* (Boston: Houghton Mifflin, 1967), p. 190. The poem "Ballad of a Landlord" was introduced by Kozol as a literary experience that would have immediate appeal to his pupils. It is not hard to see why the school authorities made an issue of this; they were probably less disturbed by the content of the poem than they were by Kozol's openly expressed opposition

to school policies and regulations. Attempts by school boards to remove certain books from school libraries and reading lists make headlines now and then, but the usual practice, certainly in the past few decades, has been to permit and indeed encourage the study of poems, plays, short stories, and novels that grapple with the controversial issues of today.

2. Ralph Waldo Emerson's essay "Self-Reliance" affirms in resonant prose the inalienable right of the individual to determine and live by his own set of values. Obviously, this right must be limited by custom or by law to accommodate the conflicting values of different individuals and groups.

3. I have been unable to trace this quotation to its source. It came to my attention in a clipping from some periodical, and my best recollection is that it was attributed to John Holt.

The value of questioning political and moral doctrines that are dominant in a culture is inherent in the democratic way of life. Teachers of literature and social studies cannot avoid discussion of fundamental moral issues. How else could they present such works as Hawthorne's *Scarlet Letter*, Dreiser's *American Tragedy*, or Ellison's *The Invisible Man?* To teach American history is to reenact the debates on fundamental political issues that shaped and continue to shape the structure of American society.

I suspect that the author of the quotation cited in the text had something else in mind, that is, indoctrinating his students with his own dogmas. This is certainly true of Jonathan Kozol, when he criticizes the "free" schools that he helped to establish for not displaying the works of Mao Tse-tung, Che Guevarra, and Lenin on their bookracks or bulletin boards.

4. Paul Goodman, *Compulsory Miseducation* (New York: Horizon Press, 1964), p. 59.

5. Paul Goodman, *Growing Up Absurd* (New York: Random House, 1960), pp. 12 ff. and chapter 2. Goodman is certainly more straightforward and open in expounding his political beliefs than are Christopher Jencks and Colin Greer. We know where Goodman stands. Greer and Jencks keep us in the dark about their political biases.

6. Goodman, *Compulsory Education*, p. 59.

7. Ben J. Wattenberg, *The Real America* (Garden City, N.Y.: Doubleday), 1974. Wattenberg presents abundant evidence of the amazing economic and social progress made by all segments of the American population—the ethnic minorities as well as the dominant groups—since the 1930s. The reality and significance of an "expanding Gross National Product" is Wattenberg's thesis. Goodman's characterization of this economic growth as "meaningless" is a value judgment that must be assessed in the light of one's definition of the good life. But, whatever one's definition may be, it cannot exclude the component of material well-being that has been achieved by America's technological progress.

8. Goodman, *Compulsory Miseducation*, p. 48.

9. Ibid., p. 66.

10. Ibid., p. 55 ff.

11. Ibid., p. 62.

12. Jonathan Kozol, *Death at an Early Age*, p. 190. "Ballad of the Landlord" is certainly not a subversive work. It represents the growing trend among black writers to speak out against injustice and discrimination long before the civil-

rights movement became a political force in the 1950s and 1960s. As a matter of fact, literary anthologies in use in the schools of Boston, New York, and most other cities contained selections from the works of the more outspoken black poets— Countee Cullen, Claude McKay, and Langston Hughes—at the time of Kozol's dismissal. The Boston school authorities, in charging Kozol with insubordination, cited the unauthorized use of the poem rather than its content. And it should be noted that this was the era of the Cold War, the McCarthy hearings, widespread dismissal of teachers charged with being or having been members of the Communist party, and the blacklisting of Hollywood writers and actors suspected of leftist sympathies.

13. Jonathan Kozol, "Look, This System Isn't Working," *New York Times* (April 1, 1971).

14. In April 1971, the public image of Richard Nixon was that of a vigorous, if rather conservative, champion of the American political system. The scandal of Watergate had not yet erupted, and perhaps the most serious criticism then being made of Nixon's policies was that he was prolonging the Vietnam War unnecessarily. Kozol's reference to Nixon as a symbol, in contrast with Gandhi and Thoreau, is therefore as much a reflection of Kozol's hostility toward the American political system as it is an expression of his disapproval of the president's foreign policy.

Kozol's indictment of the nation's educational system as being responsible for the moral climate in Washington and elsewhere that would permit a Nixon to abuse his power fails on two counts. First, it must be remembered that the investigation of Watergate by the Senate Judiciary Committee, strengthened by the vigilance of a free press, proved that the American political system is capable of self-renewal in a time of crisis. Second, it should be noted that the "population like the one that elected him" also elected Woodrow Wilson and Franklin D. Roosevelt to the presidency.

15. Kozol, "Look, This System Isn't Working."

16. Jonathan Kozol, *The Free Schools* (Boston: Houghton Mifflin, 1972), pp. 59–62.

17. Ibid., p. 70.

18. Jonathan Kozol, "Politics, Rage, and Motivation in the Free Schools," *The Harvard Educational Review* (August 1972), p. 418.

19. Ibid., p. 419.

Chapter 12. THE PENDULUM SWING

1. See "The Missing School Yardstick," by Gene Maeroff, in *The New York Times* (March 19, 1975). The letters to the editor appeared during the following weeks.

2. Fred Hechinger, "A Program That Flunked," *The New York Times* (December 10, 1972).

3. Seymour Lachman, address before the City Club, New York City, February 9, 1973.

4. *The New York Review of Books* (December 13, 1973).

5. Fred Hechinger, *The New York Times* (November 16, 1975).

6. Sidney Hook, quoted in *The New York Times* (November 16, 1975).

7. Sidney Hook, *Encounter* (January 1972), in a review of Ivan Illich's *Deschooling Society*. As early as 1946, Professor Hook had come to grips with the problem of

the relevance of the standard curriculum to the needs of society. In his book *Education for Modern Man* (New York: Dial Press, 1946) he took the Deweyan position that the content of the curriculum should be "relevant to the fundamental problems of the age—to the social, political, intellectual, and, if we like, the spiritual questions posed by our time and culture." At the same time, Hook rejected the concept of relevance that was later to be advocated by the Owl Critics. To those who see only the present moment as the proper focus of curriculum, he offered this admonition: "Relevance here becomes the pretext under which every passing whim, fancy, or predicament in the social scene stakes a claim for inclusion in the curriculum of studies."

8. Donald Barr, *Who Pushed Humpty Dumpty?* (New York: Atheneum, 1971), p. 104.

9. Harry Broudy, *The Real World of the Public Schools* (New York: Harcourt, Brace, Janovich, 1972), chapter 4.

10. Broudy, 'Why the Schools Are Unresponsive," in ibid., chapter 2.

11. Ibid., p. 41.

12. Paul Copperman, *The Literacy Hoax* (New York: William Morrow & Co., 1978), p. 61.

BIBLIOGRAPHY

A. CRITICS AND REFORMISTS

Blake, Robert W. "The New English is Cool," in *The English Review,* official journal of the New York State Association of Teachers of English, April 1970.

Friedenberg, Edgar Z. *Coming of Age in America.* New York: Random House, 1963.

————. *The Vanishing Adolescent.* Boston: Beacon Press, 1964.

Goodman, Paul. *Compulsory Miseducation.* New York: Horizon Press, 1964.

————. *Growing Up Absurd.* New York: Random House, 1960.

Greer, Colin. *The Great School Legend.* New York: Basic Books, 1972.

Holt, John. *How Children Fail.* New York: Putnam, 1964.

————. *The Underachieving School.* New York: Pitman Publishing Co., 1969.

Hunter, Evan. *The Blackboard Jungle.* New York: Harper & Row, 1964.

Illich, Ivan. *Celebration of Awareness: A Call for Institutional Revolution.* Garden City, N.Y.: Doubleday, 1970.

————. *Deschooling Society.* New York: Random House, 1971.

Jencks, Christopher. *Inequality: a Reassessment of the Effect of Family and Schooling in America.* New York: Basic Books, 1971.

Kaufman, Bel. *Up the Down Staircase.* New York: Prentice-Hall, 1965.

Kelley, Earl C. *The Workshop Way of Learning.* New York: Harper, 1951.

Kohl, Herbert R. *36 Children.* New York: New American Library, 1967.

Korzybski, Alfred, *Science and Sanity,* Lancaster, Pa.: The International Non-Aristotelean Library Publishing Co., 1933.

Kozol, Jonathan. *Death at an Early Age.* Boston: Houghton Mifflin, 1967.

————. *The Free Schools.* Boston: Houghton Mifflin, 1972.

McLuhan, Marshall. *Understanding Media.* New York: McGraw-Hill, 1965.

Postman, Neil, and Weingartner, Charles. *Teaching as a Subversive Activity.* New York: Delacorte Press, 1969.

Rogers, Carl. *Freedom to Learn.* Columbus, Ohio: Merrill, 1969.

Silberman, Charles E. *Crisis in the Classroom.* New York: Random House, 1970.

Toffler, Alvin. *Future Shock.* New York: Random House, 1970.

B. GUARDIANS AND DEFENDERS

Barr, Donald. *Who Pushed Humpty Dumpty?* New York: Atheneum, 1971.

Bestor, Donald. *The Restoration of Learning.* New York: Alfred A. Knopf, 1955.

Broudy, Harry S. *The Real World of the Public Schools.* New York: Harcourt, Brace, Janovich, 1972.

Bruner, Jerome. *The Process of Education.* Cambridge: Harvard University Press, 1960.

Copperman, Paul. *The Literacy Hoax.* New York: William Morrow & Co., 1978.

Dewey, John. *Democracy and Education.* New York: MacMillan, 1926.

Hofstadter, Richard. *Anti-Intellectualism in American Life.* New York: Alfred A. Knopf, 1963.

Hook, Sidney. *Education for Modern Man.* New York: Dial Press, 1946.

Koerner, James D. *The Case for Basic Education.* Boston: Little, Brown, 1959.

Lynd, Albert. *Quackery in the Public Schools.* Boston: Little, Brown, 1950.

Rickover, Hyman D. *American Education, a National Failure.* New York: Dutton, 1963.

Wattenberg, Ben J. *The Real America.* Garden City, N.Y.: Doubleday, 1974.

C. Guides and Lamplighters

Arnold, Matthew. "Culture and Anarchy," an Essay in Political and Social Criticism. In *Matthew Arnold, Prose and Poetry,* edited by John Bryson. Cambridge: Harvard University Press, 1967.

Ashton-Warner, Sylvia. *Teacher.* New York: Simon & Schuster, 1963.

Bacon, Francis. "Of Studies." In *A Century of English Essays,* edited by Ernest Rhys. New York: Dutton, 1959.

Barzun, Jacques. *The Teacher in America.* Boston: Little, Brown, 1945.

Bernstein, Abraham. "Letters on English and Reading," a series of monthly pamphlets issued by the Department of Education, Brooklyn College, beginning in March 1971.

Burgess, Anthony. "An Open Letter." *The New York Times Magazine,* November 22, 1972.

Fries, Charles C. *American English Grammar.* New York: D. Appleton-Century Co., 1948.

LaBrant, Lou. *We Teach English.* New York: Greenwood Press, 1951.

Leacock, Stephen. "Oxford as I See It." In *My Discovery of England.* New York: Dodd, Mead & Co., 1922.

London, Perry. *Behavior Control.* New York: Harper & Row, 1969.

Nurnberg, Maxwell, *What's the Good Word?* New York: Simon & Schuster, 1942.

Wells, H.G. *Experiment in Autobiography.* Philadelphia: J.B. Lippincott & Co., 1934.

Wise, James Waterman. *The Springfield Plan.* New York: The Viking Press, 1945.

INDEX